Guide to Doing
Business in Mexico

Guide to Doing Business in Mexico

Gray Newman

Anna Szterenfeld

McGraw-Hill, Inc.

New York   San Francisco   Washington, D.C.   Auckland   Bogotá
Caracas   Lisbon   London   Madrid   Mexico City   Milan
Montreal   New Delhi   San Juan   Singapore
Sydney   Tokyo   Toronto

Library of Congress Cataloging-in-Publication Data

Newman, Gray.
    Guide to doing business in Mexico / Gray Newman, Anna Szterenfeld.
      p.   cm.
    ISBN 0-07-009339-3 (hc)   ISBN 0-07-046378-6 (pbk)
    1. Investments, Foreign—Mexico. 2. Mexico—Industries.
    3. Mexico—Economic conditions—1982- I. Szterenfeld, Anna.
    II. Business International Corporation. III. Title.
    HG5162.N48 1993
    332.6'7373072—dc20   92-22656
                                            CIP

Previously published in hard cover as *Business International's Guide to Doing Business in Mexico*

First McGraw-Hill paperback edition, 1995.

  2 3 4 5 6 7 8 9 0 DOC/DOC 9 8 7 6 5 4 3   (HC)
1 2 3 4 5 6 7 8 9 0 DOC/DOC 9 8 7 6 5   (PBK)

ISBN 0-07-009339-3 (HC)
ISBN 0-07-046378-6 (PBK)

The sponsoring editor for this book was David Conti, the editing supervisor was Kimberly A. Goff, and the production supervisor was Donald F. Schmidt. This book was set in Baskerville by Carol Woolverton.

Printed and bound by R. R. Donnelley & Sons Company.

 This book is printed on recycled, acid-free paper containing a minimum of 50% recycled de-inked fiber.

Contents

▼

Preface

A new frontier is opening for businesses operating in Mexico. Long-standing barriers to trade, investment and capital flows have fallen, and further liberalization is expected under a North American free trade agreement. This dramatic opening, coupled with the recovery and growth of Mexico's domestic economy, presents international firms with new opportunities for expansion and profit. Recognizing these prospects, companies today are rethinking Mexico's role in their global strategies for manufacturing, distribution, marketing and financing.

This new book examines the landmark changes under way in Mexico's business environment and their implications for international companies. It is also designed to help corporate decision makers develop an effective response to the challenges and opportunities currently emerging in Mexico. The content is based on extensive research and interviews conducted with government officials, economists, industry specialists and executives of over 30 leading firms. It also draws on Business International's decades of experience in monitoring developments and trends in the Latin American business climate.

Part I, "The New Mexico," reviews the country's changing competitive environment and examines the progress made toward the establishment of a North American free trade agreement, also addressing how such an accord will affect different sectors and companies. In addition, Part I describes how major international firms are repositioning business plans and strategies for the Mexican and the North American markets.

Part II, "Operating in Mexico Today," examines in greater detail the fast-changing regulatory climate in the country, reviews Mexico's economic recovery and expected trends for the 1990s and offers unique insights into Mexican politics and their effect on business.

Part III, "Sector Profiles," takes a systematic look at how major segments of the Mexican economy—including agriculture, automobiles, petrochemicals, computers, maquiladoras and services—will fare as a result of liberal investment rules and free trade.

The book was written by Business International's Mexico-based analysts and US team of Latin American experts. The principal authors were Gray Newman, senior analyst (Mexico City) and Anna Szterenfeld, editor, Latin American Publications (New York). Other contributors were Marc N. Scheinman, consultant (New York); William Neuman (Mexico City), Holly Neumann (Mexico City) and Mimi Cauley de la Sierra (Mexico City). It was edited by Anna Szterenfeld and copyedited by Selene A. Steese.

Business International would like to thank all the corporate and government officials whose generous assistance made this book possible.

Guide to Doing Business in Mexico

PART I
The New Mexico

1
Introduction: Mexico's Modernization

Mexico is undergoing a fundamental transformation in economic strategy and in its relations with the international community. Beginning in the second half of the 1980s, the government moved to change what had been a highly protected, inefficient and overregulated economy into one substantially more open to trade and private foreign and domestic investment. At present, Mexico is viewed by many top analysts and international executives as ready for the same takeoff that characterized the economic miracles experienced in the 1980s by the four "Asian Tigers"—South Korea, Singapore, Hong Kong and Taiwan. Strong political leadership, widespread structural and regulatory reform and revitalized economic growth are changing perceptions of multinational managers concerning business opportunities in Mexico.

Largely through the issuance of presidential decrees, reform of select legislation and membership in the General Agreement on Tariffs and Trade (GATT), Mexico has radically revamped—and often reversed— many of the most important rules governing the economy and business operations in the country. Before entering GATT in August 1986, the country had one of the most closed markets in the world, where high tariff walls and prior import permits were the norm rather than the exception. Moreover, the government dominated many critical economic activities, either through nationalization or state monopolies, such as those in telecommunications (through Teléfonos de México [Telmex], the state telephone company); the airlines (Aeroméxico); banking

(Banamex, Bancomer, Banca Serfin, etc.); food distribution (Con-asupo); and the petroleum and petrochemicals industry (Petróleos de México [Pemex]). When the government did not participate through ownership, it exerted a powerful hold over the economy by tightly regulating industries and services and restricting the degree to which foreign investors could participate in domestic activities.

From 1973 to 1989, most businesses were restricted to 49% foreign participation, with the express purpose of lodging control in the hands of Mexican nationals. Cumbersome bureaucratic procedures, government restrictions on products that could be manufactured by foreign firms, price controls, limitations on technology transfer contracts and other regulations created formidable obstacles for foreign businesses operating in the country.

Tight controls over foreign investment, industrial development and foreign trade produced serious economic distortions: undercapitalization, dependence on foreign commercial bank financing, limited product offerings at inflated prices, widespread use of outdated technology and reduced trade opportunities. These factors contributed to the grave economic crisis Mexico experienced beginning in 1982 and continuing throughout the decade. This crisis was characterized by a halt in economic growth and investment, an inability to meet foreign debt obligations, declining export prices and soaring domestic inflation. It produced, in turn, a sharp decline in job creation and in the general standard of living and prompted enormous capital flight and outward migration.

The Open Economy: Trade, Technology and Capital

Impelled by severe economic stagnation to undertake long-term economic restructuring, policymakers began formulating a new economic strategy in 1985. Starting with the administration of Miguel de la Madrid (1982–88), and especially since Carlos Salinas de Gortari took office in December 1988, the government has been initiating policies aimed at dropping trade barriers as rapidly as possible, improving the competitiveness of domestic industry, shrinking the role of the state and modernizing and globalizing the economy.

Mexico's restrictive regulatory framework has been dramatically altered to favor private initiative. The country has abandoned its former import-substitution development model and is phasing out subsidies to local industry. Privatization has become the order of the day as the government divests itself of numerous state entities, both large and small. Foreign investment rules now permit 100% foreign ownership in most sectors. Deregulation has swept across numerous areas of the economy, from trucking to computers. Trade has been vastly liberalized and free trade negotiations with the US and Canada initiated. Most important, Mexico's political leadership has committed the nation to securing a prominent role in the global economy, making a return to protectionist patterns difficult. The key changes in Mexico's economic and business environment in the last few years are summarized in this section:

• **Trade liberalization.** Trade barriers have been broken down, opening Mexico's market to foreign—especially US—industrial and consumer goods. In 1986, Mexico joined GATT and made a commitment to reduce informal trade barriers. Official reference prices were eliminated, and prior import permits abolished for 95% of all imported items. Subsequently, the maximum tariff rate was reduced to about 20% (from 100% previously), with just 10% charged for many goods. Mexico's trade-weighted average tariff is currently about 11%—low by developing country standards.

Bilateral trade between the US and Mexico has soared since these changes occurred. From 1987 to 1990, American exports to Mexico grew at the rate of almost 32% p.a., whereas total trade between the two countries increased approximately 23% p.a. over the same period. Today, Mexico is the third-largest market for US goods in the world. A free trade agreement will lead to still greater trade flows.

• **Inflation reduction.** In 1987, the government initiated a trilateral price and wage agreement between government, business and labor leaders (the Pact for Economic Solidarity) aimed at reducing unacceptably high inflation. The immediate results were impressive: The inflation rate dropped from 159.2% in 1987 to 51.7% in 1988. This accord, now called the Pact for Economic Growth and Stability, achieved an inflation rate of 19.7% in 1989 and 29.9% in 1990. Inflation in 1991 dipped even further, to 18.8%. Fiscal reform and controlled government spending are also helping to maintain inflation at manageable levels.

• **Renegotiation of the foreign debt.** The 1990 renegotiation of Mexico's external liabilities under the US-sponsored Brady Plan—making Mexico the first Latin American nation to achieve negotiated debt reduction—has cut its net external transfers to an average of 2% p.a. of GDP from 6% previously. The debt agreement has freed considerable resources for domestic needs and for the support of economic revitalization, as well as bolstered economic restructuring efforts.

- **Privatization of state enterprises.** The state has scaled down its participation in some sectors and completely withdrawn from others. For example, it has reduced its activities in the food processing, secondary petrochemicals and automotive industries. About two-thirds of the 1,155 government entities existing in December 1982 were sold to private entrepreneurs, merged or closed altogether by mid-1991. State enterprises sold include the telephone company Telmex, the airline Aeroméxico and companies in the tourism, banking, steel and petrochemical sectors.

- **Deregulation.** More than 25 different areas of the economy have already been—or are scheduled to be—deregulated. The government has ended restrictive domestic regulation in the petrochemical, trucking, telecommunications, financial services, agricultural and food distribution industries, allowing private and foreign participation in many areas of the economy for the first time. The result has been modernization of these sectors and fresh opportunities for foreign firms.

- **Reform of foreign investment rules.** Foreign investment conditions were relaxed in May 1989 through a change in the regulations governing the 1973 Foreign Investment Law. Investment procedures have been streamlined and made more transparent. Prior approval requirements have been eliminated for many investments, and foreign firms can now hold 100% equity in most sectors. Conditions in specific segments covered by industrial development plans, such as computers and automotive products, have been made more conducive to foreign investment through recent sectoral decrees. It is expected that the 1973 Foreign Investment Law will be revised in conjunction with free trade talks.

- **Enhanced intellectual property protection.** In the past, the lack of protection for proprietary technology acted as a disincentive to new investment and meant that most Mexican goods were produced with obsolete technology. In the case of the pharmaceutical industry, for instance, insufficient patent protection impeded foreign company executives from launching breakthrough drugs in Mexico.

  Technology transfer rules were greatly liberalized in 1990. Most important, a landmark intellectual property law was passed in June 1991, strengthening patent protection for processes and products already covered while extending such protection to many products and industries that did not receive patent coverage under previous legislation. Trade secrets were granted coverage for the first time. In addition, a revised copyright law was approved in July 1991, granting explicit protection to computer software and sound recordings, as well as beefing up enforcement provisions.

- **Improved financial environment.** With progress in easing the foreign debt burden, reduction in domestic inflation and increased investor confidence, the cost of local money in Mexico has declined significantly. Capital taken out of the country in the 1980s has begun to be returned. Mexican companies—both state-run and private—have been able to tap into international capital markets for financing. Mexico was the largest recipient in Latin America of fresh capital flows in 1990, with a total of $8.4 billion. The companies that have placed bond issues abroad include Pemex, Telmex, Cemex (the cement manufacturer) and Vitro (the glass producer).

- **Economic revitalization.** After almost 10 years of economic stagnation and decline, Mexico's GDP has returned to a strong growth trajectory. It increased 2.9% in 1989, 4.4% in 1990 and 3.6% in 1991. The real take-off, however, is projected for 1992–1995, when growth is estimated to average 5–6% p.a. Expansion is being supported by strong investment and by a major reduction in inflation.

- **Recovery in consumer purchasing power.** Economic expansion is permitting both wages and jobs to increase gradually. Consumer purchasing power is reviving and, along with it, possibilities for consumers to choose from a much wider selection of products than ever before, especially in the food, beverages, apparel and textiles, electronics and automotive categories. Although retail sales languished in the US in 1990, the retail business boomed in Mexico, largely because of the availability of imports not previously marketed in the country. For example, 1990 was the first year in a decade that Mexicans could purchase imported cars, thanks to reforms in the decree regulating the automotive industry.

There are also qualitative changes in consumers' perceptions of what kinds of products best fit their changing life-styles. The new openness of the borders is creating habits and attitudes that frequently reflect preferences for products and services associated with foreigners, mostly from the US. These specific tastes will have profound implications for corporate planners formulating marketing strategies for Mexico.

Mexico's Future Thrust

For many observers, there is no better time than the present to consider Mexico as a site for investment. Economic liberalization is creating sizable business opportunities for both Mexican and foreign companies. These opportunities will multiply as the business climate continues to improve as a result of greater economic stability and further deregulation of the economy. One of the most important boosts for foreign investor confidence—and for the permanence of the current reformist policy direction—will be the signing of a trilateral free trade agreement between Mexico, the US and Canada, which could occur during 1992 or early in 1993.

Progress in the free trade negotiations will stimulate new investment and help the country achieve even higher levels of growth in this decade and beyond. In addition, the talks will encourage foreign firms to reevaluate their Mexican operations and look to the country as a central sourcing site for the North American market. Greater domestic operating freedom, combined with progressive integration with the US economy, will also enable multinational companies to rationalize their production in Mexico and incorporate their operations in the country into their global strategies.

Despite these promising considerations, there are risks for business in Mexico. Some are macroeconomic: Inflation, for example, is still far higher than in fully industrialized countries. The slow pace of peso devaluation relative to inflation leaves companies concerned about possible exchange rate shocks. Other risks are social and political. Mexico's political and legal institutions have lagged behind the modernization and liberalization of its economy. A closed political system—dominated by a single and extremely powerful political party—may not be compatible with an open economy, and transition to a more democratic political system may not go smoothly. Finally, poverty, public health and educational deficiencies, as well as the chasm between Mexico's indigenous population and its urban culture, are social problems that will be difficult to confront, but may have to be solved to maintain the momentum of economic revitalization into the 21st century.

Risks aside, today Mexico is clearly one of the world's most exciting business prospects. Because much of the fervor the country is generating stems from its possible integration into a North American free trade area, the next chapter focuses on the free trade agreement.

2

Moving Toward a North American Free Trade Area

The initiation in 1991 of negotiations for a free trade agreement (FTA) among the US, Mexico and Canada is the culmination of intensive diplomatic and business activity on both sides of the US-Mexico border. Presidents George Bush and Carlos Salinas de Gortari have forcefully endorsed such an agreement because they believe it will enhance the competitive advantages of both countries. More specifically, in conjunction with Canadian support, an FTA could measurably help North America in responding to the challenge presented by other leading global trading blocs, the most important of which are the European Community (EC) and the Pacific Rim.

The Bush team sees President Salinas's administration as a model for other Latin American nations that are becoming newly industrialized. Under Salinas, Mexico has reduced its inflation rate dramatically, reactivated long-stagnant economic growth, imported record amounts of US capital and consumer goods and liberalized foreign investment and trade rules. For the US, Mexico is now the third leading trading partner—third as an export destination and fifth as a source of imports. Between 1985 and 1990, US exports of consumer goods to Mexico tripled, while exports of capital goods doubled.

Mexico's maquiladora (in-bond) industry has become extremely important to US companies. Thanks to almost 1,800 US-owned maquiladoras operating in Mexico (as of mid-1991), which reexport US-made components in finished-product form, US industry has been able

9

to compete more effectively against foreign competitors in the US market.

Although an FTA is important to the Bush administration, it is even more critical for Salinas. The US is *first* for Mexico as an export destination, source of imports and source of foreign direct investment. Furthermore, the Salinas government sees an FTA as the best way to codify its policies to modernize and liberalize Mexico and to ensure that these reforms will survive Salinas's term of office and be maintained by future Mexican administrations.

Although an FTA is vigorously championed by the presidents of both countries, its value for the US has been challenged by organized labor, environmentalists, manufacturers and agricultural producers who fear that such an agreement will have a negative—not positive—impact. Whatever the final shape of the FTA, it will have a significant effect on US businesses (some more than others). The objective of this chapter is to provide corpolate decision makers with solid background information and analyses with which to evaluate the impending trilateral FTA. The following issues are reviewed:

• Events that led up to FTA negotiations;

• Trade and investment opportunities with Mexico, based on recent trends;

• Overall advantages and disadvantages of an FTA; and

• Pros and cons of an FTA for specific sectors.

Milestones: Preparing for Free Trade

The following developments and events represented milestones in Mexico's move toward modern trade reform, which, in turn, paved the way for negotiations for a more comprehensive FTA:

(1) Mexico joins the General Agreement on Tariffs and Trade (GATT) in August 1986.

Having begun to liberalize its foreign trade regime in 1985, Mexico's accession to GATT provided an even clearer signal to the international community—and to the US in particular—that it was prepared to jettison its import-substitution-oriented trade regime. In its place, the country adopted a liberal growth model based on export promotion and development. Upon joining GATT, Mexico pledged to reduce its maximum tariffs from 100% to 50% and to eliminate prior import permits and licenses that previously prevented foreign companies from competing effectively against their heavily protected Mexican counterparts. Three years later, after signing a bilateral trade and investment understanding with the US, Mexico unilaterally lowered its maximum tariff to 20%. The US government applauded this initiative and petitioned Mexico to bind its tariffs at this rate.

By 1991, on a trade-weighted basis, the country's average tariff was down to about 11%. Duties are assessed on the cif (cost of goods, insurance and freight) value. A 0.8% customs processing fee is added to the cif value, and another 15% national value-added tax is applied to the cumulative cif and processing fee total. Although the addition of the 15% national tax more than doubles the average cost of importing goods into Mexico, it is not considered a trade barrier because it is levied indiscriminately on both domestic and imported goods.

Mexico now has one of the lowest and most liberal tariff schedules among newly industrializing countries—the lowest in Latin America, in fact. GATT membership and the lowering of tariffs foreshadowed greater changes ahead.

(2) A US-Mexico Bilateral Framework Understanding is signed on November 6, 1987.

This first trade and investment understanding between the US and Mexico (the "Framework of Principles and Procedures for Consultation Regarding Trade and Investment Relations") established a mechanism for the two countries to consult with each other on trade issues, resolve potential trade disputes before they occur and negotiate ways to eliminate existing foreign trade barriers. The signing of the understanding generated enormous goodwill among Americans and Mexicans and created the first bilateral mechanism for discussing trade issues on a regular basis, with action agendas aimed at reducing conflict in some of the most disputed areas, such as steel and agricultural trade.

(3) An Understanding Regarding Trade and Investment Facilitation Talks (TIFTs) is signed by the US and Mexican presidents on October 3, 1989.

The TIFTs understanding was signed during President Salinas's first trip to the US. It went beyond the previous Framework Understanding by putting into place a process for negotiating comprehensive trade and investment issues and programs. Instead of only consulting with each other after independently gathering data, both sides, the US and Mexico, agreed to share data before discussions began. Mutual (joint) binational study teams replaced national ones. Under the new understanding, negotiations are held only after the teams have adequately discussed the major issues, in order to avoid "surprises."

The TIFTs have had a number of important outcomes. For Mexico, the talks have yielded greater access for steel and textile exports to the US. Benefiting the US, they have led to a series of presidential decrees, most notably the Automotive Decree of 1989 and the Computer Decree of 1990, which liberalized foreign investment regulations. Banking and insurance regulations have been made less restrictive, as well. In addition, two months after the visit by Salinas during which the TIFTs understanding was signed, Mexico lowered its tariffs beyond the level it had promised when it became a GATT signatory in 1986.

(4) Mexico commits to a free trade agreement in June 1990.

In early 1990, Salinas visited several European capitals. Ostensibly, the purpose of his trip was to obtain foreign investment commitments. He quickly learned that there was minimal interest in Mexico and that most attention focused sharply on Eastern Europe, which was then undergoing convulsive movements to free itself from Communist rule. This trip to Europe convinced Salinas to pursue an FTA to cement ties with the US, and he soon made it clear to President Bush that he was personally committed to joint negotiations.

For Salinas, the logic had become clear. Europe was preoccupied with its unification and the elimination of internal trade barriers targeted for 1992. More important, Eastern Europe seemed destined to become the low-cost production center that would spur future European growth. Salinas felt that Mexico needed to tie its future to the US and Canada.

At a summit meeting in June 1990, Presidents Bush and Salinas gave the go-ahead for negotiation of a comprehensive FTA. The two leaders called for a "gradual and comprehensive" transition to free trade in goods and services via the following objectives:

- Phaseout of import tariffs;
- Elimination or reduction of nontariff barriers, including import quotas, licenses and technical barriers to trade;
- Establishment of clear, binding protection for intellectual property rights;
- Creation of fair and expeditious dispute-settlement procedures; and
- Creation of means to improve and expand the flow of goods, services and investment between the two countries.

(5) The US commits to a free trade agreement in August 1990.

On August 8, 1990, Ambassador Carla Hills, the US trade representative, and Jaime Serra Puche, the Mexican minister of commerce and industrial development, jointly recommended that FTA negotiations be initiated. President Bush publicly accepted the recommendation and in turn announced that he would notify Congress (in September) of the readiness of both countries to enter "fast-track" negotiations for an FTA.

(6) Canada announces support for a North American FTA in February 1991.

In September 1990, Canadian Trade Minister John Crosbie stated that Ottawa would seek to enter the negotiations as a full partner. Mexico was not initially enthusiastic about Canada's participation, primarily because trade between the two countries is minuscule versus that between Mexico and the US. Mexico was also concerned that Canada

---

FTA "Fast-Track" Timetable

• The US administration is required to give Congress a 60-legislative day notification period that it is seeking "fast-track" negotiating authority. President Bush notified Congress on September 25, 1990, of this intention. The 60 days expired at the end of February 1991. However, the authority granted to Bush to use the fast-track procedures was set to expire on June 1, 1991.

• On March 1, 1991, Bush formally submitted a request to extend fast-track authority for two years, giving Congress until May 31, 1991, to deny fast track by majority vote.

• In May, because neither house of Congress voted by majority against fast-track procedures, authority was automatically extended, freeing the administration to negotiate a comprehensive FTA.

• Current plans call for the negotiations to be concluded during 1992, whereas actual implementation would start at the beginning of 1993.

• Once negotiations are basically finished, President Bush will give Congress 90 calendar days' notice in advance of signing the agreement. (The 90-day consulting period permits Congress to suggest changes that Bush can take back to the negotiating parties.)

• President Bush will then sign the FTA and send Congress a draft implementing bill.

• Congress then has 90 legislative days to vote on the bill in its entirety—"yes" or "no"—with no congressional right of filibuster or amendments.

might complicate the process by bringing up unresolved issues from its earlier bilateral FTA talks with the US.

Mexico's fears were allayed at a January 1991 summit meeting of the three nations. Canada agreed to the basic outline for the talks and said it would not hold up the process. On February 5, 1991, the US, Mexico and Canada issued a joint communiqué announcing that the FTA talks would be trilateral, aimed at "fostering sustained economic growth through expanded trade and investment," in a market with 360 million people—40 million more than the EC—and output of $6 trillion p.a. They also agreed that the new accord would remain separate from the FTA between the US and Canada.

(7) **The US Congress extends fast-track negotiating authority to the Bush administration in May 1991.**

Under the fast-track provision of the 1988 Trade Act, the administration is empowered to negotiate an FTA (or other trade agreements) without the fear that Congress will subsequently alter the agreement. The provision binds Congress to vote to approve or disapprove the FTA in its entirety without any changes.

Trends in US-Mexico Trade and Investment

According to official figures released by the US Department of Commerce, US-Mexico trade totaled $56.98 billion in 1990 (customs value), which made Mexico the third leading trading partner to the US. Canada ranked above all other countries in bilateral trade with the US ($169.4 billion), whereas Japan placed second ($135 billion). From 1987 to 1990, US-Mexico trade increased by 68.5%, or at a rate of 22.9% p.a. During the same period, US exports to Mexico grew much faster than imports from Mexico. The result was a dramatic improvement in the US trade balance.

Specifically, US exports to Mexico rose by 95.7% from 1987 to 1990, or at a rate of 31.8% p.a. In dollar figures, the increase was from $14 billion to $27.5 billion. In addition, there was a rise in imports. From 1987 to 1990, US imports from Mexico increased by 49.2%, or at the rate of 22.9% p.a. The dollar value of these imports grew from $19.8 billion to $29.5 billion.

In 1990, the US had a $2 billion trade deficit with Mexico, or approximately one-third of the $5.7 billion deficit recorded three years before. The reason behind the boom in US exports has been the liberalization of Mexico's trade and investment agreements and mandates under the

Table 2-1. Distribution of US Trade With Mexico, 1989
(% of total)

SITC Category	Imports	Exports
Food and live animals	8.9	8.3
Beverages and tobacco	0.9	0.1
Crude materials, except minerals	2.5	6.2
Mineral fuels, lubricants and related products	16.2	3.0
Animal and vegetable oils, fats, waxes	0.1	0.6
Chemicals and related products	2.2	9.1
Manufactured goods	20.2	22.6
Machinery and transportation equipment	44.5	45.0
Commodities	4.5	5.1

SOURCE: OECD, *Foreign Trade by Commodities.*

Salinas administration (see Chapter 6 on the status of the regulatory environment for doing business in Mexico.)

US exports to Mexico are dominated by autoparts, electronics, grain (soybeans, corn and sorghum) and plastic products. Major US imports from Mexico include petroleum, automobiles, televisions, silver, tomatoes, coffee and cattle.

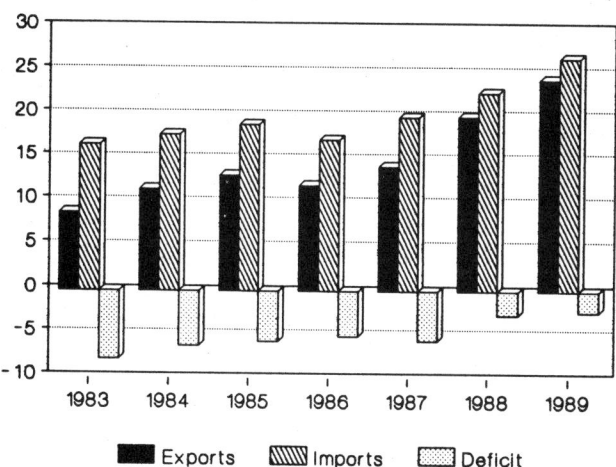

Source: US Commerce Department

Figure 2-1. US trade with Mexico ($ billions). *(Source: US Commerce Department)*

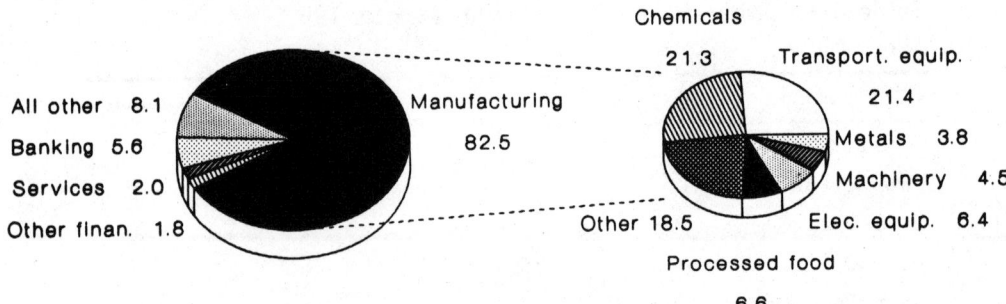

Chemicals

21.3   Transport. equip.

All other 8.1   Manufacturing   21.4

Banking 5.6   82.5   Metals 3.8

Services 2.0   Machinery 4.5

Other finan. 1.8   Other 18.5   Elec. equip. 6.4

Processed food

6.6

Figure 2-2. US investment in Mexico, 1989 (by sector—% of total).

The rapid growth in US exports to Mexico indicates that even without an FTA, significant increases will continue to occur given the enormous needs of Mexico's government to rebuild infrastructure after almost a decade of recession and slack investment. It is also clear that Mexicans prefer products manufactured in the US, both in the capital-intensive and consumer goods industries.

President Salinas has openly courted the foreign business community and given special attention to the relationship between the US and Mexico. Even though new direct foreign investment reached $2.6

Table 2-2. Distribution of Canadian Trade With Mexico, 1989
(% of total)

SITC Category	Imports	Exports
Food and live animals	8.7	20.7
Beverages and tobacco	1.0	0.1
Crude materials, except minerals	5.6	30.8
Mineral fuels, lubricants and related products	4.7	0.6
Animal and vegetable oils, fats, waxes	—	0.4
Chemicals and related products	1.2	4.3
Manufactured goods	11.6	15.0
Machinery and transportation equipment	66.4	26.5
Commodities	0.8	1.5

SOURCE: OECD, *Foreign Trade by Commodities.*

Table 2-3. Foreign Investment in Mexico
($ millions)

	1987	1988	1989*	% of total
United States	13,716	14,958	17,354	62.6
Great Britain	987	1,755	2,009	7.2
West Germany	1,446	1,583	1,798	6.5
Japan	1,170	1,319	1,439	5.2
Switzerland	918	1,004	1,094	3.9
France	596	748	857	3.1
Spain	603	637	746	2.7
Canada	289	323	381	1.4
Sweden	297	330	364	1.3
Netherlands	184	273	355	1.3
Italy	39	41	47	0.2
Others	682	1,113	1,300	4.7
TOTALS	20,927	24,084	27,744	

*estimates
SOURCE: Secofi.

billion in 1990 and continued to grow in 1991, much greater amounts will be needed to achieve the levels of development and the rates of growth that the Mexican president envisions for his country in future years. Recent events, such as the majority purchase of Teléfonos de México (Telmex, the Mexican telephone company) for almost $2 billion by a joint venture led by France Telecom and Southwestern Bell (US), suggest that some of the liberalizing decrees passed during 1989–1990, as well as Mexico's privatization efforts, are already producing the desired results.

The dominant US investors in Mexico are also those involved in the majority of export and import activity. General Motors, Ford and Chrysler are the acknowledged leaders in foreign direct investment, while General Motors and Ford also rank first and second in exports from Mexico to the US. Motorola and Hewlett-Packard (electronics); Kodak (film and electronics) and Xerox (electronics); Deere & Co (agricultural machinery) and Cummins Engine (auto parts) are other leading US firms both producing goods in and trading with Mexico.

Opportunities for US Exporters

Since 1990, the US embassy in Mexico City has focused a great deal of attention on identifying major prospects for US businesses that export their products to Mexico. The following are a list and analysis of these opportunities, by sector and subsector, along with the projected growth rates for each. The forecasts for US exports are also expressed as Mexican imports from the US. (This material was drawn from the "Fiscal Year 1991 Mexico Country Marketing Plan," prepared by the commercial section of the US embassy.)

(1) **Automotive and electronics.** Although these sectors were not mentioned specifically by the embassy, exports of US components to these two areas of the Mexican economy are expected to enjoy continued rapid growth, particularly for maquiladora operations and new automotive engine facilities such as the one that Ford is retooling in Chihuahua (see Chapter 8 on the automotive sector). In 1990, Mexican exports of vehicles alone increased approximately 41% as Mexico shipped 276,859 cars and light trucks abroad. Most went to the US, which means that about 50% of the content of those vehicles was US-manufactured, i.e., Mexican imports of American inputs. The rate of growth for the next three to four years will most likely be 15–20% p.a., including autoparts. The electronics sector, however, is expected to grow more slowly, except in the area of computers (see Chapter 10 on the computer industry in Mexico).

The automotive sector in Mexico is dominated by the US "Big Three" car companies: Ford, General Motors and Chrysler.

(2) **Computers, peripherals and software.** Major subsector opportunities are seen in CAD/CAM software, data transmission equipment and peripherals.

• 1990 estimated sales of US exported merchandise: $349.1 million.
• 1990 estimated Mexican market: $1.1 (embassy figure) to $1.5 billion (estimates by industry experts).
• Projected rate of growth, 1990–1992: 20% p.a. for US producers.
• Very rapid growth is projected in this area because of the April 1990 Computer Decree, which removed impediments to market penetration by foreign exporters. Companies that are producing in Mexico have an advantage because the decree allows them to

(Continued)

import their own products more cheaply than those manufacturers who do not produce in Mexico.

Leading manufacturers in this sector are the US firms IBM and Hewlett-Packard.

(3) Industrial plant design, engineering and maintenance equipment and services. The subsectors in this area that hold the most promise for US exporters and suppliers are engineering services in environmental and quality control areas and hardware and spare parts for machine tools.

- 1990 estimated sales of US exports in Mexico: $400.5 million.
- 1990 estimated Mexican market: $685.9 million.
- Estimated rate of growth: 12% p.a. for US exporters.
- Most of these services and products will be utilized to maintain and upgrade existing industrial facilities. Opportunities will proliferate for the formation of joint ventures, both in the public and private sectors. Consulting, engineering and plant maintenance services will be needed most in the following areas of the economy: metal foundries, electronics, chemicals, metallurgy, pollution control, pulp and paper, agriculture, food processing, pharmaceuticals, textiles, port and road development and petroleum and petrochemicals.

(4) Telecommunications equipment and services. The subsectors with the best opportunities are telephone equipment, satellite communications and equipment, fiber-optic equipment, customer premises equipment and data transmission equipment and services.

- 1990 estimated sales of US exports: $97.1 million.
- 1990 estimated Mexican market size: $452.8 million.
- Estimated rate of growth for US exporters, 1990–1992: 10% p.a.
- As evidenced by the recent privatization of Telmex, the telephone company, improving telecommunications is top priority for the Mexican government. The Salinas team is well aware how critical this sector is to business growth.

(5) Machine tools and metalworking machinery and equipment. The most promising subsectors are numerically controlled machine tools, metalworking tools for the automotive sector and metal presses.

- 1990 estimated sales of US exports: $229.5 million; 70% export share.

(Continued)

- 1990 estimated total Mexican market size: $334.4 million.
- Estimated rate of growth for US exporters, 1990–1992: 12% p.a.
- New automotive and steel projects will drive this sector.

(6) Petrochemical equipment. The sectors slated for growth are MBD technology and equipment, along with petroleum environmental-control equipment.

- 1990 estimated sales of US exports: $270 million.
- 1990 estimated sales for entire Mexican market: $320 million.
- Estimated rate of growth for US exporters, 1990–1992: 5% p.a.
- Although the rate of growth expected is only 5% p.a., the actual size of the investments Mexico will have to make during the next five years to attain this rate is very large. Fourteen petrochemical products that were formerly controlled by Pemex, the state-owned oil monopoly, may now be produced by private companies. This reclassification of petrochemical products (from basic, which are controlled by the government, to secondary, which are open to private investors) is expected to attract $5 billion in fresh foreign investment by 1995.

(7) Process-control equipment. The most promising subsectors in this area of the economy are quality control equipment, process controls for the petroleum and gas industries and process controls for the food processing sector.

- 1990 estimated sales of US exports: $332.7 million.
- 1990 estimated Mexican market sales: $454.1 million.
- Estimated rate of growth for US exports, 1990–1992: 5.3% p.a.

(8) Oil and gas field machinery and equipment. Opportunities will be greatest in offshore exploration equipment and geological analytical equipment.

- 1990 estimated sales of US exports: $162.2 million; 24.2% export share.
- 1990 estimated Mexican market sales: $1.08 million.
- Estimated rate of growth for US exporters, 1990–1992: 2.5% p.a.

(9) Pollution-control equipment and related instruments and services. Water-purification equipment and automatic automobile emission-control analyzers are expected to be the most promising products.

- 1990 estimated sales of US exporters: $14.5 million.
- 1990 estimated Mexican market sales: $207.6 million.
- Estimated growth for US exports, 1990–1992: 20% p.a.

(Continued)

(10) Hotel and restaurant equipment. The best subsectors are hotel management services and hotel personnel training services.

- 1990 estimated sales of US exporters and providers: $40.3 million; 79.8% export share.
- 1990 estimated sales in Mexican market: $220.6 million.
- Estimated growth rate for US exporters and providers, 1990–1992: 15% p.a.

(11) Plastics production machinery and equipment. The subsectors within this industry that show the most promise are injection-molding machines, extrusion equipment, blow-molding machines and plastic resins.

- 1990 estimated US export sales: $30.9 million.
- 1990 estimated Mexican market size: $96.6 million.
- Projected growth rate for US exporters, 1990–1992: 5% p.a.

(12) Mining and construction machinery and equipment. Best subsectors: underground mining machinery and equipment; crushing, pulverizing and screening machinery; hoists, cranes and monorails; and industrial trucks and tractors.

- 1990 estimated sales of US exporters: $51.3 million.
- 1990 estimated Mexican market size: $76.5 million.
- Estimated growth rate for US exporters, 1990–1992: 9% p.a.

Weighing the Impact of an FTA

Advantages

The relative importance of the trading relationship between the US and Mexico, as well as the difference in the relative size of their economies—Mexico GDP is less than 4% that of US GDP—means the effects of an FTA will be much greater for Mexico than for the US. Moreover, relatively low trade barriers already grant significant trade benefits between the two nations, limiting additional benefits to be gained from free trade.

Still, an analysis by the US International Trade Commission concludes that an FTA "will benefit the US economy overall by expanding trade opportunities, lowering prices, increasing competition and improving the ability of US firms to exploit economies of scale. Since these gains are likely to outweigh the costs, the US economy will probably gain on net."*

For US and other foreign companies, the benefits of an FTA must be viewed not simply as those that would result from the elimination of tariffs, but as a continuation of a process of integration between the two economies that has been under way for several years. By furthering this integration—and placing it within a legal framework—as well as supporting the market reform efforts being pursued by the Salinas administration, the FTA will provide additional advantages for both nations. Some of these advantages are as follows:

• **An FTA will increase demand for US products in Mexico.** Economic reforms in Mexico have spurred both economic growth and a rise in imports, most of which (nearly 70%) come from the US. An FTA would encourage greater investment and raise Mexico's domestic growth rate, thereby increasing the benefits to the US. In addition, reforms associated with free trade will improve sales prospects for previously controlled sectors. For example, the liberalization of Mexico's automotive and computer sectors will enable multinational companies in these areas to export more products from the US to Mexico.

• **Certain industries are expected to gain substantially more.** An FTA will have a greater impact on some US industries and companies than it has on the overall US economy. Several types of firms will reap the most benefits, including those concentrated in the border region; those that will gain from the removal of specific trade and investment barriers; those that require a strengthening of intellectual property laws; and those in a position to take advantage of Mexico's accelerated economic growth. These include companies in autoparts, telecommunications equipment, financial services and parts of the agricultural industry.

US **auto parts** manufacturers now have the opportunity to control 100% of their investments in Mexico via trust arrangements, which will make possible the consolidation of this inefficient industry. Joint ventures will become more important as well. An FTA, by further liberalizing trade and nontrade barriers and investment regulations in the sector (including export performance requirements and local-content rules) would bring in large amounts of US investment and, along with it, the modernization of the entire automotive industry as it plays a

---

*US International Trade Commission, "The Likely Impact on the United States of a Free Trade Agreement With Mexico," USITC Investigation No. 332-297, February 1991.

larger role in the integration of the North American manufacturing and marketing. In 1990, for instance, Ford announced a $700 million investment in its Chihuahua plant that will produce up to 20% of all Ford four-cylinder motors for North America. Mexico is already the US's leading supplier of wire harnesses and the third supplier of auto parts after Canada and Japan. It is bound to play a greater role as remaining controls are gradually lifted and competition with Japanese producers heightens in coming years.

The recent privatization of Telmex, the phone company, will appreciably affect Mexico's telecommunications. The expansion and improvement of telephone services will bring in foreign capital and lead to new demand for US telecommunications services. An FTA would complement these changes and considerably increase exports of US information and data processing equipment and software to Mexico.

Financial services and insurance companies could also benefit from an FTA. In 1990, rules governing the sector were loosened to attract greater foreign investment and modernize banking practices. Removal of the remaining nontrade barriers and foreign ownership restrictions could lead to a significant rise in services trade with the US and an increase in US investments in banking and insurance. Such changes should follow shortly after the completion of the privatization of Mexico's commercial banks in 1992.

Whereas many US **agricultural** producers will be adversely affected by the FTA (see section on disadvantages in this chapter), some producers will benefit from a market opening, particularly producers of cattle (livestock) and poultry; dairy products; deciduous fruit trees; oilseeds; grain and feed; and alcoholic beverages. These sectors are currently the source of trade friction, since US producers have distinctive competitive advantages in these areas of the economy but face entry barriers in Mexico.

• An FTA would give many of the reforms undertaken by the Salinas government the status of law. Under Mexican law, the FTA would have international treaty status, equivalent to Mexican federal law issued by Congress. Any federal law conflicting with the FTA would be overridden. The provisions could not be amended without the consent of the treaty's other parties. This assures a level of permanence and continuity that could not be achieved solely through legislation. Under an FTA, foreign investors would have the security of knowing their investments were protected by law, and this would produce a sense of permanence to liberalization in Mexico.

• **An FTA would permit US manufacturers continued access to a pool of relatively cheap labor that would, in turn, allow them to increase in-**

vestments in Mexico in labor-intensive operations. These operations are the kind that have fueled maquiladora growth. Maquiladoras, which are becoming increasingly large, modern enterprises that work in tandem with their production-sharing partners in the US, would continue to be popular under an FTA.

• **US jobs might be increased in certain sectors, or at least fewer would be lost under an FTA than if production were transferred to the Far East.** Experts claim that for every $1 billion in exports, 40,000 US jobs are created. This means that since 1987, more than 520,000 jobs were produced in the US as a result of expanded exports to Mexico. Moreover, it can be argued that even when labor-intensive manufacturing facilities move to Mexico, about 50% of the components incorporated into the final products are US-sourced. If similar jobs were transferred to the Far East, US components would probably not be utilized. Considering the forecasts for brisk export growth to Mexico over the next few years, it is likely that many new employment opportunities will be created in the US. These will tend to be high-skill-level jobs, whereas the new positions created in Mexico will be primarily at low-skill levels.

• **An FTA will enable the US to compete more effectively against other regional trading blocs, notably the EC and the Pacific Rim.** This will occur via a further lowering of production costs and an exploitation of the complementary elements of the US and Mexican economies. In the automotive industry, for example, integrating Mexican production with US manufacturing and marketing strategies has provided important competitive benefits. Low-cost, high-quality products assembled in Mexico and reexported to the US have permitted Ford, General Motors and Chrysler to compete with Japanese imports by producing niche vehicles that otherwise would have been much more costly.

• **An FTA would induce further US and foreign investments in Mexico and would make it possible to give strategic objectives a North American focus.** Because an FTA will be negotiated across the board and phased in over several years, the comprehensiveness of such an agreement, along with Canadian participation, will lend an urgency and permanence to it that individual accords among specific industries do not permit. An FTA among Mexico, the US and Canada would make North America the largest free trade community in the world. The total trade for 1990 among these three partners was about $230 billion, total GDP was more than $6 trillion and the combined population was greater than 362 million.

For Mexico, an FTA's advantages will include a strengthening of eco-

Table 2-4. Key Country Indicators, 1989

	Mexico	Canada	US
Population (millions)	81	26	251
GDP (US$ billions)	215	560	5,515
Per capita GDP (US$)	2,654	21,177	21,992
Per capita energy consumption (kg oil equivalent)	1,305	9,683	7,655
Calories per capita (daily)	3,132 '	3,462	3,645
Imports from other two as % of total	69.8	64.8	23.7
Breakdown:	Canada 1.8	Mexico 1.2	Mexico 5.6
	US 68.0	US 63.6	Canada 18.1
Exports to other two as % of total	70.5	71.1	28.4
Breakdown:	Canada 1.2	Mexico 0.4	Mexico 6.9
	US 69.3	US 70.7	Canada 21.5

SOURCE: Banco de México, International Monetary Fund.

nomic restructuring, industrial modernization, greater access to foreign markets, technology transfer, increased foreign investment, infrastructure development and enhanced employment prospects.

Disadvantages

The FTA could, however, potentially create problems in certain areas, including:

• **Mexico's low-wage labor could spark job losses or downward pressure on wages in labor-intensive industries.** Unions, especially the United Auto Workers (UAW) and the American Federation of Labor and Congress of Industrial Organizations (AFL-CIO), have argued that an FTA will lead to substantial job losses in the US and to a lower standard of living for workers. As a result, the unions have identified the FTA as their major issue for 1991. They are adamantly opposed to it and are lobbying Congress against it.

Although the unions' broadside against an FTA is exaggerated, an accord is likely to dislocate jobs in some industries. Most likely to be negatively affected are highly labor-intensive industries such as household glassware; footwear; textiles and apparel; some types of auto parts; and fruits and vegetables. There will be little or no effect on overall employment levels in the US, however, and no effect in more capital-intensive sectors.

• **Specific agricultural sectors will need to be restructured.** In testimonies before the US Congress, many experts on US agriculture have asserted that negotiations in this area under an FTA will be the most difficult. In the fruit and vegetable trade, Mexican exports are already subject to very high tariffs during the "high" winter season in the US—the period in which tariffs reach 25%—because American growers are at their low production point. The Florida Fruit and Vegetable Growers Association has emphasized before Congress that it would be extraordinarily burdensome to compete with Mexican fruits and vegetables if current tariffs are reduced, let alone removed entirely.

The categories and types of products most affected will be citrus fruits, avocados, tomatoes, cauliflower, fruits in general, nuts and food processors. Representatives and lobbyists from these sectors maintain that vastly cheaper Mexican labor and the higher health standards upheld by US growers make it impossible for US producers to face Mexican competition.

• **The effects of an FTA will fall unevenly on the US.** Border states like Texas and Arizona will benefit much more than the states in the Midwest. Some evidence suggests that smaller US firms in the Heartland might lose some jobs in the labor-intensive areas, while businesses in the Southwest border states, linked geographically and economically to Mexico, are likely to grow significantly.

• **Greater environmental damage and lower safety and health standards are a risk.** Environmentalists have joined forces with labor in lobbying against an FTA with Mexico, because they believe that Mexicans have much lower environmental standards for their industry. They argue that under an FTA it will be extremely difficult to control "polluters" on the border; to them the FTA would be tantamount to sanctioning damage to the border environment and will make it much more difficult to police the maquiladoras, which they cite as serious violators.

In addition, the environmentalists and organized labor are concerned with workplace safety and health inspection standards in the food industry (see box).

US "Greens" Flex Muscles

Environmental politics has entered the trade arena. By mounting a formidable challenge to the George Bush administration's plans to open talks with Mexico on a free trade agreement, US environmentalists seem to have ensured that ecological considerations will become part of US trade policy. Besides the FTA, this may include both future GATT negotiations and discussions under Bush's Enterprise for the Americas Initiative framework. "The arena of international agreements is the new frontier of consumer and environmental work," says Lori Wallach, a lobbyist with the Washington-based Public Citizen's Congress Watch. High-ranking GATT officials confirm that environmental matters are likely to become a major element in the next round of multilateral trade negotiations, which will probably begin at the end of the 1990s.

The environmental lobby is asking some tough questions concerning the effects of a US-Mexico FTA on the environment. After years of development, the border region is suffering from serious air and water pollution. Most pollutants come from in-bond plants making auto parts and assembling consumer electronics. Against this backdrop, environmentalists raise the following concerns:

• **Mexico's already damaged environment could be further compromised by local companies rushing to take advantage of access to US markets.** Stepped-up production by steel makers, chemical manufacturers, timber firms, mining companies and farmers seeking to increase exports of winter produce could further denude the Mexican landscape and add to water, air and soil pollution.

• **US firms may head south of the border to evade rigorous domestic standards, such as those governing waste removal. This could provide a competitive advantage over companies remaining at home.** A 1990 Mexican government study revealed that more than 1,000 US-owned plants now in Mexico generate toxic waste, but only 30% have reported, as required by law, how they dispose of it. Only 19% could show they handle the wastes correctly.

• **Mexico will not have the funds to counter a new assault on its environment.** In 1990, critics point out, Sedue, Mexico's environmental protection agency, had a budget that was only a fraction of what some US states spend on environmental enforcement.

(Continued)

• **Harmonizing environmental standards to avoid trade-pattern distortions could lead to looser US regulations.** Regulations that could be affected include those governing pollution, food products, safety and health.

Environmentalists want assurances that Mexico will hold US investors to rigorous standards and that neither natural resources will be depleted nor the atmosphere fouled to win short-term economic gains. All this "ties into the notion that we don't want countries dealing with us to do so at the expense of environmental values," says Frank P. Grad, professor of environmental law at Columbia Law School.

Labor enters the debate

On May 31, 1991, the Bush administration released an "action plan" for negotiating the FTA. The plan was part of its lobbying effort to get Congress to approve an extension of fast-track negotiating authority. It aims to counter the fears of environmental and organized-labor groups that are either trying to block an FTA or seeking assurances that environmental safeguards and job-security commitments will be included in a final agreement. Bush's document proposes the following:

• **An adequate transition period for the elimination of tariffs and nontariff barriers.** A 10-year phase-in period was provided under the US-Canada FTA, but some US industries, such as horticulture—one of the most vulnerable to competition, according to the US Department of Commerce—have requested a period as long as 15-20 years.

• **The right to increase or reimpose tariffs temporarily** in response to a substantial rise in imports that threatens to harm a specific industry.

• **An increase in the 50% domestic content rule** in existence under the US-Canada FTA, and its extension to Mexico.

• **Adequate funding for programs to provide job training** to US workers displaced by foreign competition.

• **Commitment to design a comprehensive environmental-protection plan for the border region,** and a promise not to "water down" existing US health and safety standards under an FTA. In addition, a study will be conducted to determine the environmental impact of an FTA.

• **Cooperation by the two governments in monitoring labor conditions** and enforcing existing labor regulations.

Trilateral FTA: An Agenda for Canadian Businesses

As negotiations for a North American free trade agreement unfold, Canadian business planners should begin assessing the consequences of new competition in their principal foreign market—the US—as well as in Canada. Because of their limited investment in and trade experience with Mexico, Canadian corporate executives need to do a quick study of the potential for job dislocation, as well as for new opportunities under a trilateral trade pact.

Mexico-Canada trade amounts to less than $2 billion p.a.—only a ripple compared with Canada and Mexico trade with the US or with Japan and newly industrialized East Asian countries. Moreover, unlike their more labor-cost-conscious brethren south of the 49th parallel, Canadian managers have not rushed to take advantage of inexpensive Mexican labor by establishing maquiladora plants or incorporate low-cost Mexican components into Canadian products; nor have they exploited the sales opportunities created by the push to modernize the Mexican economy. In fact, Canada ranks only eighth among foreign investors in Mexico, having less than $800 million at play.

Taking action for the future

Trade experts assert that, with the advantages of free trade, Mexico-based production could pirate Canadian market shares in both the US and Canada if Canadian firms do not step up their trade with and investment in Mexico now. Free trade will afford Mexico-based producers considerable new opportunities in sectors in which the US or Canada currently maintain high tariffs on some products, or in sectors where they use some other device to restrain imports—e.g., textiles, apparel, footwear, leather goods, furniture, petrochemicals, plastics, steel, nonferrous metals, telecommunications equipment, home appliances, cosmetics, recreational boats and fishing equipment. Canadian producers in many of these industries are already reeling from free trade with the US following the signing of a Canada-US FTA in 1989.

Like their US counterparts, Canadian manufacturers requiring moderately trained labor and competing directly with suppliers in East Asia may find that Mexico offers the best options for competitive production and sourcing. Some suggestions for Canadian firms are listed on pages 30 and 31:

(Continued)

- **Get in early.** Japanese and European reluctance to jump into Mexico presents a window of opportunity for Canadian firms. Canadian industries could be threatened as free trade encourages greater foreign investment in Mexico by the Japanese, Germans and others. To date, skepticism about the durability of Mexican economic reforms has kept Japanese and European investors on the sidelines as US MNCs have profited from Mexico City's liberalization efforts. The FTA would allay their fears and could foster a wave of investment by companies outside North America.

- **Consider forming an alliance with a US firm already in Mexico.** Such an alliance would compensate for lack of experience in the country. Canadians will find that experience in other Caribbean and Latin American markets may not carry over easily to Mexico, as Mexico is culturally unique and is developing its own special brand of free market economics. Prompt action is needed, however, for Canadian firms to get a leg up on Japanese multinational firms that may find Mexican ways as inscrutable as North Americans find Japanese business customs. By joining forces with US companies, Canadians may find friendly guides to a country eager to diversify its economic relationships, but not in the direction of the Asian superpower.

- **Take advantage of Mexico's appetite for North American goods and services.** The process of economic modernization will pick up steam after the US recession ends and tariffs begin to drop. Mexico will present important market opportunities for many durable goods and industrial-consulting services, including oil and gas machinery and equipment; quality control systems; pollution-control equipment; engineering services; machine tools; and metalworking machinery. These are all areas in which Canadian firms possess significant capabilities. Mexicans, unlike their counterparts in East Asia, have eagerly snapped up US goods and services, and these preferences should easily extend to Canadian products. Moreover, Mexico's desire to diversify its trading partners may give Canadian suppliers an advantage over other producers, especially if they begin developing Mexican markets before the recession ends and free trade begins.

- **Prepare some speedy and thorough analyses in advance of formal trade negotiations.** The scope of the market adjustments and opportunities created for Canadian companies under a trilateral FTA will

(Continued)

be influenced by the way in which the treaty is structured and implemented. Technical details such as a tariff-cutting timetable and general safeguards and rules regarding foreign investment screening will be critical. Both the US and Canadian negotiating teams will depend heavily on private sector consultations to alert them to the particular concerns of domestic industries. If Canadian businesses do not take action soon, however, their inexperience in Mexico could prove to be a definite liability in the free trade talks, since US companies will be better able to identify specific objectives for negotiators.

The Logic of an FTA

The signing of an FTA with Mexico appears to be inevitable. Rejection of the free trade agreement would have to be based on politics, since the Mexican economy is much too small to produce the kind of job dislocations in the US that organized labor is fearing. The Mexican economy has become increasingly integrated into the manufacturing and marketing strategies of major US firms, and the competitive advantages that such integration produces, particularly in labor-intensive operations, are growing more important as foreign competition in the US intensifies.

Moreover, trade with Mexico, which has grown rapidly in recent years, is critical to US economic growth. Although the US had a $2 billion trade deficit with Mexico in 1990, this deficit is substantially lower than it was three years earlier and is minuscule when compared with the US deficit with its other two leading trading partners. In 1990 the US had a $42.7 billion trade deficit with Japan and a $13 billion deficit with Canada. If the US content of maquiladoras imports is included, the US does not have a deficit with Mexico at all.

An FTA would allow the US, Mexico and Canada to further exploit the synergies among the three economies. Such an accord would send a clear message to North America's competitors throughout the world that it is ready to strategically defend its business interests. The region would then be in a position to retaliate if other trading blocs should legislate trading rules that discriminated against the US.

If an FTA is defeated, the US will simply have lost a powerful opportunity to forge a continental identity that acknowledges the complementarity of the US and Mexican economies, i.e., capital and labor intensiveness. There are also significant political benefits that each will derive from such an agreement. Mexico will not only gain access to more US capital investment, thereby spurring domestic growth and lifting living standards, but it will also have its political role in the new North America legitimized. The Bush administration will have established stronger ties with an ally, an achievement that could be presented to the US public as creating a new source of economic growth for business and as a triumph for North American diplomacy as well.

Even though the merits of an FTA outweigh the disadvantages, this does not suggest that negotiating such an accord is easy. Different industries and interest groups are affected in distinct ways and are striving to retain their own specific advantages or cushion the negative impact that an FTA might have on their sectors. Other, forward-looking companies are seeking to take full advantage of the new operating conditions in the "new" Mexico. The implications that an FTA holds for different corporate strategies for Mexico are discussed in the next chapter. Company case studies provided therein, along with sectoral profiles contained in Part III of this book, are designed to help corporate decision makers decide for themselves how their businesses will fare and how they should respond to the opportunities opening before them.

3
Corporate Strategy in the New Mexico

Spurred by a rash of probusiness and market reforms in Mexico, executives from multinational firms are busily revamping their global business strategies in anticipation of the emergence of what is likely to become the largest free trading area in the world, encompassing Canada, the US and Mexico.

Designing the correct strategy, whether for production or marketing, will be a complex task. On the one hand, executives will have to realize that, for decades, many of their Mexican subsidiaries have been cut off from the international market and the technological forces that are strengthening competitors and shaping production and distribution patterns in other parts of the world. As a result, many Mexico-based operations do not have the levels of production, technology or product quality they would need to effectively compete in a global market without significant restructuring. On the other hand, Mexico can offer firms substantial cost savings through access to inexpensive labor and ready supplies of energy, raw materials and semifinished inputs. Also, within the context of a free trade agreement, companies will have unobstructed access to the world's largest marketplace.

For the first time, international executives are able to make Mexico-based operations an integral part of their sourcing, production and marketing strategies for North America and the rest of the globe. For example, Mexican enterprises can serve as reliable nodes in cross-border manufacturing logistics networks, with companies placing operations in Mexico to maximize cost efficiencies. In many cases, these will be operations that contain a significant labor element. In other instances, besides having an important labor component, the ventures will be located in Mexico to take advantage of a particular market. Management may decide, for instance, to establish a finishing operation on Mexico's west coast to serve the Asia-Pacific region.

The inclusion of Mexico in companies' global strategies will change not only what corporations produce in that country—and how they produce it—but also the nature of operations in other regions. Many firms will want to relocate divisions or plants to Mexico to take advantage of what such a site has to offer. This shift in orientation will provide the possibility of vastly increasing production scales, as well as allow Mexico-based operations to fully participate, for the first time, in efficiency-maximizing production planning, such as just-in-time operations.

Besides production advantages, the new Mexico will offer fresh marketing opportunities. The North American free trade agreement (FTA) will bring an additional 80 million consumers into the region's marketplace. Of course, with 80% of revenues in the hands of 10% of the population, income distribution in Mexico is sharply skewed toward the low end. Although this mix should slowly change as Mexican labor becomes more fully integrated into the North American-wide manufacturing production systems—bringing about a higher standard of living for workers—executives will have to devise creative marketing strategies to be able to reach Mexico's highly segmented markets.

At the same time, competition for Mexico's broader and more dynamic market will become fierce in the absence of trade barriers against companies in North America. Many items will no longer be produced in Mexico when they can be imported less expensively. The market will be exposed to more sophisticated, higher-quality products than had previously been thought possible. The number of different firms operating in Mexico via local manufacturing or distribution operations will increase tremendously, as will the array of products from which Mexicans will be able to choose. Consequently, the same customer-statisfaction standards prompting improvements in product quality and driving marketing campaigns in industrialized countries will have to be employed in Mexico as well.

Fresh Approaches to the Mexican Market

MNC planners are now poring over strategy papers trying to devise the best approaches to what are apt to be fiercely competitive Mexican and North American markets in the 1990s. Although strategies differ, virtually all executives interviewed agree that, from now on, Mexico must be viewed within the context of their companies' larger North American operations. They foresee country markets in the region melding and creating nascent markets, new customers and intensified competition. The tactics for meeting these challenges range from rationalizing marketing and manufacturing activities to increasing the focus on customer needs and reorganizing to meet those needs more efficiently and profitably.

Executives point out several key factors as shaping their firms' strategies in today's Mexican business environment, including:

- Economic reactivation after a decade (the 1980s) of stagnation;

- Increased competition, both domestic and foreign;

- Distinct pressures to maximize value and minimize costs on a global basis;

- A need for flexible and fast sourcing, production and distribution;

- A critical need to source intraregionally to improve market share and profitability;

- A shift in supplier relationships, reflecting open borders and increased competition;

- Improved intellectual property protection;

- Changing, more sophisticated consumer purchasing habits;

- An urgent push to improve quality; and

- Competitive shakeouts among companies and industries.

Checklist: Preparing for an FTA

Companies must consider external and internal factors when revising corporate investment, manufacturing and marketing strategies in response to developments in Mexico. External factors include customer needs, tastes and customs; political stability; economic issues such as price controls; legal factors, e.g., foreign investment regulations, taxation and intellectual property protection; and concerns such as labor, energy and construction costs and availability of raw materials.

(Continued)

Internal factors include various elements of a competitive strategy, including product specialization (linewidth, targeted customer segments and geographic coverage), brand identification, distribution channel selection, product quality, technological leadership, degree of vertical integration, cost position, service, leverage and relationships with the host government and parent company.

Companies should ask some of the following questions when assessing the impact of a free trade agreement on their business:

(1) What can or should be done to prepare for a free trade agreement?

(2) Should we rationalize our production strategy for North America? Why and how?

(3) What is our lowest-cost production point?

(4) Where are our lowest-cost suppliers?

(5) How can we maximize our current capacities?

(6) Which operations may become redundant?

(7) Should we concentrate production in one country?

(8) How large is the potential new market?

(9) What new products can we introduce in each country?

(10) Where are distribution networks the strongest?

(11) What can we do to improve the supply and quality of inputs and packaging materials?

(12) How can we best defend a product in the local market?

(13) What are the advantages and disadvantages of working with other affiliates?

(14) What are our complementary strengths?

(15) How can we coordinate marketing efforts?

(16) What differences in market tastes will inhibit rationalization of production throughout the area?

(17) How do transportation costs stack up?

(18) Do we have any new competition and, if so, what is it doing?

(19) How can we better monitor the competition?

(20) How will pricing change once the borders are completely open?

Profiting From the New Environment

Companies will adopt a variety of approaches toward today's business environment in Mexico. For some, strategy will involve a more long-term commitment to manufacturing in Mexico, perhaps making it a site for global sourcing. For firms in labor-intensive industries, relocating product lines to the country to take advantage of its low-cost structure will be preferred, especially once an FTA is in place. Other firms may choose to cancel investments or downsize operations in Mexico in the wake of the lifting of import restrictions, and opt instead to service the market through distributors. Many companies will use a mixture of approaches. Some operations may close down while others are strengthened. Certain products will be imported and others made locally, based on cost effectiveness.

Some of the ways in which companies are responding to Mexico's market reforms and preparing for the North American regional market are discussed below and on the following pages.

Implementing quality-improvement programs

Companies operating in Mexico's protected markets did not always have strong incentives to achieve world quality standards prior to the import opening. In the last several years, firms have focused on improving not only the quality of the product, but also its packaging, distribution and associated customer service. Often, companies are sourcing abroad as a way to upgrade product quality. With a further drop in duties on goods imported from the US, this practice is likely to increase.

In the view of one executive with Mexico's Grupo ICI, subsidiary of Imperial Chemical Industries (ICI), the British chemical company, "total quality is the most important force shaping the marketplace of the 1990s." Factors contributing to total quality include product excellence, responsiveness to consumer needs, organizational strength, strong relationships with suppliers, effective cost reduction and improved employee motivation.

A commitment to quality will be of particular importance under the FTA. According to the ICI executive, meeting international standards for product quality will be crucial for local as well as mutinational companies in Mexico in developing and maintaining a competitive edge. "After the FTA, labor-intensive companies with top-quality products and excellent customer service will continue to be successful," predicts the executive. "But firms that do not produce high-quality items and that require leading edge technology will not succeed unless they source the technology abroad and pay royalties, or merge or form joint ventures with other companies that have such technology."

Emphasizing customer satisfaction

Customer satisfaction will be essential to success in the new marketplace. Marketing strategies will have to be revamped to better target customers and identify their needs, and client service will have to be upgraded.

Cummins Engine (US) is one company whose dominant market position is being threatened by market liberalization and trade reform. Stressing product quality and service are important aspects of the company's competitive strategy, and it is adjusting its distributor agreements to enhance these key elements. In one case, the firm moved to transfer business away from a distributor that was not responding to corporate demands. Greater use of computerized systems is also being used to support the company's strong service network (see case example in this chapter).

Creating a Customer-Oriented Culture

As markets globalize and competition for consumer dollars intensifies, companies should keep in mind the following:

- Old rules no longer apply;
- World-class quality and excellent customer service are essential to success;
- Globalization will create new customers and new competitors;
- No single company can profitably compete for all customer groups;
- Softening national borders does not necessarily mean that customer needs in different countries are the same;
- Companies must rethink who and where their customers will be, and what products and service they will need;
- Concentrate on carefully targeted markets and customers;
- Reorganize to meet customer needs efficiently and profitably;
- Place customers' interest first, the company's second;
- Ask customers what they want;
- Treat local customers with the same deference as those outside the country;
- Monitor customer satisfaction on an ongoing basis; and
- Keep in touch with customers regularly.

Source: Grupo ICI.

Intraregional sourcing

As economic and trade barriers fall, new business opportunities are being created. Liberalized foreign investment regulations, privatization and reduced government intervention, not just in Mexico, but throughout Latin America, are leading companies to reassess their investment strategies. Regional rationalization of operations and markets is becoming increasingly desirable as a means to achieve economies of scale, increase efficiency, decrease cost and cover all markets in the region. According to one executive with a chemical company, "If you're competing on a regional scale, it will not work if you have different strategies for different countries. Companies are looking to globalize and increase volume in their production unit by taking advantage of economies of scale, which means rationalizing operations—for example, having one plant instead of three to supply the entire region."

Developing new and closer relations with suppliers

Along with the opening of the borders for finished consumer goods, restrictions and duties on imported ingredients or components have also been reduced. Although some companies have begun to source outside of Mexico, many prefer to work with the existing network of local suppliers. Company X, a subsidiary of a major food processing company, has begun to import some of its ingredients but has placed special emphasis on working with its local suppliers. "We are competing in an open market, so we insist on international prices for raw materials. We believe that local suppliers can be competitive in price and quality, but we have to convince them that the rules of the game have changed," explains the firm's director general.

One benefit derived from working more closely with local suppliers has been the discovery of new products that the subsidiary can purchase on behalf of its parent company. "We are actively considering a number of products that we may source to our parent company or to other US companies because of the time we spent with our suppliers," adds the director general.

According to an executive with Grupo ICI, companies will increasingly look for suppliers who can do more than just deliver essential goods in a timely manner. Suppliers will have to be partners in implementing total-quality programs and developing products that satisfy customer needs. "Manufacturers are going to be looking very carefully at opportunities to acquire—or form joint ventures with—suppliers of key raw materials, producing a cost-effective vertical integration," he says.

Upgrading technology at Mexican operations

Recently liberalized technology transfer regulations will allow greater investment in up-to-date technology and development of new products.

For many years, investors had asked for expanded protection for industrial designs, utility models, trademarks, service marks and trade secrets, as well as stiffer penalties and enforcement. Now, investment has been greatly facilitated by a new law governing industrial property rights, passed in June 1991. The legislation provides a much broader scope of patent coverage and other protection than existed under the previous law. In addition, a new copyright law was passed in July 1991, granting expanded protection for software producers, the recording industry and other holders of copyrights.

Learning to survive competitive shakeouts

One effect of regionalization and more open borders will be amplified competition among both companies and industries, with more losers likely to emerge than under the old business environment. Those companies with superior technology, market position, cost structure or other key factors should survive, whereas others may be forced to merge with other firms or be liquidated. Executives point out that firms in several sectors are potentially at risk, including those that produce agricultural equipment, consumer goods, chemicals, electronics, pollution-control equipment, processed food, tires and toys.

Sonoco Products (US), the paper- and plastic-products manufacturer, has adopted a range of strategies to help it survive competition not just in Mexico but throughout Latin America. Among these tactics are acquisitions, vertical integration, cost reduction, diversification, upgrading technology, revamped strategic planning, regional integration and enhanced competitive intelligence (see case example in this chapter). Other companies have strengthened their positions by rationalizing production and divesting uncompetitive businesses, or by forming strategic alliances.

Forming a North American division

Hewlett-Packard is one company that is reorganizing its corporate structure in line with the trend toward regional markets. Hewlett-Packard Intercontinental, the corporate division that currently coordinates operations outside of the US and Europe, has created a subdivision called Hewlett-Packard Americas. Under the scheme, all activities in the US, Canada and Mexico will soon be reporting to a single office. Eventually, all Latin American operations will be included, and the intercontinental arm will be replaced with three separate divisions: Americas, Europe and Asia-Pacific (see case example in Chapter 10).

Setting up a world-class manufacturing center

Manufacturers in many industries, notably the automotive, electronics, apparel and other firms producing in Mexico's maquiladoras, have selected Mexico as a base for global sourcing. The US consumer goods manufacturer Black & Decker, which rationalized its global manufacturing operations several years ago, operates a global manufacturing center for clothes irons in Mexico. The facility, which today is the company's lowest-cost, top-quality production site, has helped boost the company's competitive position worldwide. Although the FTA is impelling the company to focus even greater attention on quality and the revamping of its operations directed at the local market, Mexico will remain a critical operation within the corporation's global strategy (see case example in this chapter).

In the automotive sector, Ford and General Motors (both US) are leaders in using Mexico as a world-class export base. Ford's success in producing world-class cars in Mexico has led competitors Nissan (Japan) and Volkswagen (Germany) to announce billion-dollar investment plans to manufacture entry-level vehicles for export. Ford's advantage, of course, is that it has already positioned itself with US consumers. In addition, under an FTA, there may be strict North American content rules of origin that will prevent Nissan vehicles made in Mexico from freely entering the US unless these requirements are satisfied.

The computer industry is following a pattern very similar to the one set by the automotive sector. Companies such as Hewlett-Packard and IBM (both US) have begun to use Mexico as the sole source for specific products or to rapidly increase their exports, particularly of microcomputers. As in the case of the automotive industry, computer manufacturers are experiencing fast growth encouraged by more liberal sectoral regulations.

Forming strategic alliances

Ford is successfully pursuing a strategy that utilizes Mexico as an export base for its entry-level vehicles, while taking advantage of the liberalization of the competitive rules in Mexico and the booming domestic market. The firm is also a trendsetter in its strategic alliance with a Japanese competitor, Mazda.

Faced with the difficulties of producing a small, entry-level vehicle—which has the thinnest profit margin—in the US, Ford formed an alliance with Mazda in which the Japanese firm was to play a leading role in the design and production of subcompacts for the global market. Given the relative cheapness of Mexican labor and the problem of making competitive subcompacts in the US equivalent to Japanese models, Ford and Mazda put their alliance to work in Mexico.

At first they produced only Mercury Tracers built on the platform Mazda used for its 323 model. Today, however, Ford manufactures Mercury Tracers and Ford Escorts in Mexico, exclusively for export to the US and Canada. Mexico is the sole worldwide source of the Tracer, whereas the country produces 15–20% of the Escort's total global output.

To complement its export strategy, Ford is importing more upscale, luxury vehicles (e.g., the Lincoln Town Car) to benefit from growing demand in Mexico. Sale of Lincolns, Explorer utility vehicles and Aerostar minivans complements Ford's Mexican domestic strategy, which has been to serve the more affluent customer.

Downsizing Mexican operations

For some companies, integrating Mexico into a global strategy will mean cutting back on local production and instead focusing on distribution of imported goods. Faced with a poor cost structure and supplier problems at its Mexican manufacturing facilities, Company B recently transformed its subsidiary into a sales and marketing operation. By sourcing from the company's other global manufacturing facilities, management has been able to fend off the threat of new competitors in the local market and boost both domestic sales volume and market share (see case study in this chapter).

Setting up a distribution operation

Mexico's import opening led Amway International (US) to set up marketing operations in Mexico, a country it had long considered promising. The consumer-products firm, which specializes in direct sales, established its headquarters in Monterrey and distribution centers in various cities. Amway has experienced faster growth in Mexico than in any of the nearly 30 countries in which it has operations (see case example in this chapter).

Taking advantage of growth in consumer demand

Firms in traditionally protected consumer product markets in Mexico have watched import competition drastically reduce their market share. Imports, however, have often stimulated consumer demand and dramatically increased the size of the market. By taking advantage of strong brand franchises—while making investments to improve quality—companies can boost sales even as their percentage of the market declines. Because per capita consumption is low in many consumer markets, complete elimination of import duties (combined with extensive growth) could fuel greater expansion for many products.

Local acquisition

US-based Quaker Oats' Mexican subsidiary, Fábrica de Chocolates La Azteca, acquired Chocolates Larin from Richardson-Vicks (US) to help complement its existing lines in the confectionery chocolate market.

The move allowed the Quaker Oats subsidiary to expand into different areas of the confectionary chocolate market and better compete against new import brands. The purchase also boosted its production capacity, thus providing economies of scale needed for Fábrica de Chocolates La Azteca to defend its competitive position.

Another company that has benefited from a local acquisition is US-based PepsiCo, Inc. In 1990, Sabritas, PepsiCo's snack food subsidiary, acquired Gamesa, Mexico's largest manufacturer of cookies and pasta. The purchase solidified PepsiCo's leading role in the $1 billion Mexican snack market by bringing together a firm that produces salty snacks (Sabritas) with a firm that produces sweet snacks (Gamesa).

A number of MNCs have also taken advantage of the government's privatization drive to purchase consumer-goods-oriented firms. Unilever (UK) subsidiary Anderson-Clayton acquired several food processing plants when Conasupo, the state-owned food distribution agency, was privatized, whereas local partners of PepsiCo and Coca-Cola bought various sugar mills from the government.

Regaining majority control

Besides considering acquisition of independent companies, foreign firms are repurchasing shares of their own subsidiaries from Mexican partners or shareholders. This has been facilitated by changes in Mexico's foreign investment rules permitting majority ownership by foreign companies.

One example is Ralston Purina, which by late 1990 had succeeded in repurchasing nearly 100% of the shares of its six Mexican affiliates (having previously held only 49%). This move has permitted the company to pursue a fresh strategy for its Mexico-based operations, founded on restructuring to build on those areas of the economy in which the company can maintain the strongest competitive advantage possible over the long term (see case example in this chapter).

Other companies that have regained majority control in their Mexican operations include the industrial company Union Carbide and the retailer Woolworth (both US). When Mexican financier Roberto Hernández and his investment house Accival sold off interests in a number of joint venture firms (in order to accumulate capital to get involved in telephone, banking and other state privatization ventures), Union Carbide bought back its shares. It was thereby able to resolve long-standing management problems at its subsidiary.

As a result of the same selling off of shares by local investors, Unilever, which was already involved in acquiring formerly state-owned holdings, purchased other Mexican-owned companies from the Visa Group, a local industrial conglomerate.

Reassessing sourcing strategies

Quaker Oats is now actively involved in identifying all ingredients being utilized in its facilities in the US and comparing their quality and cost with those inputs available in Mexico. The performance of both the Mexican and US manufacturing operations will be assessed by the same standards, which are based on where the product can be produced most cost efficiently, according to the director general of Fábrica de Chocolates La Azteca, the company's Mexican subsidiary. "We are evaluating the opportunities to export semi-processed raw materials from Mexico that could be integrated into US processing," he says.

Spurred by free trade, another global food products company, Company A, is undergoing a similar process. It is using a product-by-product approach to identify the comparative strengths and weaknesses of its operations in Mexico and the US. The analysis will later be applied to Canada as well. Company A management already envisions certain cost advantages in using US operations to supply northern Mexico, while leaving the plant in Mexico City to handle the rest of the country (see case example in this chapter).

Entering a new market through a joint venture

Market liberalization is encouraging the entry of new players in several sectors, many through joint ventures. The government is even encouraging highly innovative joint ventures in the agriculture sector. In a unique alliance arrangement, foreign-owned agribusiness firms are joining forces with holders of collective land parcels, or ejidos. Gamesa, Mexico's largest cookie and pasta producer—acquired by PepsiCo in 1990—is raising beans and wheat on 5,000 acres of land that consist mostly of ejidos. Because private firms cannot directly manage ejido lands, a complicated structure was set up to permit Gamesa to associate with ejido farmers (ejidatarios) in the form of a trust, with a nonprofit organization that oversees production and several government agencies as additional partners. The project permits Gamesa to source agricultural inputs from an efficient production unit that would otherwise not have existed (see case example in Chapter 7).

Alliances are helping firms to capitalize on neglected market niches. To this end, Herman Miller Inc., the giant US furniture company, and Swiss-Mexican entrepreneur Heinz Righetti formed a joint venture, Herman Miller Righetti (HMR). HMR is now one of Mexico's leading designers of office furniture, benefiting from the size and experience of the US partner and the local staff's knowledge of the market (see case example in this chapter).

Joint ventures may become a popular way for Canadian firms, anxious to take advantage of a North American free trade agreement, to enter Mexico. Such alliances will help Canadian firms compensate for lack of experience in the country, since Canadian executives, unlike their US counterparts, have not previously rushed to take advantage of inexpensive Mexican labor. Even though some Canadian businesses have operations in Caribbean and other Latin American markets, their experience there may not easily be transferred to Mexico, which is culturally unique and developing its own brand of free market economics.

Subcontracting with another firm
For some firms, subcontracting with a Mexican or other foreign company is the easiest way to take advantage of the benefits of manufacturing in Mexico. This option has been popular in the maquiladora sector for many years, with firms specializing in subcontracting located from Tijuana to Matamoros. With the benefits of free trade, more US companies interested in getting into Mexico but wary of or unable to make a direct investment are likely to consider this option. Many firms that initially operate through subcontracting later make a further commitment and set up their own manufacturing facilities.

Globalizing brands
Mexican consumers are demonstrating a growing preference for international—particularly US—brands, which have strong recognition as a result of purchases by Mexicans in the border region. With the greater integration of the US and Mexican markets, many companies that traditionally had different brands for both markets have adopted a policy of global brands. Ralston Purina, which recently acquired 100% ownership of its Mexican subsidiary, decided to change the name, packaging and appearance of its brands in Mexico to match those marketed in other parts of the world (see case example in this chapter).

Reexamining areas under price control
A number of basic consumer goods are still subject to strict price controls. MNCs often shy away from production of these goods because of the lack of pricing freedom. In most controlled areas, however, imported products can be sold in Mexico without any price constraints, creating an unusual paradox. With an FTA, price controls may be lifted completely, providing opportunities for firms to produce locally rather than import.

Relocating operations to Mexico
This may become a popular approach taken by Asian—mostly Japanese and Korean—firms to ensure access to the expanded North American market. Some Japanese companies (e.g., Nissan) are already planning major expansions in Mexico, which will enable them to bypass trade barriers against the importation of Japanese automobiles into the US.

Korean firms such as Samsung and Goldstar, which operate assembly plants in Mexico, are discussing new investments to avoid being locked out of the benefits of free trade. Hyundai, the automotive manufacturer, recently invested $30 million in a factory to assemble truck flat beds and containers—making it the largest Korean investment to date in Latin America. Daewoo Electronics installed a new $18 million television factory in 1991, and plans to later expand operations to include personal computers, microwave ovens, video recorders and other household appliances.

Responding to the Challenges and Opportunities of an FTA

(1) Implement a quality-improvement program;

(2) Establish a customer-oriented culture;

(3) Seek out opportunities for intraregional sourcing;

(4) Develop new and closer working relations with suppliers;

(5) Upgrade technology at Mexican operations;

(6) Learn to survive competitive shakeouts;

(7) Form a North American division;

(8) Examine the role of Mexican operations in a strategy for the Southwest US;

(9) Relocate operations to Mexico;

(10) Downsize Mexican operations and focus on distribution;

(11) Set up a distribution operation for the first time;

(12) Monitor synergies with other sectors;

(13) Take advantage of growth in consumer demand;

(14) Consider local acquisition;

(15) Regain majority control of your subsidiary;

(16) Reassess sourcing strategies;

(17) Enter a new market through a joint venture;

(18) Subcontract manufacturing to another party;

(19) Form a strategic alliance;

(20) Consider globalizing brands; and

(21) Reexamine areas under price controls.

Case Example

Mexico as a Global Production Base: How Black & Decker's Operation Boosted Its Global Position

Black & Decker's (US) global manufacturing center for clothes irons, located in Querétaro, serves as an example of how Mexico's inexpensive labor and other advantages can boost a company's competitive position. Mexico recently replaced Singapore as the company's lowest-cost, top-quality production site. Below, management highlights some of the benefits of operating in Mexico and sheds light on how it is preparing for heightened competition under a free trade agreement.

The need for greater economies of scale impelled Black & Decker (B&D) to rationalize manufacturing in the mid-1980s. Apart from a few assembly operations or facilities for local markets, the firm's worldwide production is now concentrated in five countries: Mexico, Italy, Singapore, the UK and four plants in the US. B&D's management zeroed in on Mexico, not only because of the country's cost advantages but also as a result of problems it was experiencing in other nations. Factors in Mexico's favor included:

• **Proximity to the US.** Mexico's location is a major trump card. It permits greater flexibility for managing inventories and satisfying customer needs. Brett Olsen, chief financial officer for B&D in Mexico, offers the following illustration: Suppose K Mart, the US retailer, suddenly changes its iron order from style X to style Y. If the irons were ordered from Singapore, it would be difficult to switch because the products would already be on a ship on the Pacific. In Mexico, however, the firm is able to achieve the same quality and quick response to customers as at its US operations, but with added cost advantages.

• **Labor pinch in Singapore.** Despite a serious labor shortfall, measures were implemented to curb an influx of Malaysian workers. A wage premium was imposed for each Malaysian employee, causing Singapore's average hourly wage to rise at an alarming rate.

B&D's long-term future is further jeopardized by a new productivity index being used in Singapore. It measures plants on the basis of output per worker to single out the most productive investments and encourage firms to relocate. Parts-assembly operations such as B&D's score well below chemical plants and oil refineries on this type of index.

• **Gloomy prospects in Brazil.** B&D has limited production in Brazil to the local market, following the elimination of a special export subsidy in 1990. Previously, each exporter received a cost rebate of up to 35%. The subsidy automatically made Brazil the lowest-cost operation for the company. Once the refund was eliminated, Brazil became a higher-cost operation relative to other facilities. Rising economic strife made it difficult to invest resources to boost efficiency, however. "How can you run an export operation when there is a dock strike every three months?" asks Olsen.

New attention to quality

Despite Mexico's comparative advantages, however, free trade presents a new set of challenges for the company. Key focuses of management concern include:

• **Achieving top quality at a low price.** B&D approaches quality and cost issues very aggressively. Management believes the company can ill afford to compete on the basis of cost alone, particularly when faced with amplified competition. In 1990, the firm embarked on two programs to boost quality and efficiency. Although Querétaro is its lowest-cost facility, management set a goal to reduce costs by 2–3%. The plant's 2,000 workers attended training sessions to acquire new problem-solving skills and learn cost-cutting techniques. The effort paid off: Management achieved its goal and reaped savings of over $6 million.

Results from a quality-improvement program were less tangible. Olsen believes quality is as much a state of mind as a specific set of techniques and finds commitment from top management essential. "Suppose a factory has a very reasonable 2% product return rate. Should management spend $100,000 to reach zero or just stay with 2%? Always invest the money," he says. "This decision will send a strong signal that management is dedicated to total quality."

• **Revamping Mexico City operations.** Besides its production facility in Querétaro, B&D has a small plant in Mexico City. The operation manufactures a wide range of products for the local market and for export to other Latin American countries. The facility is undergoing a major facelift to become a world-class operation, a change aimed at enabling it to survive import competition. Currently, the plant is shielded by a 20% duty. Once the borders are completely open, there will be nothing to prevent a Mexican distributor from buying products in the US for duty-free resale in Mexico. The company's goal is to get the Mexico City facility to provide the same quality product as manufactured in the US for the same cost or less.

• **Cultivating new suppliers.** A scarcity of suppliers is a pervasive problem for foreign companies operating in Mexico. Free trade, however, will offer the opportunity to seek outside sources. B&D now uses a Querétaro supplier whose prices are 10% higher than its US counterparts. A 12% import duty makes it cost efficient to buy from the local firm, however. Once free trade is a reality, local suppliers will have to match the price and quality of their northern competitors or risk losing business.

Case Example
Moving Away From Local Production: One Firm's Strategy to Win Sales in Mexico

Although for some companies Mexico offers competitive advantages as a global production site, for others integrating the Mexican operation into a worldwide strategy will mean moving away from local production and targeting Mexico's market potential. Company B, a large consumer goods manufacturer recently reorganized in Mexico with just such a strategy in mind, aimed at reaping greater economies of scale at other global production centers while boosting local sales. With the new organization, Company B is poised to meet the challenges and opportunities presented by a free trade agreement.

Management recently transformed its Mexican manufacturing operation into a sales and marketing company. The Mexican subsidiary is now sourcing products from existing global manufacturing centers in the US, the UK and France and has refocused local resources on cultivating the market. The change is paying off. Despite the arrival of roughly 20 new competitors in Mexico over the past few years, Company B's sales volume and market share grew substantially in 1990.

Opting for imports

According to the general director of Company B, the operation faced a serious dilemma before it reorganized in 1990. Operating costs were rising dramatically because of problems with suppliers, labor and outdated technology. Prices for raw materials were climbing, even though the quality was often shoddy and shipments were late. Productivity was diminishing. These issues and other idiosyncracies of Mexico's operating environment inhibited management's ability to achieve the quality levels attainable in the US and Europe.

"The choice was either to invest the time, energy and money to overhaul the manufacturing operation over the next five years—and hope for efficiency—or to source our product from the company's global manufacturing centers in the US, the UK and France. For us, the decision was obvious," says the general director. Just as with other MNCs, Company B is moving toward global manufacturing centers, where one country supplies products for worldwide operations. For management, it did not make sense to revamp the Mexican plant when the company can now import world-class quality products from other existing plants. In fact, operations in other countries, such as Canada, the Netherlands and Germany, have also moved away from manufacturing and created marketing companies.

The change has enabled management to concentrate on the market rather than exhaust resources worrying about late shipments of low-grade raw materials and infrastructure problems. Company B is eager to cultivate, in particular, an emerging institutional market, including schools, hotels, restaurants and other service establishments. With duty-free entry of imported products under a free trade agreement, costs will also come down.

Creating a new organization

Company B's new marketing company is organized into four groups: large retail chains, wholesale distributors, small retail stores and institutional clients. Each division focuses on understanding the peculiarities of the Mexican market and distribution chain in its area. Managers maintain regular contact with clients, including communication and visits to divisions and individual store and department managers, as well as to the clerks and salespeople behind the counter. Remarks the director, "Our strategy is not to have demand 'pull the product' through the distribution chain but to have the products already there."

Under the new organization, job responsibilities in the manufacturing plant have changed drastically. Rather than assemble the product, workers now handle decorations and specific add-ons. Initially, there was some opposition, but now, says management, employees are earning more and doing more creative work. Consequently, resistance has dissipated. In fact, the change is paying off internally and externally: With one exception, Company B is the only firm in the market that achieved an increase in sales volume and market share in 1990. Without disclosing any figures, the director says the increase was "substantial."

Case Example

Regaining Majority Control: Ralston Purina
Takes Advantage of the New Investment Climate

The Mexican subsidiary of Ralston Purina, the large US-based pet-food and animal feed producer, has a history typical of many foreign-owned companies in Mexico. Following the passage of the 1973 foreign investment law, which limited foreign ownership to 49%, the firm sold off its majority-control interest to Mexican investors on the local stock market in 1979. The move, although not specifically mandated by law (a grandfather clause would have applied), was necessary to obtain approval of the Foreign Investment Commission for expansion plans. Firestone, Scott Paper, Union Carbide and many other US MNCs did the same in order to provide their Mexican operations with greater flexibility.

Less than 10 years later, under favorable investment conditions and a more liberal government policy toward majority foreign ownership, Ralston Purina took back majority control of its holding company, Industrias Purina SA (IPSA). In 1988 it purchased a large block of shares held by Sociedad Industrial Hermes, a Mexican industrial conglomerate, and the following year issued a tender offer to repurchase the remaining outstanding shares. By late 1990, Ralston Purina had reacquired virtually 100% of the shares of IPSA and obtained approval from the National Securities Commission (CNV) to delist.

The purchase of the stock held by the Mexican conglomerate was friendly, according to Ralston Purina. "Hermes wanted to pursue other interests, and we wanted to regain control for strategic purposes," explains Juan Gargallo Costa, IPSA's president and director general. The move has permitted the company to pursue a new strategy for its Mexican operations, based on restructuring to build on those areas where the firm can maintain the strongest competitive advantage over the long term.

Focusing on core businesses

The company is now actively pursuing this strategy, based on emphasizing its core businesses. This has required three initial changes: (1) divest some businesses; (2) purchase 100% control over other businesses being operated as partnerships; and (3) reduce heavy debt previously accumulated by the Mexican company. Lance, a Mexican milling and cookie business, purchased in 1979 by Ralston Purina, was sold off, as was Pilgrim's Pride, a poultry company. At the same time, Ralston Purina bought out its partners in Purina del Pacífico, an affiliate serving the feed market in northwest Mexico.

After reducing its debt, selling off some businesses and acquiring other joint ventures, management embarked on an ambitious investment plan designed to better equip the company for the new business environment in Mexico. Although the idea of a North American free trade agreement still appeared to be only a remote possibility, the firm was preparing for Mexico's insertion in a more global environment by taking measures such as:

• **Making new investments and improving quality.** A new pet-food facility was built in Cuautitlán next to an existing animal feed plant. Even though both plants operate separately, locating them side by side creates obvious synergies. The Ciudad Obregón facility was augmented, and animal food mills were retooled to improve quality. In Monterrey, a new facility was also built next to an existing one. The recently opened plant produces Sup-r-block, an animal feed concentrate.

• **Globalizing brands.** At the same time it invested in the manufacturing plant, the company decided to pursue a new marketing strategy to better compete with the fledgling Mexican market for animal food imports. Part of this strategy was to globalize brands. The brand, packaging and ingredients now sold in Mexico are the same as those sold in South Korea, Spain or the US.

The decision to completely overhaul the name and appearance of Ralston Purina's pet food brands was risky in the short term, according to Gargallo Costa. The Mexican subsidiary had the brand leaders in all segments of the Mexican pet-food market before the change. Gargallo claims the transition was successful and that the company has retained its market share.

Why take the risk? "We are in a better position now than before," explains Gargallo. "If you are convinced that a global market is coming, then you had better have the cost structure and the right products to succeed. In a closed market you may be the best on the block, but not the best in the world. When the borders open and the product offering increases, you have to raise your quality."

The local subsidiary replaced all but two of its existing animal food brands. "You can't generalize on the decision to adopt global brands," warns Gargallo. "It is very complex. In our case, we decided to retain two existing brands for very specific market segments to position ourselves against a competitive product."

• **Rationalizing production.** With the opening of Mexico's economy to imports, Ralston Purina has also adjusted its production in Mexico. Production of some products has been phased out, and other products are imported from plants in the US. Some product lines continue to be produced in Mexico because of advantages from lower costs for labor, transportation and raw materials, to existing plant infrastructure. "The issue is how to structure your production base to provide the best product for the consumer at a cost that you can live with," adds Gargallo.

Case Example

Rationalizing Production and Sourcing: How a Major Food MNC in Mexico Charts a Course for Free Trade

Many multinational companies are mapping out strategies for a trilateral free trade agreement, even though most executives believe full implementation of such an accord is several years away. Company A, a large European food conglomerate, is using a product-by-product approach to identify the comparative strengths and weaknesses of its operations in each country. Affiliates in the region—which have operated autonomously in the past—are also working together to develop ideas and design a unified strategy.

Planning for the future

According to a director with Company A's Mexican subsidiary, free trade with the US will offer many new opportunities, particularly since food markets in industrialized countries are saturated. "It is a tough fight to squeeze one point of growth in these mature markets," says the director. "Acquisitions are often the only way to master any jump in sales and market share. Strong growth is possible in the developing countries, however. The potential in nations such as Mexico makes it imperative to get ready for free trade."

Still, free trade will also present challenges. Competition will heighten once the borders are fully open and products flow freely. "Unfortunately," says the executive, "many Mexican firms do not realize how dramatic the changes will be; they are not doing anything except worrying and talking about the threats of free trade."

Despite the fact that Company A has ample resources to weather any competitive threat, it is taking a proactive stance in planning for the future. The director emphasizes that management is looking closely at every operation because the implications of free trade can be different for each product. In order to formulate an appropriate response, Company A is conducting an in-depth analysis of its current manufacturing and marketing strategies in both the US and Mexico.

Company A is also examining each product in the context of variables such as consumer tastes and needs, customer service, labor content, efficiency of existing manufacturing processes, availability of raw materials and infrastructure. The analysis focuses primarily on identifying synergies between US and Mexican operations and will later look at operations in Canada as well. Company A has already taken advantage of some synergies between its US and Canadian operations resulting from the 1988 US-Canada FTA.

Below and on page 54, Company A sheds some light on how its preliminary review of its businesses is already uncovering potential opportunities in key areas:

• **Linkage with the US operation: cold-meat products.** This is one area where Company A's Mexican operations could clearly benefit from linkage with the US business. Cold cuts for the Mexican market are processed in central Mexico. It is expensive, however, to transport the meat via cold storage to northern Mexico. In fact, the government allows

Company A to charge a higher price for some products because of freight costs. Coincidentally, Company A's US cold-meat production is in the southwest. Free trade could provide cost advantages by enabling the US operations to supply northern Mexico, leaving the plant in central Mexico to handle the rest of the country.

• **Sourcing out of Mexico for the region: fruit juices.** Notwithstanding economies of scale, management clearly wants to take advantage of Mexico's moderate climate and fertile land by producing tropical fruit juices for the region. This will probably not include orange juice, however, which is already processed efficiently in Florida and Brazil.

• **Distribution of imports: confectionery goods.** Company A's Mexican subsidiary recently started to import sweets from the US. The products are selling well, although on a limited scale. An FTA would eliminate the duties Company A pays on the sweets, making it even more attractive to distribute them to a larger market. Given strong competition in confectionery products, the company is analyzing how duty-free imports might alter its position. The executive considers the following questions: Will we need to lower prices by the amount of the duty, or can we keep prices the same? What is the risk of other Mexican firms going to the US and buying the sweets from wholesalers? How will they price them? The executive notes that it is always easier to defend a product in a closed market. An FTA will alter the competitive landscape, making it crucial to keep abreast of market dynamics.

• **Introduction of new products to the US: instant soups.** Company A's Mexican operation excels in the production and marketing of instant soups. Management may decide to transport this success across the border by introducing the products in the US.

• **Use of new suppliers: packaging.** Considerable cost-cutting benefits are possible in this area. In Mexico, packaging inputs are often expensive and of questionable quality. The elimination of duties would let Company A cultivate outside suppliers for materials.

Building team effort

Company A's worldwide businesses, which span 130 countries, operate with considerable autonomy. With free trade, however, each North American branch will have to sacrifice some independence. The subsidiaries are already working together to discuss how different products may be affected and what might be the best strategy for each. Their product-by-product approach is facilitated by a restructuring of the US operations. Company A recently reorganized by creating a separate company for each key product line.

Case Example

Entering New Markets: How a US-Mexico JV Cornered a Niche in the Furniture Market

Anxious to gain access to a budding market in Mexico and capitalize on a neglected market niche, US furniture systems giant Herman Miller Inc. and Swiss-Mexican entrepreneur Heinz Righetti joined forces in 1981 with the formation of Herman Miller Righetti (HMR). The joint venture (JV) weathered Mexico's decade-long economic crisis and, bolstered by the recent market opening, is now one of the country's leading designers of office furniture systems.

HMR sales have grown more than 30% p.a. over the last three years, according to Gilles Vignal, the company's general manager. The firm hopes to reach $10 million p.a. in sales in the near future. All parties involved in the venture stressed good internal communications as the key to the company's success.

Joint venture negotiations began in 1980, when Righetti—a Swiss national and design industry veteran who has lived in Mexico about 30 years—went shopping for a US partner to expand into the underdeveloped Mexican design market. Righetti hit on Herman Miller as his first choice and made contact, despite the fact that the company had never made a JV alliance before. Righetti insisted on a joint venture relationship, believing this would guarantee Herman Miller's long-term commitment to the project.

Bill Mitchell, Herman Miller's vice president of Latin American and Asian sales and an HMR board member, says it was the personal contact with Righetti that convinced the firm to consider the venture. Herman Miller has long had licensees in Latin America, but Mitchell stresses that the joint arrangement gives the firm far more control.

Power sharing for mutual benefit

Ownership in HMR is divided 49% to 51%, with Righetti holding the majority share. (Until 1989, Mexico's investment law restricted foreign ownership to a maximum of 49%.) Righetti makes it clear, however, that from the start control has been shared equally by the partners. "We did this to make Herman Miller more comfortable," he says.

Vignal calls the company "a gem, the best of both worlds." It benefits from the size and experience of the US partner and the local staff's knowledge of the Mexican market. The JV agreement provides for the supply of parts and finished product from Herman Miller, as well as a trademark license, technology transfer, training and service. Herman Miller also has right of first refusal on any new design elements produced by the Mexican firm.

HMR has benefited from Mexico's 1987 entry into GATT and the subsequent opening of the borders. The company previously manufactured or locally sourced 93% of all inventory, but now it imports 50% from Herman Miller, taking advantage of the US partner's greater production capacity. Most imported items are finished metal goods—both parts and end products. All wood processing is done in-house, along with the manufacture of panels and work surfaces.

The company has two manufacturing facilities, a main plant in Mexico City and a secondary facility in Ciudad Juárez. The Juárez plant was installed to service the area's growing in-bond industry. The increase in imports from the US will give HMR room to expand in the market without having to increase existing production capacity.

HMR's day-to-day management is the responsibility of Vignal and his Mexican staff. Still, Vignal says that he is on the phone at least three times a week with Herman Miller's headquarters in Zeeland, Michigan, and talks daily with Righetti. Righetti, HMR's CEO, plays a key role in policy decisions and the formation of long-term strategies. HMR's Mexico City plant also maintains a direct computer link to Zeeland to track orders and shipping. The partners stress this blend of autonomy and consultation. "If you want a good joint venture, have someone who's really responsible for management in the company, rather than doing it piecemeal from the partner's home offices," says Vignal.

Opportunities: a two-way street
Mitchell says that the US parent company is satisfied with the existing relationship and doubts that changes in the investment law allowing 100% foreign ownership of firms in Mexico or the possibility of a US-Mexico free trade agreement would significantly alter the company's status. "Who has the majority share is not as important as a good working relationship," he says. Righetti does say, however, that new possibilities under an FTA would have to be considered. He speculates that if the FTA is approved, Herman Miller might eventually open up new production facilities in Mexico, in coordination with HMR.

Although HMR depends heavily on Herman Miller for supplies, the possibility exists for a two-way exchange. Vignal has long wanted to supply Herman Miller with high-quality Mexican textiles easily accessed by HMR. He says the biggest obstacle to such an arrangement is a generalized perception in US industry that Mexican inputs are of low or irregular quality. Mitchell says, however, that Mexico's improving economic climate might eventually convince the US partner of the reliability of Mexican sources.

Paradoxically, the joint venture has opened up new markets for Herman Miller in the US and in Mexico. In one instance, an HMR contract with General Motors of Mexico led to a contract with the auto manu-facturer's US parent. The same has happened with other MNCs, includ-ing Ford and American Airlines, according to Vignal.

Even though nearly all of HMR's production is directed at the domes-tic market, the company occasionally fills gaps in Herman Miller's ex-port capacity. In two recent cases, the Mexican firm shipped products no longer manufactured by the parent to clients in Australia and the United Arab Emirates.

Although both partners and manager Vignal say the joint venture has been a positive experience for all parties, they admit the relationship has had its ups and downs, especially during the darker days of Mexico's economic crisis. Righetti says the worst times came in 1982–1983, when the Mexican economy collapsed and dollars were hard to acquire. This made it difficult for HMR to purchase inputs from Herman Miller. Now, however, with economic prospects improving, the partners indicate that the relationship is closer than ever.

Case Example

Setting Up a Distribution Operation: How
Amway Adapted Its Direct Sales System to Mexico

Changes in Mexican government attitudes toward foreign capital led US company Amway International, in June 1990, to set up operations in Mexico, a country it had long considered a strong potential market. The consumer products firm, which specializes in direct sales, chose the northern industrial city of Monterrey for its headquarters, while estab-lishing distribution centers in several cities and contracting legal and public relations services in Mexico City. Mexican operations have grown rapidly, and Amway Mexico is now moving ahead with plans for expand-ing into agricultural production and manufacturing.

Amway has grown faster in Mexico than in any of the nearly 30 other countries in which it has operations. First-year sales are now estimated at $15–20 million, more than double original projections. Amway Inter-national recorded worldwide sales of $2.2 billion in 1990.

The company was aided in its rapid start by a unique organizational structure and extensive sales network. In the first months of Amway op-erations in Mexico, approximately 15,000 company salespeople from the US and other countries came to Mexico to recruit distributors lo-cally. As of early 1991, the company had about 65,000 distributors regis-tered in the country.

Although headquartered in Monterrey, Amway has contracted legal representation and public relations services in Mexico City. "It's import-

ant to obtain in-country services—lawyers and accountants who understand the local government structures," says Managing Director Russ
Hall. "In Mexico, things happen more on a one-on-one basis with state
agencies. Personal relations are important. It isn't something where you
just fill out a form and enter it into a computer."

Adjusting to local ways

To make the Amway system successful in Mexico, the company was
forced to modify it to conform with local legal and other standards.
Management was also challenged by a general lack of service infrastructure in several key areas. Roadblocks the company faced included the
following:

• **Need to modify organizational structure to meet legal requirements.**
Complying with Mexico's latest foreign investment regulations has been
relatively trouble free for the company. By being careful to meet basic
investment, financing and long-term foreign currency balance requirements, the firm has been able to keep contact with government regulators to a minimum.

One difficult legal task, however, was to modify the company's organizational system to comply with Mexico's strict labor laws. "We had to
make sure that there was absolutely no labor connection between
Amway and it's individual distributors" to avoid responsibility for social
security payments and income tax withholding, explains Warren Kauf-
man of Goodrich, Riquelme & Assoc., a Mexican law firm that deals
mostly with MNCs and handles the Amway account. As part of the revised method of operating, each Amway distributor in Mexico must register as an individual business. Amway assists new distributors in meeting
these requirements.

• **Need for marketing assistance.** Besides buying products from the
home office in Ada, Michigan, the Mexican subsidiary receives extensive help through an international division created to support foreign
markets. Advisors are sent to Mexico to work with staff on questions
such as marketing, research and development and lab testing of products under local conditions.

Amway Mexico has been aided by an open-door policy, which gives it
direct access to all levels of the parent company to help it deal with problems encountered in areas such as supply and manufacturing.

• **Inadequate payment system for distributors.** This has been the firm's
number one stumbling block. In the US, Amway receives advance payment from distributors through a computerized direct-debit banking
system—a system that, in Mexico, exists only in Mexico City and is only
available to certain companies.

The government's decision in May 1989 to privatize the banking system, however, has created a new attitude among Mexico's bankers. "A year ago we couldn't even get anyone to hold a meeting to discuss it. Now we have contact with several banks on this," says Hall. The company has found Banco Serfin to be especially receptive to its needs and now hopes to establish a direct-debit payment system with the bank's help. "Serfin has been very aggressive. They understand the need to adapt their system to support higher-level technology."

• **Underdeveloped national shipping and delivery systems.** In the US and Europe, Amway International uses home delivery to get products to individual distributors. In Mexico, however, there are no existing shippers that offer adequate delivery service. As a partial solution, the company has set up eight distribution centers—where distributors collect product shipments directly—in six cities and plans to move into at least four new cities within half a year.

To overcome the lack of development in home delivery services, Amway has worked closely with Estafeta, the Mexican express delivery company. The company is now able to deliver products in two to six days to those areas not served by its own distribution facilities.

• **Inadequate communications systems.** The firm uses a rapidly expanding toll-free telephone system to receive orders from its distributors. In spite of the service's notorious inefficiency, however, the company has had few problems. Still, the cost involved is considerable, since Telmex, the newly privatized telephone company, does not offer a discount rate structure for toll-free line users. The company has also experienced delays in acquiring a dedicated lease line for computer communication between the Monterrey office and outlying distribution centers.

• **Official red tape.** Other delays have been caused by the registration process for imported products, both for trademark registration and government health authorization. The average lead time in Mexico has been three months, compared with one month for the company's European affiliates.

• **Too much success, too soon.** Paradoxically, the company has actually experienced difficulties as a result of its rapid growth. "To be honest, we weren't prepared for so much demand," admits Marketing Director David Casanova. The firm was forced to double its initial staff and accelerate the development of its fledgling product distribution system through Estafeta.

Amway does not expect a free trade agreement between the US, Mexico and Canada to solve its service problems. According to Hall, a trade accord would not lead Amway Mexico to revert to distributors in the US. "The pulling back of management into the US isn't the goal of a free trade agreement. The idea is to be able to move around better in this country."

Future production plans

Early success in Mexico has led the company to consider expanding into production. Amway has purchased farm land for the production of Acerola cherries, used in the processing of vitamins. Mexico's Bancomext export bank referred the company to advisors, who helped in the selection and purchase of the required land. Export of the fruit to the company's processing plant in California is expected to begin in mid-1993.

Amway is also moving ahead with plans to establish a maquiladora in Tijuana for the manufacture and export of home water-processing systems. In addition, the firm is giving some thought to sourcing raw materials from Mexico for US manufacturing operations. Once its Mexico operations are well established, Amway will consider offering products specific to the Mexican market.

Case Example

Focusing on Quality and Customer Service: How Cummins Engine Is Coping with New Competition

Many multinational companies have ambitious plans for integrating Mexico into their global production systems and capitalizing on the upcoming free trade agreement with the US and Canada. Firms already in Mexico, however, must also scramble to protect market share, reshape domestic distribution arrangements and improve customer service as Mexico opens to much tougher competition.

The Cummins Engine Co (US) entered Mexico after World War II with its first international distributorship. The firm has since grown to dominate the domestic heavy-duty engine market with a 100% share and holds a 60% share of the medium-duty engine market. Cummins Engine sells a full range of its product line in Mexico, including domestic- and foreign-produced small, medium and large truck and bus engines and associated products (e.g. filters, turbochargers, generators, radiators and electronic controls).

Today, market liberalization and trade reform are challenging the firm's dominant position, compelling changes in marketing strategy and in relations with distributors, such as:

• **Cummins in Mexico must now compete with imported engines and auto parts.** The border was opened to imported diesel engines in 1990 and passenger buses in 1991 and will be opened to heavy-duty trucks in

1993 and medium-duty trucks in 1994. Furthermore, any firm that already supplies parts and services in Mexico can now import them as well. Already, Navistar has brought its engines to Mexico, and Caterpillar will probably be next.

• **The national trucking industry has been deregulated.** Increasing competition among fleets is forcing fleet managers to reduce operational and maintenance costs. To meet manager demands, Cummins must ensure that its distributors increase efficiency and maintain a high level of service while reducing prices and service charges.

• **Some of Cummins's US distributors are selling parts across the border.** This practice, which violates territoriality agreements, undermines the firm's Mexican distributors. Cummins is attempting to resolve the problem through price adjustments and programs that transfer payment to the Mexican distributor for US exports.

• **The company must now provide service in Mexico for US-sourced products.** As North American truckers and trucks gain increasing presence in Mexico, Cummins's local distributors will need to service all US products, whether or not they are offered for sale in Mexico, whereas US truckers will have to rely on the Mexicans since, at least initially, few of the US trucks will have access to service shops operated by their companies.

Pressuring distributors
To face the new competition, Cummins will depend heavily on a well-established distribution and service network run by independents. The company also has two other competitive strengths: economies of scale developed through its long experience in Mexico and a head start in integrating its Mexican operations with its North American ones.

Although superior service is critical to the company's competitive strategy, it also may be a weak spot, since it provides less immediate payback for distributors while requiring more effort than sales. Yet service is key to customer satisfaction and a guaranteed customer base in the future. To shore up this side of the business, Cummins will:

• **Encourage distributors to maintain quality.** Agreements with distributors have been revised to compel enhanced quality and service. This increases pressure on distributors to amplify investment. In one case, the company transferred business away from a distributor that was not responding.

• **Combat off-brand imports.** A key problem facing all engine manufacturers in Mexico is off-brand imports. Distributors are able to purchase off-brand parts, sold in some cases by the original manufacturer, at prices lower than those of the Cummins brand. Cummins has begun to reduce its parts prices in response.

• **Use the power of computers.** Although trade liberalization has threatened Cummins's market share to some degree, computerization (and the large capital outlays needed to automate) has blocked some competition and enhanced the position of the company and its distribution network. For example:

(1) Independent shops do not have the capital to invest in expensive testing equipment to regulate engine electronics. They are losing out to the Cummins network.

(2) Among the larger truck and bus fleets, on-board computers are being used to measure engine performance. In the company's view, this will enhance the use of Cummins's service network and parts.

(3) Recent government measures are forcing truck companies to maintain, for the first time, strict accounting records. Distributors, through the Cummins computer system, provide on-going records smaller firms are not able to supply.

(4) The company will soon develop a nationwide computerized network that will provide instant information from the distribution channel to the factory and warehouse, yielding just-in-time benefits and reducing warehousing costs. Other companies, especially parts importers and dealers with less-developed national networks, will be forced to carry larger inventories and, consequently, higher expenses.

More eyes on quality

Underlying all the changes is Cummins's emphasis on quality control. The company's quality-control program is based on use of district field service engineers, who perform ongoing assessments of engines. When they spot a problem in repair records, they report it, and the part is changed, either in design or service.

To convince larger clients of the superiority of its original brand equipment, the firm performs fleet tests using both original and off-brand material. A recent test demonstrated improved efficiency afforded by Cummins ring liners to a client. A similar test was run on Cummins Premium Blue Oil, designed especially for truck engines.

Unfortunately, whereas larger end users can be persuaded using such strategies, smaller users often sacrifice long-term utility for short-term price advantage. In some cases, Cummins's distributors, seeking to increase profits or responding to local competitive pressures, may use competing parts in engine installations and repairs.

Case Example
The Japanese View:
Mitsui Sees the FTA as 'Pure Opportunity'

Large Japanese trading companies, having gained a foothold in Latin America in recent years, are among the companies most likely to benefit once North American free trade is fully implemented. Mitsui de México, with $500 million in sales in 1990, is one of the leading Japanese trading companies operating there. Mitsui management sees the free trade agreement as "pure opportunity."

In the late 1980s, when Mexico's economic future was still far from apparent, Mitsui took an aggressive stance toward making a long-term commitment toward conducting operations in the country. The firm enlarged its resident Japanese staff from 12 to 18 employees, at a time when other Japanese trading companies were holding the line or, in some cases, cutting back. In addition, Mitsui has laid the basis for a sound position in a growing Mexican economy, partly through participation in a pair of mixed government-private sector investment firms. Mitsui has a 10% share in Mexiplus, an investment promotion company that has spearheaded several major projects, including the Altamira tank terminal. Mitsui also has an 8% share of Impexnal, an export promotion company set up by Bancomext, the state export bank.

In recent years, Mitsui de México's parent company has given consideration to a proposal by its US subsidiary for the merger of US, Canadian and Mexican operations into one affiliate. Even though the Tokyo parent has decided to shelve the idea for the time being, the company is actively analyzing the implications of an FTA on its overall North American business.

"I believe that the decision will eventually be taken to move toward integration," says Mitsui de México General Manager Goichi Shimojo. He says that the North American FTA would be a major impetus to the company's own regional integration. In fact, in 1991, for the first time, Mitsui de México attended the annual meeting of North American general managers as a full participant.

Seeking out synergies

Following a directive issued by Mitsui USA to offices throughout the country to prepare for opportunities presented by an FTA, meetings were set up in 1991 among the Mexico staff and representatives of the Los Angeles, Seattle, Houston, Chicago and Vancouver, Canada, offices. Shimojo describes these meetings as "get-to-know-you" and brainstorming sessions. "By sharing information on local operations, we get ideas for new business possibilities," he says.

Each of Mitsui's three North American affiliates is participating in the study on the consequences and effects of an FTA. Mitsui de México is looking at several possible areas of company expansion under such an agreement, including the petrochemicals, petroleum, autoparts, garments and shipping sectors. Thus far, the company's analysis indicated the following trends:

• **Auto parts and the garment trade should represent new areas of activity for the company.** A likely scenario would have Mitsui financing expansion by existing producers, in exchange for control of export operations—with an eye toward taking advantage of more favorable tariff structures under an FTA.

• **The free trade agreement may open up opportunities in Mexico's state-controlled petroleum sector.** This sector has undergone some liberalization under the Salinas administration and may open further to foreign participation under a free trade agreement. According to Shimojo, "We are very much interested in investment and financing in the oil and petrochemical sector. We are ready to work with Pemex in any respect." The company lost a recent bid for the turnkey construction of a facility for an aromatics chain for Pemex in Cadereyta, Nuevo León.

The firm also hopes to capitalize on continued Japanese government support to Pemex (Petróleos Mexicanos, the state-owned oil company). In 1990, the Japanese government announced two major loans to fund Pemex's "environmental program"—one for $500 million, in addition to another $315 million package. Mitsui is preparing proposals in conjunction with other foreign companies to provide equipment and heavy machinery for these projects.

• **Increased trade among Canada, Mexico and the US would translate into an expansion of Mitsui's shipping and transportation operations.** The company traditionally concentrates on shipping support activities, including warehousing and customs brokerage. Shimojo reports that his firm might consider direct investment in the trucking sector under a free trade agreement. Although the Mexican trucking industry underwent a long overdue deregulation in 1989, a further opening is still a possibility, especially if an FTA were to give carriers greater cross-border access.

In 1991, Mitsui invested in the construction of a tank storage terminal at the Gulf port of Altamira, in the state of Tamaulipas. Although the company has no further plans for port infrastructure investment at the moment, future activities would probably focus on the pacific ports of Lázaro Cárdenas, Manzanillo and Ensenada.

• **An FTA would bring more Japanese firms into Mexico, meaning more business and financing opportunities for Mitsui.** Contracts initiated by Mitsui USA have also brought business to the Mexican multinational firm. In 1990, it financed 15% of a $160 million purchase of General Electric (US) locomotives by the Mexican railway parastate. The rest of the deal was financed by the US Eximbank.

Japanese want stability

Shimojo believes the primary benefit of a trilateral free trade accord to Mexico would be an increase in the country's credibility in the eyes of foreign investors and greater stability in economic policy, giving prospective foreign investors assurance as to the lasting effects of Salinas's modernization program. "Japanese investors want a steady policy—stable, unchangeable, consistent," he says.

Case Example
Designing a Regional Strategy: How Sonoco Is Positioning Itself for the Future

With Mexico having taken the lead several years ago in moving toward market reforms, multinational companies with strong operations there have begun to look for ways to capitalize on the liberalization that has spread to much of the rest of Latin America and to reposition themselves for long-term growth. One firm, Sonoco Products Co, has been preparing to face the challenges of the next decade by revamping many of its planning, marketing, quality, pricing, acquisition and human resources strategies for Latin America.

Sonoco is a US manufacturer of paper and plastic products for industrial and consumer packaging, with sales of $1.7 billion p.a. Its Latin American businesses account for $52 million p.a. in sales, 75% of which are in Mexico. Consequently, the company maintains its corporate headquarters in that country, from which it manages its other operations in Colombia, Venezuela, Argentina and Puerto Rico.

With so much of its business concentrated in Mexico, Sonoco Latin America has had to study the implications of the economic opening and other challenges presented by the structural reforms occurring there in recent years. To strengthen its position for the future, the company has adapted its regional strategy to these changes. According to the company's president for Latin America, the company aims to change the corporate mind-set from inward to outward directed, to learn to operate in a more competitive environment in which "monopolies are no more" and to develop into a provider of world-class products that are able to compete globally.

Surviving competition

The newly competitive environment within Mexico and the rest of Latin America is forcing companies to adopt new ways to cope with slow economic growth and the removal of protection for local manufacturers. Sonoco has implemented a number of strategies to continue growing in the face of competition. These include:

- **Gaining market share through improved competitiveness.** The company aims to offer better value at the same price, "which is better than offering the same value at a lower price," says the president. To achieve this, Sonoco will use technology and technical service advantages from its parent company to improve products and service and will concentrate on quick deliveries. The goal is to gain volume by absorbing demand growth rather than by simply taking market share away from competitors.

- **Penetrating local markets through related products.** "This is the best time to pursue technology transfer to develop new products," says the president, "especially if these reduce costs or improve competitiveness for exports."

- **Targeting acquisitions.** Sonoco has been able to take advantage of both the privatization trend and the fact that many competitors and related businesses in Latin America are having difficulty surviving recession. In 1985, the company acquired Gargo, a Mexican state-owned firm that produces clay-coated board and folding boxes, thereby doubling Sonoco's production capacity and substantially diversifying output. Later in that year, Sonoco acquired 100% ownership of a related new industrial product in Mexico, permitting another 50% increase in production capacity and product diversification. In 1988, again in Mexico, it broadened its product line by acquiring a heavily indebted competitor and was undergoing similar acquisition negotiations in Colombia and Venezuela in 1990.

- **Vertical integration.** The parent company has a competitive advantage worldwide in quality, reliability and cost because of its aggressive strategy of vertical integration. Sonoco Latin America, likewise, has been able to maintain production and consistent quality, in spite of cyclical scarcities of raw materials, because of its willingness to invest vertically in wastepaper collection, paperboard manufacturing and production of adhesives, all for conversion into final products. This has given the firm a considerable competitive advantage.

- **Creative cost reduction.** According to company management, as inflation comes under control in many countries and as more countries open their borders, price increases will become increasingly ineffective as a tool to improve the bottom line. Consequently, the company is looking to cut costs through raw materials imports, head-count reduction and emphasis on fixed costs. In countries where Sonoco has small operations, it is considering sharing physical facilities with another company, sharing top management with another business and hiring part-time outside services for staff operations (e.g., accounting, auditing, industrial engineering and legal).

• **Diversification.** This is indispensable when a company has a very concentrated customer base in Latin America, since wild swings in demand can create havoc with revenues. Diversification limits vulnerability to such demand fluctuations. As a result, it has been one of the goals of Sonoco's acquisitions in Latin America.

• **Revamping strategic planning.** Sonoco's strategic planning process for Latin America is being updated to take liberalized foreign investment rules, new export opportunities, import competition, development of trading blocs, privatization and the other changes in the Latin American business environment into consideration.

• **Regional integration.** If vertical integration was critical in the 1980s to ensure supply and quality, in the 1990s firms will need to integrate regionally to compete in cost. As a result, Sonoco is looking for "clusters" of countries that can be integrated. With tariff reductions implemented or planned in many countries, lower-priced, higher-quality raw materials can now be produced in one country in large volumes and then imported by the smaller operations.

Sonoco's strategy in northern South America, the Caribbean and Central America is to source from one country for the others. By the end of 1990, wastepaper was collected in each country, but there was just one world-class paper mill to serve all of the small conversion operations. In addition, adhesives were slated to be produced in only one country.

• **Adapting to regional and global markets.** In the past, when markets were local and closed to foreign competition, it was sufficient to know the local competition and try to be superior to them in product, quality and service. Technological improvements were made exclusively to satisfy local end users, who usually were not exporters.

In the future, however, markets will not be exclusively local. Competitive intelligence will grow increasingly complex, and quality and technology will have to satisfy regional and global markets. In light of this, Sonoco is working on ways to improve its competitive intelligence capabilities, use the best production technology and achieve the best quality to match the stricter standards developing in the region. "If our customers have turned to exports, we as suppliers must measure up to new standards. It we do not, customers will have many alternatives to import."

Achieving globalization
At the same time the company is moving away from a local and toward a regional focus, it is also striving to develop a global orientation. To this end, all regional divisions are now required to present strategic plans that include an analysis of regional and global business opportunities and potential threats. Also, the US and international managers are participating in roundtable discussions with the commitment to find ways to globalize each individual product or family of products.

Mexico is a key country in Sonoco's strategy to globalize and to achieve greater integration with the US. Sonoco has established a maquiladora in Monterrey, which will be used to help the firm "learn to export" to the US. A task force made up of managers from several divisions is analyzing export opportunities. The plan is to manufacture in Mexico, with marketing to be handled by the corresponding Sonoco division in the US, although the company is also looking at sourcing opportunities from the US into Mexico. Another task force is studying the prospects for sourcing the future requirements for some Sonoco products in the US from Mexico.

Sonoco is also considering investing in Brazil, which it sees as the other Latin American investment site that must be viewed in a world context. The company is studying a number of issues: Should Brazil be considered exclusively as an internal market opportunity? Is Brazil a viable sourcing point for world markets? How will Brazil compete with other rapidly developing countries (from the global perspective) by the year 2000?

Sonoco is also monitoring Asian investment in the Western Hemisphere's Pacific Rim and studying which areas—Canada, the US, Mexico, Central America, Colombia or Chile—will have the competitive advantage as a sourcing base 10–20 years in the future.

PART II

Operating in Mexico Today

4
Assessing the Political Outlook

When he took office in December 1988, President Carlos Salinas de Gortari was dismissed by some observers as an inexperienced technocrat who would have trouble governing the country. Mexico was then experiencing considerable social and political discontent after nearly a decade of falling living standards, exacerbated by its traditionally closed political system. Salinas's election was followed by allegations of vote-rigging, which badly impaired his perceived legitimacy. Despite these handicaps, however, he has demonstrated remarkable political acumen and is proving to be the most forceful and competent Mexican president in many years.

Salinas has carefully balanced major economic reforms aimed at modernizing the economy and cutting back government regulation with more spectacular moves designed to gain popular support. During his first two years in office, he adroitly blended the announcement of plans to privatize Telmex, the state telephone company, and denationalize the commercial banking sector with the jailing of corrupt leading public figures from unions, the security forces and the business community. He has injected much dynamism into the liberalization begun by his predecessor, Miguel de la Madrid (1982–88). At the same time, Salinas has gained the support of the middle classes and foreign investors and kept the stabilization program, the Pact for Economic Stability and Growth (PECE), on course.

Despite the remarkable reforms occurring in business and the economy, political change is not following the rapid pace of economic modernization. *Consequently, familiarity with the long-ruling Institutional*

Revolutionary Party (PRI) and its various components, as well as the mechanics of Mexican politics, is critical to a successful business endeavor in the country.

Understanding the Political System

Salinas's ascension to power marked nearly 60 years of uninterrupted rule by the PRI—the party that has produced every Mexican president since the end of the Mexican Revolution in the 1920s. Since its founding (under its original name, the National Revolutionary Party) in 1929, the PRI has dominated Mexican political life, hammering out a consensus on political decisions based on a system of consultation and reciprocity among different political and interest groups.

At the heart of Mexico's political system lies the concept of one-party rule. Still, within the omnipresent and powerful PRI, a wide variety of groups have managed to coexist and, in fact, the party owes much of its longevity to an ability to assimilate these diverse groups.

The PRI has no single party line or ideology. It supported, for example, the nationalization of Mexico's commercial banking system under then-President José López Portillo in 1982 and now supports the banks' privatization under the current government. Although the party adopts much of the rhetoric of each successive administration, it would be a mistake to assume that it is merely an electoral vehicle for the current president. The PRI machinery remains the single most powerful institution in Mexico apart from the president, and can also place strong limits on the president's actions.

Inside the Party

The PRI is composed of three major groups: workers, represented by the Confederation of Mexican Workers (CTM) and led by 91-year-old Fidel Velázquez; peasants, represented by the National Peasant Confederation (CNC); and the lower and middle classes, represented by Une (formerly the National Confederation of Popular Organizations, or CNOP). The president, however, wields enormous power, as do state governors.

Among the three pillars of the PRI, the CTM is by far the strongest and most vocal. It currently represents nearly six million workers, who account for nearly half the unionized work force. Its leader, the labor chieftain Fidel Velázquez, has been in power almost as long as the PRI has existed. Nonetheless, labor's power is limited. It did not support the decision to select Salinas as the party's candidate for the presidency in 1988, and some labor leaders discreetly support the opposition to the

PRI. Frictions between labor and Salinas are rarely revealed to the public, however, except as veiled comments and signals.

Still, the fact that the struggle between labor and the administration is dealt with as an internal party problem does not make it any less significant. It is part of one of the most important ongoing battles in Mexican politics today: the decade-and-a-half fight between traditional PRI bosses and a group of younger, usually US-educated, bureaucrats known as the "technocrats." The Miguel de la Madrid administration and Salinas's arrival to power in 1988 marked an important victory for the

---

Mexico's Political Structure

Present government: Carlos Salinas de Gortari of the Institutional Revolutionary Party (PRI) was elected in July 1988 with 50.4% of the vote, according to the official count. Electoral fraud was allegedly used to achieve this bare majority. His party controls both houses of Congress and all but one state. He has achieved remarkable success in implementing market-oriented reforms that contradict much of the traditional PRI party line. He took office for a six-year term on Dec. 1, 1988.

Parliamentary Forces

	Chamber of Deputies		Senate	
	Seats	%	Seats	%
Institutional Revolutionary Party (PRI)	320	64.0	61	95.3
National Action Party (PAN)	89	17.8	1	1.6
Party of the Democratic Revolution (PRD)	41	8.2	2	3.1
Party of the Cardenist Reconstruction Front (PFCRN)	23	4.6	—	—
Authentic Party of the Mexican Revolution (PARM)	15	3.0	—	—
Popular Socialist Party (PPS)	12	2.4	—	—
Total	500	100.0	64	100.0

NOTE: This breakdown reflects the current number of seats held by each party following the August 1991 mid-term elections.

Next elections: Presidential and legislative, August 1994.

technocrats, who often have limited political and party experience and are distrusted by the long-standing party bosses.

Companies operating in or interested in doing business in Mexico should be aware of these two groups and their relative power. The presence of the party stalwarts and the technocrats helps to explain how revolutionary rhetoric often espoused by the PRI (and even by Salinas at PRI events) can coexist with the administration's market-oriented policies, including privatization of state-owned enterprises, reduction of protectionist trade barriers and the embracing of a free trade agreement with the US. The struggle between these two groups may also help explain what appear to be inconsistencies in Salinas's modernization plan.

Despite Salinas's departure from many traditional Mexican policies, which supported strong state intervention in the economy and viewed foreign investment with suspicion, he still forms part of a system that does not completely share his market-oriented views and can still limit his ability to implement change. For example, although the retention of Petróleos Mexicanos (Pemex), a state monopoly in the oil sector, runs counter to much of the current administration's thinking, significant changes—at least those that may be evident to the public eye—cannot be expected under the current political conditions.

FTA: Salinas's Attempt to Extend His Influence

Investors must also realize that Salinas and the PRI face very different timetables. As the president's six-year term (Dec. 1, 1988 to Nov. 30, 1994) proceeds, it will be more difficult for him to make major changes that the PRI might view as detrimental to its long-term stability. There is a risk that Salinas's reforms will be halted or slowed down. This risk explains in large part the reason for the current administration's decision to embrace free trade agreement talks with the US and (somewhat more reluctantly) with Canada.

A free trade agreement is seen as the best guarantee that the reforms being set up today by Salinas will outlive his term. (Reelection is not permitted under the constitution.) Although each Mexican president has enormous power to change the direction of government, officials hope that a free trade agreement will place certain constraints on future leaders who will hesitate to reverse such a legally binding accord with the US. The trade pact is also designed to provide investors with greater confidence in the long-term direction of Mexico's economic policy. Although attention is currently focused on Salinas's six-year presidential term—which has inspired a rise in short-term investor confidence—officials hope that a free trade agreement will enable both policymakers and investors to break with the six-year horizon, and domestic and foreign investors to engage in longer-term planning.

During the course of the free trade negotiations, it will be important to monitor how far Salinas will go in opening up areas of the economy still closed to foreign investment and what techniques will be used to support such an aperture. During his first two years in office, the presi-

---

Major Cabinet Members

(1) Director General of the Technical Secretariat of the Presidential Cabinets: José Córdoba Montoya

(2) Secretary of Finance and Public Credit: Pedro Aspe Armella

(3) Secretary of Commerce and Industrial Development: Jaime José Serra Puche

(4) Secretary of the Interior: Fernando Gutiérrez Barrios

(5) Secretary of Foreign Relations: Fernando Solana Morales

(6) Secretary of Ecology and Urban Development: Luis Donaldo Colosio Murrieta

(7) Secretary of Labor and Social Welfare: Arsenio Farell Cubillas

(8) Head of the Department of the Federal District (Mayor of Mexico City): Manuel Camacho Solís

(9) Attorney General of the Republic: Ignacio Morales Lechuga

(10) Secretary of Communications and Transportation: Andrés Caso Lombardo

(11) Secretary of Public Education: Ernesto Zedillo Ponce de León

(12) Secretary of Agriculture and Water Resources: Carlos Hank González

(13) Secretary of Energy, Mining and Parastatal Industry: Fernando Hiriart Balderrama

(14) Secretary of the Controller General of the Federation: María Elena Vázquez Nava

(15) Secretary of Health: Jesús Kumate Rodriguez

(16) Secretary of Tourism: Pedro Joaquín Caldwell

(17) Secretary of Agrarian Reform: Victor Cervera Pacheco

(18) Secretary of Fishing: Guillermo Jiménez Morales

dent relied heavily on changes in administrative regulations and on the mechanism of trusts as the means to allow greater foreign investment in Mexico.

For instance, instead of changing the 1973 Foreign Investment Law, the government issued new regulations to the existing law in 1989. In 1990, rather than changing the mining law, the administration likewise issued new, more liberal regulations. In both cases, liberalized administrative rules have facilitated foreign investment in Mexico, but do not constitute lasting modifications as would a change in the underlying laws. A new intellectual property law and a new copyright law, passed by Mexico's Congress in June and July 1991, respectively, represent some of the few areas where the underlying law will have been changed, rather than only the accompanying regulations.

Political Stability:
Status Today and Future Risks

Mexico still enjoys one of the most stable regimes in Latin America. Salinas's ability to surpass his narrow technocratic background as secretary of programming and budget during the de la Madrid administration bodes well for continued stability, and there is little doubt that he will complete his six-year term in 1994. He will play a major, and probably decisive, role in the selection of his successor, as have all presidents since the 1930s.

In fact, political stability has improved dramatically since Salinas took office. Although most of his reforms have had little beneficial effect on the average citizen, two major factors that threatened political stability in 1988 are no longer as important. First, inflation has declined drastically, from a high of 159% in 1987 to 51.7% in 1988 and just 18.8% by 1991. Second, the two major opposition parties have experienced internal difficulties, which leave them weak and poorly positioned to address the general public's concerns. The combination of more favorable economic conditions with the weakness of the two major opposition parties has reduced much of the pressure for political change in the country.

Within the PRI, there are few signs, despite the rhetoric, of a real democratic opening. At its last National Assembly, held in September 1990, the party implemented only minor changes to its structure and platform. What appeared to be a truce in late 1990 between Salinas and hard-line members of the PRI—who oppose a rapid political opening—should help the traditionalists feel more confident that, despite the president's economic reforms, free and fair competition is not coming soon to the political sphere.

Plans to revise the party's statement of principles have also been postponed. Although Salinas reduced the strength of the three sectors—representing labor, peasants and the lower and middle classes—within the party's assembly, he accepted their existence, calling for party affiliation on a voluntary and individual basis as well. The president's inability to reform the PRI poses one of the most serious challenges to political stability and gives rise to serious questions when looking to the 1994 presidential succession process.

The Opposition and Elections

The principal opposition parties in Mexico are the right-wing National Action Party (PAN) and the left-of-center Party of the Democratic Revolution (PRD). The PAN is associated with the Catholic Church and has its strongest support in northern Mexico. Its 1988 presidential candidate, Manuel Clothier, obtained 17% of the vote, according to official results. The PAN, although often critical of the PRI and Salinas's handling of electoral matters, has aligned with the PRI on two crucial matters—passage of a constitutional revision to permit the privatization of banks and a change in the electoral system—when the PRI needed a two-thirds majority in the Congress, which it does not enjoy now. Contributing to the PAN's recent weakening is the fact that much of Salinas's economic program corresponds closely to the free-market-oriented philosophy espoused by the PAN for years.

The PRD was formed after 1988 by supporters of Cuauhtémoc Cárdenas, whose coalition of parties garnered 31% of the controversial presidential vote in July 1988. The PRD has accused the government of widespread fraud in the 1988 electoral process and in vote counting and tabulation. The party is made up of two principal groups: ex-PRI members who left the PRI along with Cárdenas (formerly a PRI senator and governor, and son of ex-president Gen. Lázaro Cárdenas) and former members of the Mexican Socialist Party (PMS), which disbanded when the PRD was formed. The PRD has maintained a much more critical stance toward the Salinas administration than the PAN and has continued to raise the specter of July 1988's vote fraud to question the legitimacy of the Salinas presidency.

Although both parties appeared to represent substantial threats to Salinas in the months before he took office, since then neither has been able to present a strong opposition. The PAN has been divided between members who are willing to align with the PRI when common ground can be found and those who believe the PAN should adopt a more stringent, anti-PRI line and even ally with the left-of-center PRD in order to defeat the PRI. Overall, the PAN has been more conciliatory than the PRD. Likewise, the PRD has been divided between the anti-PRI members (most of whom have emerged from the PRI) and a faction willing to work with the administration (mostly from the PMS). Unlike the PAN, the PRD has been more stridently anti-Salinas.

Of the two opposition parties, the PAN has clearly gained the most politically since 1988. Its first big win was the governorship in Baja California in 1989—the first victory of an opposition gubernatorial candidate to be recognized since the formation of the PRI in 1929. In contrast, the PRD has been subject to an intense campaign of repression, including assassination of several of its politicians, jailings and fierce attacks on its leaders and sympathizers. The PRD has also had few electoral victories in proportion to what appeared to be a substantial level of support for Cárdenas in 1988. This poor showing has caused considerable disillusionment within the party, with some groups calling for the PRD's complete withdrawal from the electoral system.

Neither the PAN nor the PRD have taken Salinas to task on the upcoming free trade talks. Although the PRD has been critical of an agreement with the US, it has not focused on the issue of a trade accord. Indeed, some of the strongest criticism of a trade pact has come from the PRI's congressional representation and from PRI-aligned labor leaders.

Key Players to Watch

José Córdoba Montoya: Director General of the Technical Secretariat of the Presidential Cabinets. Born in France of Spanish parents but now a nationalized Mexican, this Stanford University-educated economist is the least visible but one of the most powerful members of the Salinas administration. Córdoba is the equivalent of a super chief of staff of the cabinet and is seen as responsible for the most significant policy decisions made by the administration, from designing the PRI's political strategy to the move to negotiate a free trade agreement with the US and Canada. Because of his immigrant status, Córdoba cannot aspire to the presidency and is thus considered to be Salinas's most faithful supporter.

Pedro Aspe Armella: Secretary of Finance and Public Credit. Aspe is the most high-profile member of Salinas's cabinet because of the key role he played in Mexico's debt renegotiation in 1989-90, his office's crackdown on tax evaders and his handling of the privatization pro-

(Continued)

gram. He is considered one of the most intelligent in the group of technocrats associated with Salinas and has been very active in a wide range of policy initiatives, many beyond the scope of the Finance Secretariat, from the budget to Pemex crude oil sales. Aspe has placed key supporters in various ministries and will probably be one of the major contenders for the presidency in 1994. There is concern that he has grown overly powerful too early in the current administration and is thus vulnerable to attack from the political opposition. Aspe is not well liked within the PRI.

Luis Donaldo Colosio Murrieta: President of the National Executive Committee of the Institutional Revolutionary Party (PRI) and Senator from Sonora. A University of Pennsylvania graduate (Masters in economics), Colosio was the campaign manager for Salinas during the 1988 presidential race and was appointed president of the PRI after Salinas took office in December 1988. He is closely identified with the president and has pushed through reforms in the PRI designed to reduce the power of old party bosses, especially those linked to the labor sector led by Fidel Velázquez. He is disliked by a large part of the PRI machinery but was reappointed to head the party in August 1990 just prior to the PRI's 14th National Assembly.

Fidel Velázquez: Secretary General of the Confederation of Mexican Workers (CTM), a position he first held in 1941, only five years after the CTM was formed. Don Fidel, as the labor chieftain is known, is surpassed only by the PRI as the longest-living institution in Mexico's modern history. He was opposed to Salinas's ascension to power but has been effectively weakened by the president. At present, Fidel is in a fierce struggle with a smaller union, the Workers and Peasants Revolutionary Confederation (CROC), which is supported by the administration and hopes to replace Fidel and the CTM as the most powerful labor organization after Fidel's scheduled retirement in 1992. No clear successor is yet visible, and his retirement or death will most likely be followed by a major restructuring of the organized labor movement.

Francisco Hernández Juárez: Secretary General of the Telephone Workers Union since 1976. Juárez is the most politically active of a trio of younger labor leaders—along with Jorge Sánchez García of the Electrical Workers Union (SME) and Homero Flores of the Air Pilots Union (ASPA)—who have maintained comfortable relations

(Continued)

with the administration. Earlier in the president's term, the newly founded Federation of Unions of Goods and Services Companies, in which Juárez plays a key role, was expected to gradually replace the Labor Congress (CT) as part of the government's plan to remove labor's old guard and replace it with younger leaders who more readily accept the president's modernization scheme. However, Labor Secretary Arsenio Farell Cubillas has recently supported both CROC and Rafael de Jesús Lozano Contreras, the new head of the Labor Congress, in hopes of developing pro-government labor leaders who are less independent than Juárez.

Cuauhtémoc Cárdenas: Head of the PRD and former presidential candidate during the controversial July 1988 elections. Cárdenas, a former PRI governor and the son of the most revered Mexican president of this century—Gen. Lázaro Cárdenas—continues to be the best-known political opponent to Salinas. Cárdenas has been busy, however, trying to hold factions of the PRD together. The party is divided internally between those more willing to negotiate with the government and hardliners who insist that negotiations with Salinas will only serve to legitimize the administration. A Cárdenas-led front (since dismantled) known as the National Democratic Front, officially came in second place in the 1988 presidential elections, although some observers believe it garnered votes roughly even with those of Salinas. The PRD has been able to mobilize sufficient force to combat selective electoral fraud practiced against it. It should prove to be the PRI's greatest challenge in the Federal District (Mexico City) and in the central states of Michoacán, México, Guerrero and Morelos in the August 1991 midterm elections.

Manuel Camacho Solís: Head of the Department of the Federal District, often referred to as the Regent or Mayor of Mexico City. His position is appointed by the president; it is not an elected post. Camacho was the Secretary of Ecology and Urban Development during the Miguel de la Madrid administration and played a key role in Salinas's presidential campaign. He is identified with the reform wing of the PRI and has been the subject of heavy criticism from the old guard in the party, which has slowed down party reform. Camacho has privately called for a greater role for the opposition and has the difficult job of controlling Mexico City, where left-of-center leader Cárdenas has strong support. How well Camacho continues to respond to the opposition will affect his political future. He is consid-

(Continued)

ered to be, along with Secretary of Finance Pedro Aspe, among the strongest contenders for the presidency in 1994.

Rolando Vega Iñíguez: Head of the Business Coordinating Council (CCE), owner of Seguros and Fianzas Atlas and part owner of the CBI brokerage house. He is former director of Banca Confia and previous president of the Mexican Association of Bankers. Iñíguez was reelected to head the CCE in July 1990, after serving in an interim capacity in 1989. He has tried to maintain CCE unity by following an independent—but not too critical—line vis-à-vis the government. Iñíguez, along with Agustín Legorreta, former head of Banamex and head of the Inverlat brokerage house and Seguros America, as well as former bank owners Carlos Abedrop, Alberto Bailleres and Pablo and Israel Brener, are all prospective purchasers of the commercial banks up for sale in 1991.

Need for Reform: The 1994 Challenge

The fact that Mexico's political system remains fairly closed, however, presents the risk of political instability. Salinas's failure to reform the PRI poses one of the most serious political problems facing Mexico today. If this issue is not resolved, it could complicate the presidential succession process in 1994.

Since Salinas assumed the presidency, he has gained a great measure of popularity he did not enjoy prior to his election. The same cannot be said for the PRI, however. Although the president has been able to link lower inflation and much-needed social programs with his personal leadership—while maintaining some distance from recent state elections where the opposition complained of fraud—the PRI's standing continues to suffer from its identification with vote-rigging and antiquated party machinery.

In the past, the PRI was used by the president in power as the conduit for social improvements ranging from new schools, roads and medical clinics to sewage systems and electrification projects. Following the reduction in government spending since the economic crisis of 1982, the PRI has watched as cutbacks in social programs eroded its popular appeal. The most serious challenge to the party, however, is a new social works program created by Salinas, known as the National Solidarity Program (Pronasol). The program is an extrasecretarial campaign that provides many of the services traditionally identified with the PRI. Salinas has taken on the program as a personal project and travels the country extensively to inaugurate new schools and water projects and hand out titles to plots of land. The PRI has not been strongly associated with the program, whereas the links between Pronasol and President Salinas have been very strong.

Unless there is a concerted effort on the part of Salinas to revive the declining image of the PRI, Mexico will be faced in 1994 with a president and a campaign that may have significant popular support, but do not possess a strong electoral apparatus within the party to prepare for the presidential succession. This has led to widespread speculation about 1994, with some officials in the Salinas administration favoring a constitutional reform that would eliminate Mexico's prohibition of reelection—a constitutional tenet that was one of the rallying cries of the Mexican Revolution. They argue that the president should not take the risk of naming a successor who could change the course of his reforms.

Although it is highly unlikely that Salinas will attempt to push through a constitutional reform to permit reelection, the fact that this possibility forms a part of the political discourse in Mexico today demonstrates the concern over 1994 elections. The challenge facing Salinas is to find a way to translate his personal popularity into support for a largely discredited party. Under a less likely scenario, he might need to take the risk of either creating a new party or putting the Solidarity campaign machinery to the test as a surrogate for the PRI.

Political Watchlist

Finalization of Free Trade Talks: Mid-1992
If negotiations between the US, Mexico and Canada go as scheduled, FTA talks could be completed in early 1992.

Labor Union Reorganization: 1992
Fidel Velázquez has indicated his intention to retire from the CTM at the end of his term. If he does not die before then, the labor movement will undergo a major transformation after his retirement. Although the government is already trying to limit the CTM's power in order to avoid a vacuum after Velázquez's departure, labor unrest will be exacerbated as new union leaders jockey for position.

Legislative Approval of Free Trade Agreement:
Late 1992 or early 1993
Although approval in Mexico of a free trade agreement is not in question, the US Congress vote will be carefully watched.

Preparation for 1994 Presidential Succession: Spring 1993

By the spring of 1993, the leading contenders for the 1994 presidential vote will be clearly identified. Cabinet changes during 1992-93 will help observers recognize the leading candidates. Until then, attention will focus on how Mexico City Mayor Manuel Camacho Solís and Secretary of Finance Pedro Aspe Armella fare.

PRI Selection of Presidential Candidate for 1994, or the Destape (unveiling): October-November 1993

Although in theory the selection process lies with the PRI, Salinas will have the decisive vote and will have already groomed his hand-picked successor from his cabinet. The decision by the PRI is traditionally made in the autumn of the year preceding the elections, which are scheduled for the summer of 1994.

Presidential Elections for the Term of Office 1994-2000: August 1994

The PRI has never lost an election since its founding early in this century, and the 1994 election is not likely to be an exception. If free trade talks go well and Mexico's economy continues to grow, the threat of an opposition victory will be extremely limited. Cárdenas will almost certainly run, however, and could benefit from a strong nationalistic vote if trade agreement problems arise.

5

The Economy on the Eve of Free Trade

Mexico is a giant in terms of population, size of economy, territory and natural resources. It is the 11th most populated nation in the world (with inhabitants estimated at 81.1 million in 1990), more than three times the size of the US's northern neighbor, Canada, and larger than any European nation. Its economy ranks approximately 15th in the world, above those of Sweden, Belgium, Austria, Taiwan and South Korea. Within Mexico's territory lie proven oil reserves of at least 65.5 billion bbl—the fourth largest in the world. The country also produces more silver, fluorite and graphite than any other nation worldwide and is a major producer of many other minerals.

Despite this wealth of resources, territory and population, Mexico has failed to achieve its development potential. The nation's third-world infrastructure and legacy of excessive state regulation of the economy have restricted economic growth. Now, on the eve of Mexico's entry into a North American free trade agreement (FTA), President Salinas is tackling the serious difficulties Mexico faces. If he is successful, the nation could join the ranks of other important, newly industrialized economic powers.

The general forecast for Mexico over the next few years is positive: increased growth fueled by greater foreign and domestic private investment spending, as well as a gradual recuperation of workers' lost purchasing power accompanying rising per capita income. There are also real risks inherent in Mexico's current economic structure, however, which could limit the country's ability to sustain stable economic growth. Mexico is still a developing country, with serious problems in areas such as infrastructure, education, income distribution, employment and agriculture, and limited experience with the market-oriented business culture that has developed in the rest of North America, Europe and parts of Asia. Furthermore, Mexico's external accounts are burdened by large foreign debt servicing obligations, in addition to growing trade and current-account deficits, which could pose serious problems to the president's goals of economic modernization and stability.

Companies willing to monitor Mexico's progress in creating a modern economy will be able to best take advantage of the country as a more stable sourcing site, a growing market for their goods and services and a centerpiece in their plans to rationalize production within the North American market. Mexico will certainly have problems in the years to come, but firms with a clear vision of the economy's strengths and weaknesses will be well positioned to analyze economic difficulties and determine if they are symptomatic of a more serious imbalance or are minor flare-ups accompanying more stable economic growth.

Fulfilling this task requires careful and consistent monitoring of Mexico's political, economic and regulatory environment. This chapter provides a brief summary of Salinas's economic reform plan, a general forecast of the consequences of a North American FTA on Mexico and a look at Mexico's current economic situation.

The Challenge of Development

Mexico's economy has undergone a radical transformation in recent years. Its domestic market has been opened to foreign-produced goods as barriers to trade, and import duties have been drastically reduced. Restrictive regulations have been relaxed to permit greater foreign investment in industry. In addition, the economy is being exposed to greater competition as state-owned industries are privatized and a deregulation campaign is put in place. The changes are especially dramatic when viewed against the decades-old backdrop of state intervention and a closed economy based on the model of import substitution. These changes are also the first signs of a policy that will further open the country's economy to a North American regional market, which will be formalized with the signing of an FTA.

Antecedents to Reform

Mexico's turnaround dates back to a shift in economic policymaking begun cautiously under Miguel de la Madrid (1982–88) and accelerated by Carlos Salinas de Gortari. When President de la Madrid took office on Dec. 1, 1982, Mexico was in the midst of its worst economic crisis since emerging from the decade-long revolution in the 1920s. The "era" of rising oil prices in the late 1970s turned out to be short lived. When the oil boom fizzled, Mexico's economy, heavily in debt to foreign commercial banks, took a turn for the worse. Just months before de la Madrid was sworn in, Mexico had devalued the peso, suspended payment on its foreign debt, imposed exchange controls, nationalized the commercial banking system and froze dollar bank deposits (which were then converted into pesos). Public confidence in the government's ability to manage the economy had hit rock bottom.

De la Madrid immediately adopted measures to increase domestic savings, strengthen nonoil exports, gradually remove trade restrictions and help the country's private sector restructure its dollar debt to avoid bankruptcy. Economic planners, however, still clung to the idea of import substitution, encouraging local manufacture of goods for domestic consumption while limiting or prohibiting imports. As late as 1984, "national integration" plans—designed to keep sectors such as the pharmaceutical and automotive industries protected from foreign import competition—were being promulgated. According to a senior official in the de la Madrid administration, it was not until a second oil price drop in late 1985–86, and a subsequent debt crisis, that the government realized more fundamental changes were needed and the pace of reform had to be accelerated.

During the last three years of de la Madrid's term of office (1986–88), the administration discarded the import-substitution model and began to do away with much of Mexico's traditional protectionist trade poli-

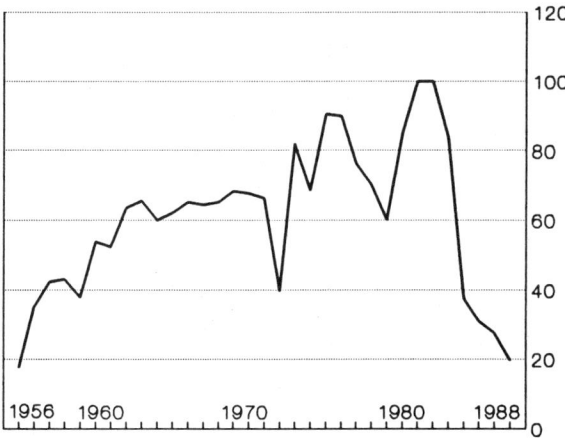

Figure 5-1. Trade opening (share of Mexican imports requiring license—%). *(Source: US Intl. Trade Commission)*

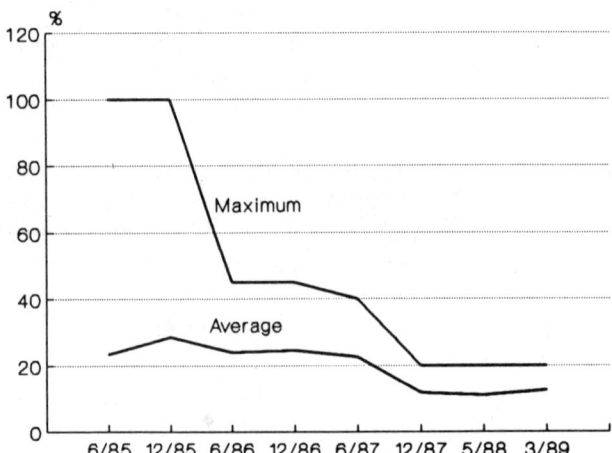

Figure 5-2. Falling import duties (% rates in effect 1985-89). *(Source: Ministry of Finance)*

cies and limitations on foreign investment. Officials adopted a policy based on trade liberalization, shrinkage of the state sector and price and wage controls (which have been extended and elaborated on by the Salinas administration). From 1986–88, Mexico joined GATT; eliminated most import licenses (in 1982 all goods required licenses to be imported and by 1988 only 21% of the value of all imports required licensing); and accelerated its plans to gradually reduce import duties. Privatization of state-owned enterprises had begun, and a social pact was reached between labor and business to hold down price and wage increases to bring inflation under control.

Although de la Madrid did much to usher in a new era for Mexico, it was President Salinas (1988–94) who solidified the previous administration's accomplishments and pushed the concept of opening (apertura) into areas of the economy that had long been considered the province of the state.

Salinas's Liberalization Thrust

Upon taking office at end-1988, Salinas enunciated an economic reform program with four major goals: (1) control and reduce inflation, (2) trim the public sector and reduce its debt, (3) liberalize trade and (4) boost domestic and foreign investment. Although some actions taken by Salinas have surprised the public, such as his decision in May 1990 to reform the constitution and reprivatize the commercial banking system, his decrees have generally been consistent with his reform plan. With some of his initiatives, it has been the timing that has caught political observers off guard. Consistency has been a hallmark of Salinas's reform program since its inception. Although it does not often state its intentions explicitly, the administration strongly believes that consistent and predictable actions (in substance, if not timing) are crucial to developing and sustaining public confidence in the economy and the government's ability to manage it. In fact, public confidence lies at the very center of Salinas's foremost goal of stable economic growth with price stability.

Tackling inflation

In order to tackle inflation—which has been the administration's number one priority during its first three years—Salinas extended a program of price, wage and exchange rate controls (called the Economic Solidarity Pact, or PSE) begun during the last 12 months of the de la Madrid administration and renamed it the Pact for Stability and Economic Growth (PECE). Through a series of pacts, signed for limited periods of seven to 14 months, business and labor representatives promised to limit or eliminate price and wage increases. In return, the government curbed price increases of public goods and services and strictly controlled peso devaluation.

The results have been a sharp initial decline in inflation, from 51.7% at end-1988 to 19.7% at end-1989. During 1990, however, as the government reduced subsidies on certain public sector goods and services and experimented with greater price relief for private firms, inflation rose to nearly 30%, with the consumer price index reaching 29.9% at end-1990. Inflation in 1991 was down again, to 18.8%.

One of the most criticized elements of the PECE has been the government's decision to control the peso's daily parity with the dollar as part of its anti-inflation campaign. Critics contend that the peso is overvalued, pointing to the growing trade deficit, and that consequently a maxidevaluation will be required. Government officials argue that a lower rate of slippage helps reduce inflationary expectations and will result in reduced inflation. Furthermore, they argue that the peso must be compared with more currencies than just the US dollar, many of which have appreciated against the dollar.

Despite criticisms that controls on prices, wages and exchange rate movements are an inefficient—or even ineffective—means of stabilizing inflation, the controls have reduced inflationary expectations and prevented Mexico from experiencing hyperinflation—which was a real danger in 1987 and early 1988. (Inflation peaked at 180% in March 1988.)

Although trade liberalization is a separate goal, the administration's anti-inflation campaign also owes much of its success to increased import competition. Many businesses in Mexico concede that import competition has been more important than price controls in limiting their ability to increase prices.

Shrinking the state sector

The growth of Mexico's public sector reached its apogee in 1982 when, in response to massive capital flight, then-President José López Portillo ordered the nationalization of the country's commercial banking system, with the exception of one workers bank and the only foreign commercial bank in operation. From that point forward, privatization became the watchword for subsequent administrations. By mid-1991, over 875 out of 1,155 state enterprises had been sold, merged, liquidated, closed or consolidated with other firms, including both national airlines—Aeroméxico (Aeronaves de México) and Mexicana (Compañía Mexicana de Aviación)—Cananea, the country's largest copper mine, hotel chains, sugar refineries, parts of Conasupo, the national foodstuffs company and, most recently, the controlling share in Telmex (Teléfonos de México), the national telephone company. The principal steel mills were sold in 1991, and by mid-1992, all of the commercial banks will be back in private hands.

Trimming the public sector has also involved reducing government spending—especially subsidies to inefficient state entities and programs—while increasing the size of the tax base. Reductions in state spending, greater tax revenues and lower interest rates have permitted the administration to reduce the public sector borrowing requirement, which dropped from 16% of GDP during 1986 and 1987 to less than 5% during 1990. A reduced internal debt has helped push interest rates further down, which in turn cuts debt servicing in what government officials call a "virtuous circle."

The restructuring of the external debt in 1990 permitted Mexico to reduce the size of the total external debt from $95.1 billion at end-1989 to less than $84 billion in late 1990. Government projections show the debt dwindling in real terms and as a percentage of GDP in subsequent years.

Lifting trade restrictions

Perhaps the most visible contrast between the Mexico of today and that of the mid-1980s is the wide variety of imported merchandise now available to the consumer. The trade opening was accelerated during the de la Madrid administration, and Salinas has continued to lower tariffs and reduce the number of goods needing prior government approval (licenses) for their import. The highest tariff is now 20%, and most tariffs are 10% or less.

The trade liberalization in Mexico has benefited the government in its fight against inflation and has forced domestic firms to become more efficient, improve product quality and rethink their production strategies in the face of international competition.

Although a North American FTA is a logical extension of Salinas's policy to liberalize trade, the accord is geared more toward providing foreign and domestic investors with clear and stable guidelines with regard to investment access to Mexico and trade access to the US. Salinas hopes that an FTA will furnish understandable rules that are not subject to sudden change and thus extend the horizon for investment in Mexico, which is often limited or clouded by fears of major policy changes after each six-year presidential term.

Boosting foreign and domestic investment

In his bid to encourage foreign investment, Salinas issued new regulations in May 1989 that permit 100% foreign ownership in nearly two thirds of the country's economic sectors. Automatic approval of foreign investments is guaranteed if certain conditions are met. In cases where the government must still approve a venture, the new regulations speed up the process dramatically. Although these guidelines represent a codification of a more liberal government policy toward foreign investment—which companies began to notice in the last years of the de la Madrid administration—foreign investors are calling for more substantive changes. Such sweeping modifications could be accomplished via a rewrite of the restrictive 1973 Foreign Investment Law to reflect the alterations made in May 1989. Revamping the law itself is expected as a matter of course in FTA negotiations.

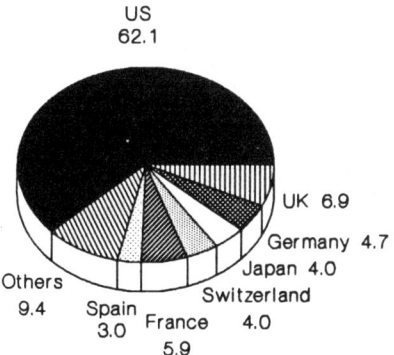

Figure 5-3. Foreign direct investment, 1990 (by country of origin—% of total). As of October 31. *(Source: Secofi)*

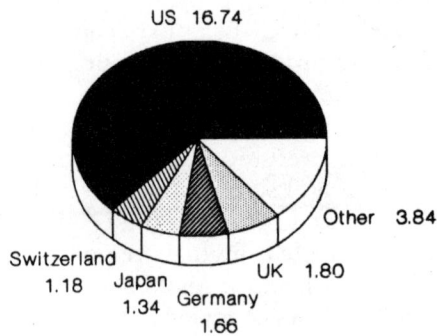

Figure 5-4. Foreign direct investment, 1990 (by sector—% of total). As of October 31. *(Source: Secofi)*

To encourage domestic and foreign investment, and as an integral part of both the trade opening and the privatization drive, the government is also attempting to deregulate many aspects of conducting business in Mexico. As a first step toward the reprivatization of the commercial banks and the eventual opening of the market to foreign financial services, the administration has given commercial banks greater freedom to decide how to allocate credit and has permitted foreigners greater access to Mexican securities. Along with the trade opening and the reduction in import licenses, the customs process has also been streamlined. In areas such as trucking, air freight and cargo handling, new regulations have broken the control of inefficient and often corrupt cartels and monopolies.

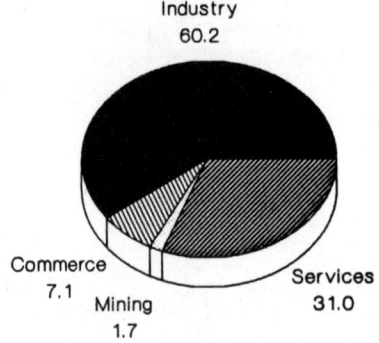

Figure 5-5. Accumulated foreign direct investment ($ billions, by country of origin). As of end-1989. *(Source: Secofi)*

An Unfinished Program

Although the pace of Mexico's economic integration within the North American market will accelerate in the coming years under the framework of the free trade agreement, large segments of the economy remain sheltered from foreign competition or are as yet unaware of the challenges that a global, or even regional, market will bring. Banking and financial services, as well as petroleum, are still closed by law. Other sectors, such as retailing, have yet to face any significant competition from abroad. Despite the heavy concentration of foreign investment in the manufacturing sector, most firms, including subsidiaries of MNCs, are just beginning to learn how to operate in a global context. Despite the size of Mexico's economy, its potential within an integrated North American market has hardly begun to be realized.

There are serious shortcomings in Mexico's infrastructure that must be resolved if greater investment and higher GDP growth are to be sustained under an FTA. Ports, railroads, highways, the postal system, telecommunications, electricity, education and water—all services traditionally provided by the government—are in need of massive upgrading. The government has made important strides: private participation in the construction and management of new toll roads has begun; the national telephone company has been privatized; and in April 1991, the Mexican Postal Service authorized a US company to operate new post offices and manage the Postal Service's express mail system. The government has already permitted other foreign companies (e.g. Federal Express—see case example in Chapter 12) to enter the air freight market to compete with the Postal Service in the areas of express mail and air cargo deliveries.

Effects of an FTA on Mexico's Economy

The pace of Mexico's economic integration with the US should accelerate over the next several years as a North American free trade agreement is negotiated and implemented. Although the FTA primarily encompasses trade issues, it is expected that investment issues—relaxation of restrictions in certain areas of the Mexican economy, in particular—will also be on the negotiating table. The impact of a North American FTA goes far beyond simply removing existing barriers to the free mobility of goods within the region. Foremost among the Salinas administration's motivations for negotiating a trade pact is the need to attract more capital investment—both from domestic and foreign sources—to finance the restructuring of Mexico's economy to permit stable growth and improved living standards.

Legal restrictions have long served to limit private and especially foreign investment in Mexico. Although many of these restrictions are being lifted, there is a more serious matter that the Salinas administration fears may obstruct large, long-term investment: the complete change of government that occurs every six years when Mexico elects a new president. Although reelection is not permitted, a president's powers are virtually unlimited during his term. The rules of the game in Mexico have changed before: The nationalization of the commercial banks in 1982 and the freezing of dollar accounts are two dramatic examples. The potential for major policy changes of this type worries many investors.

Salinas's decision to reverse many long-standing nationalistic policies has been greeted with praise by many foreign and domestic investors. Still, a doubt remains: could not his successor revert back to the previous model based on closed borders and suspicion of foreign investment? Support for the FTA is designed to respond to that fear and to create a climate of permanence in which investments can be planned.

The FTA, the administration argues, should strengthen foreign investors' confidence that the course being adopted by the Salinas government will survive in future years. Also, a free trade accord will provide investors with greater certainty that goods produced in Mexico will have access to the US and Canadian markets. Although an FTA does not guarantee a lack of protectionist sentiment in the US Congress, it does make it less likely that such sentiments will change the rules of the game. Likewise, whereas an FTA—which will be a treaty under Mexican law—could be abrogated, it would be more difficult for future Mexican presidents to alter a treaty than to change a law or executive decree.

Among the major effects of a free trade accord on Mexico will be the following:

Rising investment. A North American FTA will encourage an increase in private investment—from both foreign and domestic sources. In fact, the dramatic growth in domestic fixed investment during the latter half of 1990 and in 1991 is partially the result of greater confidence among domestic investors that some form of trade accord is inevitable. (Effort to improve quality in the face of import competition is also a reason for the sharp rise in investment spending.) The rise in investment will be motivated not just by the advent of more permanent rules of the game; investment will be the natural response to greater demand for Mexican products in the US and Canada as their prices fall and as tariffs are reduced and eventually eliminated. Increased investment in Mexico will also result in greater demand for imported machinery and capital goods, which should help companies achieve more efficient production and higher levels of productivity.

Rationalized production. This process, which has already begun in Mexico's manufacturing sector since the borders were opened to foreign-produced goods, will become more widespread. Some local industries (e.g. stereo equipment) will virtually close down because of competition from better-quality, lower-priced imports. Other industries, however, will find a comparative advantage to production in Mexico— whether it be the manufacture of a completed product or of certain components. In the autoparts industry, one leading exporter to the US has already begun reevaluating production to limit itself to certain components that can be added to a final product.

Rising wages. The cost of labor in Mexico should rise as free trade stimulates economic activity. As capital (in the form of new machinery and more advanced technological processes) enters Mexico as the result of a more stable investment climate, labor should become more productive and consequently, better paid. Wage rates are not likely to rise as dramatically as some analysts have suggested, however. Although an increase in demand for labor and higher productivity is an expected effect of a North American FTA, Mexico has a very large labor pool that is unevenly distributed throughout the country, thus limiting wage hikes. Increased migration from southern Mexico (the poorest region) to central and northern Mexico, where many new companies are likely to establish their operations (to better serve both the central Mexican and southwestern US market from a single production site), will help slow the rate of rises in real wages.

Accelerated GDP growth. Investment will fuel GDP growth to levels above 5% p.a. in coming years. Bottlenecks may develop in some areas, however (e.g. petrochemicals and financial services), unless the government relaxes restrictions on foreign or domestic investment. Although imports and exports are expected to increase dramatically, import growth will probably be higher than export growth (as is currently the case) during the next five years as a result of the need for capital goods in Mexico to help industries recover after a long period of weak investment. Even when overall GDP growth in Mexico was much lower, imports grew faster than exports. With greater investment needed to compete with foreign goods and to supply a rapidly growing domestic market (which will have little idle plant capacity), imports, primarily of capital and intermediary goods, will continue to rise.

Ballooning current-account deficit. Strong growth in investment spending, much of it on imported capital goods, suggests that Mexico's current-account deficit will continue to grow over the next several years. The deficit does pose certain dangers to Mexico: The country will be very dependent on large capital inflows in order to finance the shortfall. Large amounts of direct foreign investment and capital repatriation will

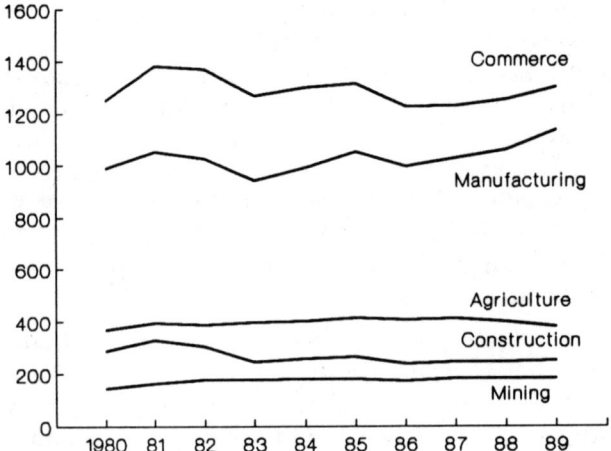

Figure 5-6. Production stagnates in 1980s . . . (billions of constant 1980 pesos). *(Source: INEGI)*

be needed, but it is projected that these inflows will be forthcoming as long as Mexico stays on course with trade and economic liberalization. Indeed, strong capital-account surpluses in both 1990 and 1991 were more than enough to meet Mexico's financing needs.

Mexico's return to international capital markets, involving both private and government enterprises, should become another important source of foreign financing. Greater liberalization of the rules permitting foreign indirect investment in the Mexican stock market, and changes to make it easier for domestic companies to seek equity financing, will also provide greater sources of financing needed for growth.

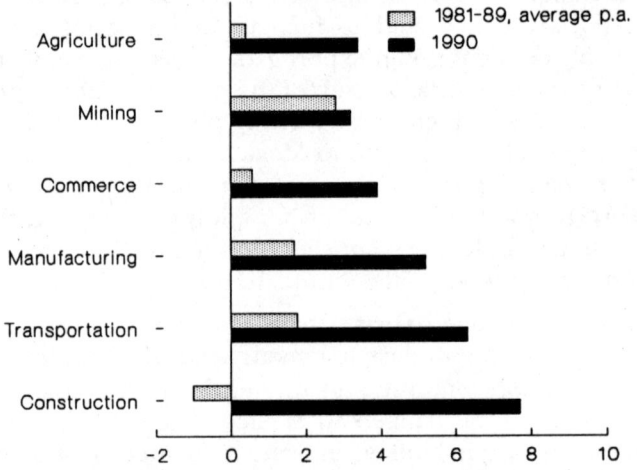

Figure 5-7. . . . . But recovers in 1990 (sectoral growth—%). *(Source: INEGI)*

Mexico's Thriving Parallel Economy

The economic crisis of the 1980s led to the emergence of a massive parallel economy in Mexico. Although the informal sector functions as a safety valve against unemployment, it also distorts government efforts at economic planning and analysis, represents stiff competition for many businesses and is a major avenue for tax evasion. In Mexico City, the proliferation of street vendors has forced officials to seek solutions, but they are handicapped by the sector's size and unique political strength.

Estimates of the informal economy's size vary greatly, but an analysis published by the private sector Center for Economic Studies (CEESP) indicates that undocumented activity adds up to 25-33% of official GDP figures; some estimates run as high as 40%. Conservative calculations place informal sector production at almost $50 billion above the official GDP of $201 billion for 1990.

All available data on the informal economy point to phenomenal growth over the last 10 years. A Banco Nacional de México study estimates that over 26% of the economically active population participated in the informal sector in 1989, up from just 4.4% in 1980. Other studies indicate that informal activity grew from 10% of GDP in 1970 to 25-30% during the 1980s.

Avoiding the tax bite and regulation

The greatest motivator of undocumented activity is tax evasion. According to one economist, the most important contribution to the informal economy—in terms of value added—comes from legitimate businesses underreporting profits for tax purposes. In 1989, unpaid taxes from underground activity in Mexico City were estimated at 70% of the total tax receipts for the year. Another study, based on 1985 data, estimated unpaid taxes nationwide at over 25% of all federal receipts.

In 1990, the government began to crack down on tax evaders, stepping up enforcement efforts and singling out several cases with high visibility. Although most business leaders recognized the need to clamp down, many executives complained about unequal treatment.

Excessive regulation is another problem. For some industries (e.g. trucking), deregulation has been positive. Restrictive and outdated rules forced a large portion of the industry into illegal activity, which created a system of corrupt trucking oligarchies with a stranglehold on freight handling in large areas of the country. Industry regula-

(Continued)

tions were revamped in 1989, however, and the Trade Secretariat reports that 35,000 additional trucks have been registered since the new rules went into effect.

Look-alikes and copycats

In at least one case, lack of regulation encouraged underground activity. Inadequate intellectual property protection and a sluggish legal system have caused the bootleg recording, video and computer software business to blossom. The National Computer Program Association (ANIPCO) reports that the illicit copying or sale of top-of-the-line software (e.g. Lotus, D-base) is on a par with legitimate software sales.

Bootleg software is cheap and readily available, with some stores openly selling pirated packages, complete with manuals, at about 10% of the normal price. Although piracy occurs at industrial levels, it has also developed into a cottage industry, with hackers taking out classified ads to promote bootleg programs.

The informal sector has also become an avenue for parallel market goods, or inferior products that compete with established brands. Makers of athletic shoes have been hurt by Asian imports of cheap footwear, many of which are underreported in customs and channeled through the informal market. Also, licensed shoe distributors complain about a lack of trademark control, with brand-name copies or look-alikes entering Mexico freely. In 1990, the government initiated a program to clamp down on low-quality imports, implementing stricter control and labeling standards.

Domestic producers also specialize in look-alikes, focusing on such products as cosmetics and shampoos. One source reports a strong demand for empty skin cream containers, sold to underground producers who market their copy-cat product through the informal sector at bargain prices.

Peddling and political might

Some workers in the underground economy conduct business above ground, e.g. street vending and other curbside operations. A 1989 study placed Mexico City's informal sector retail sales for that year at about Ps1.2 trillion ($453 million). Reportedly, street vendors realize profits as high as 55% on sales of imported items such as electrical equipment and appliances. Established merchants complain of unfair competition from vendors who operate without being regulated or paying taxes. The Federal District assembly is under a great deal of pressure to regulate the sector.

(Continued)

Although peddlers are nothing new in Latin America, Mexico's vendors are unique because they represent a powerful, organized political force—one allied with the ruling party. The majority of street vendors in Mexico City and throughout the country are required (often by force) to become affiliates of the Institutional Revolutionary Party (PRI), usually through its lateral merchant associations or popular organizations.

In the past, the PRI has used this relationship to mobilize support and garner votes. Now, however, the informal sector is using it for political leverage in confronting government regulatory efforts. Vendors recently demonstrated to protest mistreatment by police, forced evictions from certain locations and other government pressures on their ever-increasing ranks.

Economic Profile and Forecast

In 1990, Mexico's economy experienced real GDP growth of 4.4%, the strongest growth registered since it entered its economic crisis in the early 1980s. Despite the US recession in 1991, Mexico posted another strong year of economic expansion with growth of 3.6%, fueled by a marked increase in investment and consumer spending.

Mexico's GDP reached about Ps668 trillion ($238 billion) in 1990. The actual size and growth rate of the economy are difficult to determine, however, given a large informal sector. Some analysts suggest that the economy is at least 25% larger than reported in official GDP statistics. There is also strong evidence that the economy grew at rates higher than officially reported in the 1980s. The informal economy is strongest in urban areas and plays a dominant role in retailing and commerce (see box on pages 97–98 and above on the informal economy).

GDP will grow rapidly in 1992–95 as investment spending remains strong, rising from to about 5–6% p.a. There are dangers, however, that the economy could overheat and that bottlenecks in areas such as transportation, telecommunications and the supply of skilled labor could develop if the growth rate is too high.

Agriculture: Dominance of the Ejido

Mexico's primary sector—agriculture, livestock, fishing and forestry—has lagged behind the economy over the past 40 years. As a percentage of GDP, it has declined steadily from more than 15% in 1960 to 7.5% in both 1989 and 1990. Agricultural production grew in 1990 by 3.4%, the first year of growth since 1987, and thanks in large part to more favorable climatic conditions. Although the sector is expected to continue its growth in 1992–95 (albeit at a slower rate, averaging 2% p.a.) and share of overall GDP appears to have stabilized, bold moves will be required to incorporate it into a North American market. While some product categories—fruits and vegetables for the frozen-food market in the US in particular—have grown substantially in recent years and attracted private investors, most of Mexico's countryside remains divided up in small land plots (ejidos).

A new scheme designed by the Agriculture Secretariat to permit alliances between the private sector and ejido farmers was begun in 1990. Then, in early 1992, the government overhauled its agrarian legislation and formally ended the nation's agrarian reform program. Besides ceasing distribution of land parcels, the new law authorized ejido farmers to rent their land or enter into joint ventures and other contractual arrangements with private investors. In addition, the law allows companies to own land for the first time since Mexico's revolution early this century. Now, with clearer rules of the game in place, agribusiness companies will be more willing to make large investments in Mexico. The agriculture sector, which has performed at levels below those of any other in Mexico's economic development, also has perhaps the greatest potential under an open market (see Chapter 7, Reforms in Agriculture).

Mining: Below Potential

Despite rich mineral resources—Mexico is the world's largest producer of silver and a leader in sulphur, lead and zinc—Mexico has not been able to revive its mining sector. During 1990, mining output was up 3.2%, but lower world prices in 1991 slowed growth. The government has moved cautiously to allow more foreign investment in mining—it is presently restricted to 34% in companies permitted to mine coal, iron ore, phosphoric rock and sulphur and 49% for firms involved in most other mining activities. Through the use of 20-year trusts, foreign companies can obtain majority control in all mining projects (except oil and uranium, which are important sources of revenue and remain limited to the state). In 1990, several foreign mining concerns obtained 100% control—part equity and part via a 20-year temporary trust. During 1992–94 the industry plans to invest about $2.1 billion in mining, although if restrictions are further relaxed for US and Canadian mining companies total investment in the sector could increase more substantially.

Petroleum: Starving for Investment

Mexico has the fourth-largest oil reserves in the world—all controlled by Petróleos Méxicanos (Pemex), the state monopoly. Oil revenues accounted for roughly 12% of the government's 1990 budget. Output rose to just over 2.5 million bpd during 1990. Exports declined from the high of 1.38 million bpd in late 1990, however, when Pemex increased export sales to respond to the Persian Gulf crisis. Exports averaged 1.36 million bpd during the first few months of 1991. In 1990, the average price for crude exports was up considerably to $19.12/bbl, a 22% increase over 1989 prices, the result of price hikes following Iraq's invasion of Kuwait. With the Mideast conflict over, prices have fallen, and Pemex is not expected to repeat 1990's revenues of $10 billion in crude and petrochemical sales ($8.9 billion in crude sales) until 1993 at the earliest.

Although Pemex was able to bring in some $3 billion more than the government had budgeted for 1990, most of the increased revenues resulted from the rise in oil prices, not from higher production levels. In fact, years of declining investment in exploration, drilling and refinery capacity have left Pemex unable to significantly raise the level of exports.

Pemex is attempting to tackle the problem by increasing investment funds—up 11.8% in real terms in the 1991 budget—and is aggressively seeking outside financing. One of the principal projects for which Pemex has sought such financing is the $807 million Cantarell project in the Campeche Sound. According to an internal study prepared by Pemex's Strategic Planning Division, the Cantarell project would provide Pemex with an additional 380,000 bpd within four years and would permit the entity to maintain current production levels for another six or seven years. Without Cantarell, Pemex studies estimate that Mexico will become a net importer of crude oil by 1997.

Despite the importance of the Cantarell project, Cantarell has had difficulty obtaining financing. When the authorities first tried to secure capital in 1990, they were turned down by the Japanese Eximbank. Following the Persian Gulf crisis, however, Pemex found new interest—this time from the US Eximbank. In November of 1990, US Treasury Secretary Nicholas Brady announced that a $1.6 billion loan from the US Eximbank would be available to help finance new petroleum exploration and drilling ventures in Mexico. (The loan proceeds will be limited to contracts with US companies.) Mexican officials later indicated that total loan proceeds from the US Eximbank may represent nearly $6 billion. The Cantarell project is expected to be a recipient of some of the loan proceeds.

Despite some press reports stating that Mexico's decision to issue service contracts to foreign companies was a major shift in policy, the country has not publicly changed its position that risk contracts are not permitted under the Mexican Constitution and that no constitutional changes will be made.

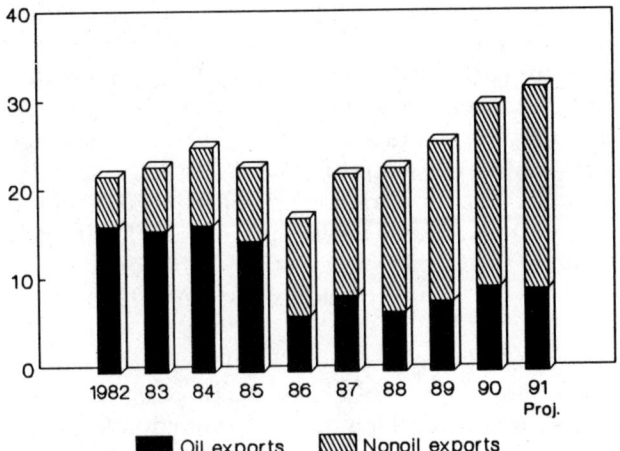

Figure 5-8. Less dependence on oil exports ($ billions). *(Source: Banco de México)*

Additional funds are coming from international capital markets where Pemex placed $450 million worth of Eurobonds during 1990. The government has also turned to foreign companies to aid in exploration and drilling. In April 1991, Pemex awarded a precedent-setting contract to Triton, a US company, to explore and drill for crude. More exploration and drilling contracts are expected.

Industry: Gearing Up for the FTA

The industrial sector (which includes mining, manufacturing, construction and utilities) represents roughly one third of Mexico's GDP. During the current economic recovery, this sector has experienced the strongest growth. Industrial production rose 3% in 1991, and is expected to grow at an average rate of some 6% during 1992–95.

The most important component of the industrial sector is **manufacturing,** which represents nearly one quarter of GDP. Manufacturing grew 5.2% in 1990 and about 4% during 1991. The strongest growth areas in the manufacturing sector in 1990 were metal machinery and equipment (12.9%), "other" industries (8.8%), basic metals (8%) and publishing (7%). Other key areas of manufacturing include automotive, food processing, chemicals and petrochemical products. Manufacturing is expected to remain one of the strongest sectors within industry over the next few years, as companies gear up production to face greater import competition and to take advantage of greater access to the North American market.

A forecast for moderate growth in manufacturing in general does not mean some sectors will not be harmed by greater integration with North America. Sectors such as electronics (radios, televisions, stereo equipment), textiles and furniture have all suffered from the trade opening experienced thus far. Whereas some areas, such as textiles, may grow under an FTA as a result of greater access to the US market, others will continue to decline and may even cease to be economically viable.

Because Mexico was traditionally a fairly closed market, little disposition to export existed—with certain notable exceptions, such as the maquiladoras, which operate under a special trade regime. Since Mexico was largely closed to imports, foreign companies wishing to sell in the Mexican market had little choice but to set up manufacturing operations in Mexico. The country has only recently opened up and begun to develop an export mentality. The result is a relatively weak export focus despite a few standouts, such as the automotive industry (vehicles, motors and autoparts), with exports of $4.5 billion that account for nearly 30% of all manufacturing exports and 25% of all nonoil exports in 1990.

Now, the industrial sector is forecast to look more like the maquiladora industry, which has enjoyed a limited type of free trade "agreement." The difference between the current maquiladora regime and the future of Mexican industry under an FTA is that whereas maquiladoras enjoyed zero duties, most of their production had to be exported and thus did not compete directly with Mexican industries. Under an FTA, import competition for domestic industries will increase.

The maquiladora industry as it is now defined is expected to show slower growth in the next few years after a strong year in 1990—up nearly 20% in terms of value added, from $3 billion in 1989 to $3.6 billion in 1990. The US recession has hurt the sector more strongly than other manufacturing sectors because of its nearly exclusive export focus. With the prospects of further relaxation of restrictions on foreign investment and zero tariffs for all industries, two key advantages to setting up a maquiladora will be lost, causing many companies to look at other forms of doing business in Mexico (see Chapter 11 on the maquiladora sector).

The fastest-growing area within the industrial sector in 1990–91 was **construction,** which grew approximately 4% during 1991, following a 7.7% increase in 1990. The high levels of growth in construction are the result of infrastructure projects—from highway and road building to maritime port construction—as well as the building of residences and hotels. The upgrading of infrastructure is one of the most critical tasks at hand, and the Salinas administration has come up with creative ways (e.g. toll roads) to permit private financing, construction and operation of infrastructure projects.

Services: Still Opening Up

The services sector represents approximately 60% of Mexico's registered economy, with the retailing, hotel and restaurant industries accounting for more than 25% of total GDP. After experiencing 3.3% growth in 1990, the sector is expected to expand an average of 4–5% p.a. during 1992–95.

Services growth has been uneven, with transportation and communications expanding fastest in 1989 (5.2%) and 1990 (6.3%). Retailing, restaurants and hotels grew by 3.9% during 1990—the same rate as the economy in general. The actual level of growth in retailing is difficult to determine, however, since this is one of the areas in which the informal economy is strongest, making official numbers highly unreliable.

Retailing, which is still virtually unexplored by foreign investors, is expected to see increased foreign interest, especially in franchises and in the Mexico City area, where nearly one fifth of the nation's population resides. **Financial services** should also receive foreign investment as insurance companies, investment banks and other financial companies are opened to foreign capital.

Tourism is one of Mexico's most important sources of foreign exchange income, although it is not the cure for the country's underdeveloped economy many officials envisioned in the early 1970s. Tourism income grew 14% in 1990, with total income reaching $3.4 billion. Foreign and local investment in Mexico's Pacific coast and Baja California resorts should continue to help boost tourist activity. Still, tourism faces certain restrictions because of years of poor investment in infrastructure and limits on foreign transportation services. Construction of complementary infrastructure—from marinas and golf courses to convention centers—has not kept up with the pace of hotel construction. Even though improvements and expansions in Mexico's principal airports have permitted the tourism industry to take advantage of liberalization in air travel (charter flights are now permitted), the poor condition of roads and other services has kept Mexico from benefiting from new rules permitting the introduction of foreign chartered bus services.

Government Spending:
Deficit Down

The budget for 1991 included Ps144.2 trillion (about $48 billion) in programmable public expenditures, a 2.3% real increase over 1990's level. Total spending, including debt servicing, was budgeted at Ps233.8 trillion (about $78 billion), a 5% real decrease from 1990. Social services, including urban development, drinking water, health, education and the National Solidarity Program (Pronasol), Salinas's anti-poverty plan, received the largest budgetary increases. Pronasol received a 41.2% real hike for 1991—the greatest increase in the overall budget, pushing it to Ps5.1 trillion ($1.7 billion). Pronasol expenditures exceeded federal funds to tourism, fishing, urban development and drinking water programs combined.

Government income of Ps142.6 trillion ($47.5 billion) in 1991 represented 27.7% of GDP and a real increase of 1.2% over 1990. Taxes and receipts from government-owned enterprises accounted for most of the income, with Pemex contributions alone amounting to nearly one third of state revenue. When the 1991 budget was drawn up in fall 1990, officials adopted what appeared to be a very cautious forecast for oil revenues: the budget carried the assumption that crude oil exports would average 1.36 million bpd at about $17/bbl p.a. during 1991. By the end of first-quarter 1991, that "cautious" target seemed less attainable. In early 1991, officials purchased options providing guarantees that despite further drops in the price of crude oil, Mexico would get a price of at least $17/bbl during the year.

The drop in interest rates during 1990 and 1991 improved the government's finances considerably. By end-1990, the public sector domestic debt had fallen to Ps134.5 trillion (about $45 billion), a 9.5% decline in real terms from the end of 1989. The administration's ability to reduce its deficit further also contributed to the drop in the internal debt. The fall in interest rates and the reduction in the size of the internal debt permitted the government to achieve the smallest financial deficit in years—3.9% of GDP in 1990. Moves to widen the tax base and decrease state subsidies helped further reduce the financial deficit in 1991, and should permit the government to achieve a surplus in 1992.

The government has also reaped the benefits of the external debt restructuring, which provided total cash flow savings of approximately $5.8 billion in 1990 and $3.8 billion in 1991. Total external debt as a percent of GDP fell from a high of 76.6% in 1986 to approximately 38.8% in 1990 and is projected to fall below 30% by 1994.

Additional funds from the sale of state-owned companies and healthy oil revenues have helped the government maintain its spending levels without serious problems. At the end of 1990, the government sold a 20.4% controlling interest in Telmex to a group of Mexican investors and foreign operating companies for $1.76 billion, followed by a public offering in early 1991 of additional Telmex shares worth an estimated $2 billion. When revenues are added from the sale of the domestic commercial banks, to be completed in 1992, total revenues from the privatizations could reach $10–20 billion. Although the eventual use of such funds has not been disclosed, they should serve as an important cushion for any budgetary problems.

Investment: Accelerated Growth

Investment was a key component behind 1990's strong economic growth in Mexico, as companies positioned themselves for greater competition under an FTA and responded to already increased rivalry resulting from previous progress in trade liberalization. It is expected to be a major component of total spending over the next several years.

Fixed investment rose by an estimated 10% in 1991 and is forecast to rise 7% p.a. on average during 1992–95. This compares with a strong showing of 13.4% in 1990. Private investment—which now accounts for nearly three quarters of all investment—should rise by similar amounts (vs 13.6% in 1990), although public sector investment spending will continue to be important.

New direct foreign investment spent in 1990 reached $2.6 billion, up from $2.2 billion spent in 1989, but much lower than 1987 levels of $3.2 billion (boosted in part by debt-for-equity swaps). During 1990, total authorized or registered direct foreign investment reached $3.7 billion, a significant increase from 1989. Not all of that was actually spent, however. There is a controversy over the method of calculating foreign investment inflows; the Foreign Investment Commission claims that direct foreign investment was greater than the amount cited by Banco de México. Although both agencies agree that investment increased in 1990, it is clear that these inflows did not meet official expectations fostered by the liberalization of Mexico's foreign investment regulations in May 1989. In fact, lower-than-projected inflows was a principal reason Mexico decided to pursue a free trade agreement. Direct foreign investment should increase substantially once FTA talks are concluded, and inflows could meet government targets of $4–5 billion p.a.

Indirect foreign investment reached approximately $14.7 billion as of June 1991, in the form of American Depositary Receipts (ADRs) issued by Mexican companies led by Telmex, neutral stock trust funds, and stock holdings and country funds, such as the Mexico Fund.

New investments by MNCs include $930 million from Volkswagen (Germany) in the next few years for automobile production plant expansion, Nissan's (Japan) $1 billion outlay for a new assembly facility, Goodyear's (US) $200 million factory expansion, Rhône-Poulenc's (France) $120 million investment in a new chemical plant, $60 million from Hilton International (US) for hotel construction, Cummins Engine's (US) $24 million investment in a plant expansion and Ford's

(US) $700 million outlay for an automotive motor plant expansion. In 1990, Ford completed a $300 million expansion of another plant that exports two models to the US. Although most new investment will enter the industrial sector—especially in automotive, autoparts and chemicals—there is a growing trend toward investment in services and the commercial sector.

Inflation: Top Priority

Inflation control remains one of the principal targets of the Salinas administration. Although it fell dramatically, from 159% in 1987 to 19.7% during 1989, inflation rose again during 1990 and closed the year at 29.9%. By 1991, it was back down to 18.8%. The PECE has been at the heart of the administration's attack on inflation. The pact has been in effect since Salinas took office and was extended in November 1991, to last until early 1993. The PECE combines fiscal austerity with controls on wages, prices and the exchange rate. During 1989, the first year the pact was in effect, few price increases were granted and the peso was allowed to devalue against the dollar at a fixed rate of Ps1 per day. (In 1988, under the PSE, the PECE's predecessor, the peso-dollar parity had remained frozen during most of the year.) Minimum wages were allowed an 8% hike in January 1989, a 6% increase in July and a 10% rise in December. The peso slippage was slowed to Ps0.8 per day in late May

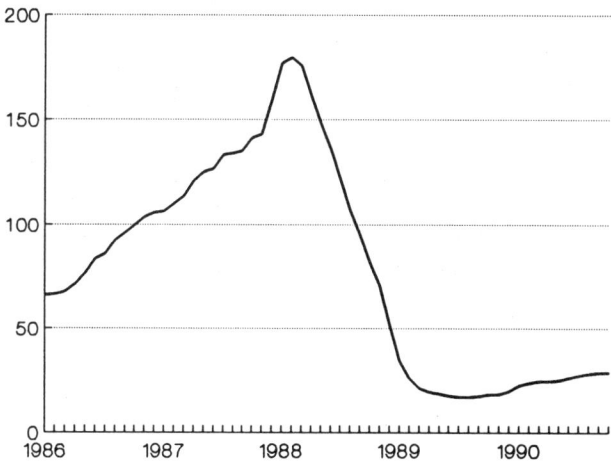

Figure 5-9. Inflation plummets, but still resistant (12-month CPI variation—%). *(Source: Banco de México)*

1990 and further reduced to Ps0.4 per day in mid-November 1990. In November 1991, it was further slowed to Ps0.2 per day.

After strict price controls in 1989, officials began to permit greater price adjustments in 1990. More than 250 price hikes were permitted that year, including prices of basic foodstuffs such as tortillas, beans, rice, wheat flour, milk and oil, and costs of public goods and services, e.g. gasoline, petrochemicals, electricity and transportation. The government appeared to be looking for ways to slowly replace the PECE's controls with a more flexible system in hopes of eventually abolishing the pact once inflation reached the levels of developed countries. Indeed, one of the key means of holding down inflation under the PECE has been mild adjustment of the exchange rate parity. Annual inflation could drop to single digits after 1992.

Interest Rates: Sharply Reduced

Interest rates in Mexico fell during most of 1990, even though inflation rose during the year. By end-1990, interest rates had fallen to their lowest level in more than a decade. The banks' cost of funds (CPP) fell to 29.23% in December and continued to drop during 1991. By the end of 1991, the CPP was 20.5%, while the benchmark 28-day treasury certificates (Cetes) rate fell to 16%. A new 364-day Cete introduced in November 1990 should help extend the investment horizon.

The drop in interest rates was a clear sign domestic investors were

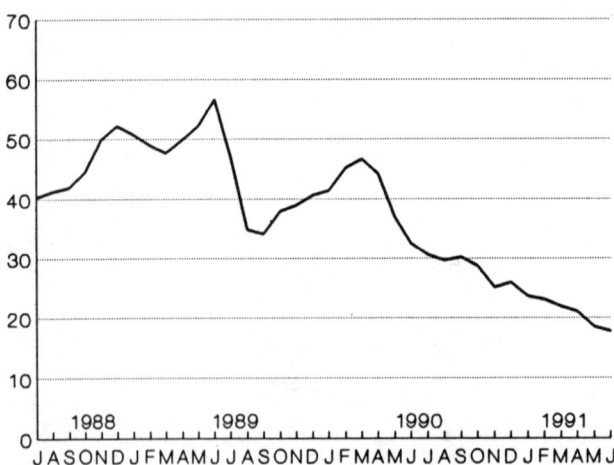

Figure 5-10. Falling cost of money [28-day treasury certificate (Cete) rate—%]. *(Source: Banco de México)*

confident that the government could maintain its exchange rate policy and that the risk of a surprise devaluation was extremely low. Given the rate of inflation, real interest rates in peso terms have been very low. Still, interest rates in Mexico are considerably higher in dollar terms than in the US, and companies operating in the country argue that domestic financing puts them at a disadvantage with other foreign competitors.

Balance of Payments:
Trade Difficulties

The economic reactivation begun in 1989 has been accompanied by a growing trade deficit. Most forecasts project a still larger deficit as Mexico integrates into a North American market. In 1989, the country registered its first trade deficit in eight years when the balance dropped to negative $645 million. During 1990, as the economy grew more swiftly and capital goods imports rose sharply, the trade balance fell to negative $3 billion.

At end-1990, imports continued to grow (27.3%) more quickly than exports (17.6%). The differences in the rates of expansion would have been even greater had it not been for the tremendous boost oil price hikes gave to export value during the year-end conflict in the Persian Gulf. Imports for 1990 reached $29.8 billion vs exports of $26.8 billion.

Of special note is the growth rate of capital goods imports, which increased 43% during 1990, double the previous year's rate. The most important growth in capital goods imports was in the second half of 1990, when the economy was expanding the fastest.

Mexico expects the trade deficit to widen further in the initial years of a North American FTA, to about $10 billion p.a. This fall will be exacerbated as companies increase investment spending and make major purchases of capital goods and equipment to prepare for a more competitive climate under a free trade pact. Even though the size of the trade deficit is worrisome, Mexican officials argue that a growing deficit is simply a consequence of economic reactivation and should not be a problem as long as investment and other sources of capital continue to enter the country.

Trade between the US and Mexico accounts for the bulk of the latter's imports and exports. Because of differences in the way trade is calculated in the US and Mexico, the US-Mexican trade profile changes depending on which system is used. Using Mexican data, total US-Mexican trade in 1989 reached $31.6 million, or 68% of $46.2 million worth of trade. (According to the US Department of Commerce, total Mexican trade reached $52.1 billion during 1989.) Mexican data indicates that approximately 70% of all Mexican exports went to the US in 1989 and approximately 68% of imports to Mexico came from the US. Data for 1990 suggest that there has been little change in the importance of the US to Mexico's total foreign trade. Indeed, with an FTA, the US— along with Canada—is likely to play an even greater role in Mexico's trade relations.

In 1990, the government changed its reporting methodology and now includes maquiladora shipments as exports. Prior to the change, value added by maquiladoras was included in the services balance as "services for transformation." The change in methodology does not effect the current-account balance, which under either system includes the in-bond contribution to the balance of payments. It does, however, almost by "sleight of hand," make the trade balance appear stronger. This report continues to use the previous methodology for forecast purposes to permit accurate comparisons to previous years. If in-bond income ($3.6 billion) is included, the trade balance for 1990 would be a positive $610 million.

The **current-account** balance, which reached negative $5.25 billion in 1990, almost doubled to negative $11 billion by end-1991, largely because of the ballooning trade deficit. The widening of the trade deficit more than offsets an increase in net transfers and a slightly declining services deficit, which have benefited from lower interest rates as a result of Mexico's foreign debt restructuring.

International reserves were estimated at nearly $17 billion at end-1991, a record high, thanks to direct foreign investment and other net capital inflows.

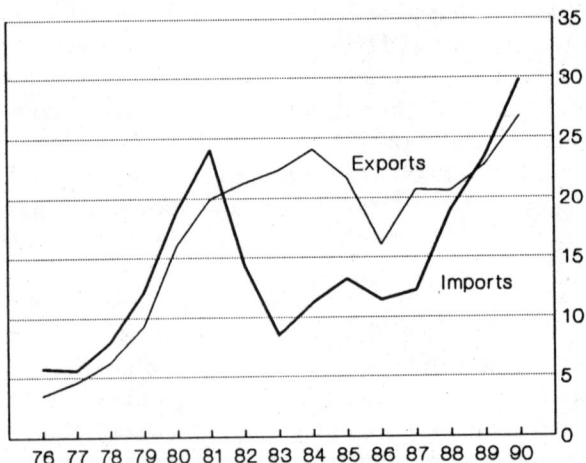

Figure 5-11. Imports overtake exports ($ billions). *(Source: International Monetary Fund)*

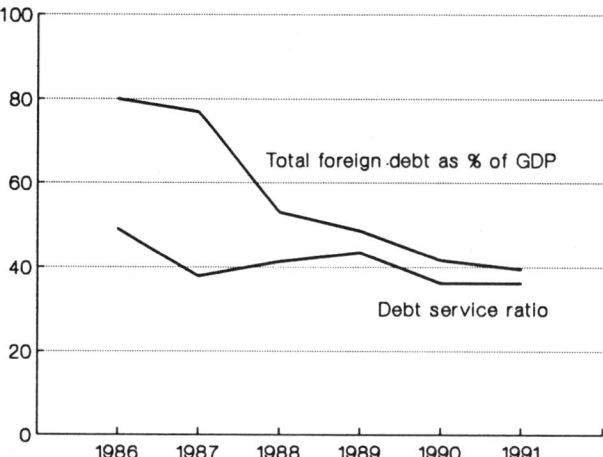

Figure 5-12. Mexico's falling debt burden. *(Source: Ministry of Finance; Business International Global Forecasting Service)*

Mexican Peso: Ongoing Controversy

The exchange rate policy as of early 1992, which limits the rate of peso devaluation to the dollar (set to slide at Ps0.2 per day), is one of the most controversial aspects of Salinas's economic program. The inflation differential between Mexico and its leading trading partners is much greater than the rate of devaluation (less than 5% in 1991). This has led analysts to contend, citing the growing trade deficit, that the peso is headed for overvaluation and that a devaluation will soon be necessary.

This argument has been countered by the Mexican government's belief that the dollar's devaluation against other major currencies has benefited the peso and reduced the risk of overvaluation, and that as long as Mexico is able to finance its trade and current-account deficits with capital inflows, there is no disequilibrium.

The exchange rate, however, appears to be a very sensitive issue for Mexican domestic investors. Past devaluations have brought high inflation and destroyed investor confidence, while doing little to stem capital flight. Currency adjustments have been considered by most Mexicans as evidence of a lack of government control. The policy of slowing devaluation significantly below the differential in the rate of Mexico's inflation and that of its leading trading partners (principally the US) has widened the trade gap, but has been crucial in maintaining domestic investor confidence in Salinas's economic program.

To the extent that investor confidence leads to increased investment and results in increased capital inflows that permit Mexico to finance the current-account deficit while reducing inflation, the present exchange rate policy can continue. Indeed, in early 1992 many analysts predicted that the government would soon fix the peso-dollar parity as part of its attack on inflation. Bringing inflation down will be more difficult than expected, but eventual success will help ease costs associated with the current exchange rate policy.

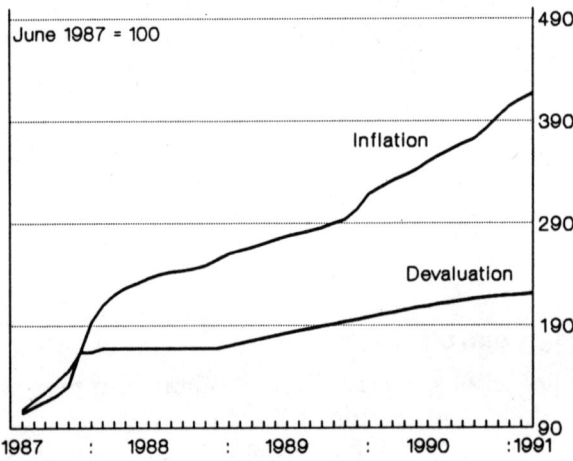

Figure 5-13. Inflation/devaluation gap widens (CPI vs Ps:$ index). *(Source: Banco de México)*

6
The New Regulatory Environment

Business operating conditions in Mexico have improved considerably in recent years, as President Carlos Salinas de Gortari's economic and industrial development model has been put in place. More stable economic conditions, combined with greater flexibility granted to foreign-owned operations, have been major factors in the improvement. In contrast to the traditional policy of maintaining extensive state regulation of the economy and limiting foreign investment, the Salinas policy team has accelerated the tendency begun by the Miguel de la Madrid administration (1982–88). This tendency is to reduce the role of the government in the country's industrial development while relying more heavily on local and foreign private investment to stimulate economic growth.

Still, doing business in Mexico provides numerous challenges, some common in the developing world and some unique to the country. This chapter introduces some of the most important aspects of Mexico's regulatory environment, along with observations from companies and analysts as to how to adjust to the business environment.

Foreign Investment Regulations

Mexico has undergone a radical change in attitude toward foreign investment in the past 10 years. In May 1989, the government passed far-reaching revisions of foreign investment regulations that reversed long-standing restrictions on foreign capital. Although the 1973 Law for the Promotion of Mexican Investment and the Regulation of Foreign Investment remains on the books, including its limits on the amount of foreign equity and the areas in which it is allowed, it has been largely superseded by the new regulations.

The 1989 rules make it easier for foreign companies to own 100% of investments in areas not specifically off limits to the private sector. Up to 100% foreign majority holdings are now possible in almost two thirds of the economy, including important sectors such as glass, cement, steel, iron and cellulose, in which foreign ownership previously had been limited to 49% or less. The areas still reserved for local or state ownership include the petroleum and primary petrochemical industries, radio, television, urban road transportation, air and sea lines, forestry and gas distribution.

The government has begun to ease restrictions in some of these reserved areas, however. In August 1989, for example, 14 basic petrochemicals (reserved for the state) were reclassified as secondary, thereby opening the industry to private and foreign investment (see Chapter 9 on the petrochemicals sector). In addition, in May 1990, the government approved a constitutional amendment permitting local private ownership of commercial banks. Majority foreign participation in the banks is still not permitted.

In order to provide investors with a comprehensive list of areas in which foreign holdings are restricted, the May 1989 regulations include six categories of classified areas: activities reserved for the state; operations reserved for Mexican nationals; enterprises in which foreign investment is limited to 34%, including phosphoric rock, sulfur and carbon mining; ventures in which foreign investment is limited to 40%, including secondary petrochemicals and automotive parts; areas where foreign investment is limited to 49%, including some mining, river and lake transportation, firearms, explosives and telecommunications; and activities in which foreign investment is permitted up to 100% with authorization from the Foreign Investment Commission (FIC), including agriculture, newspaper and magazine publishing, construction and educational services.

In all other areas not included in one of the six categories classified, up to 100% foreign participation is permitted. Furthermore, no prior authorization is required if the project meets the following conditions:

(1) Investment during the preoperative period does not exceed $100 million.

(2) The project is funded with financial resources brought in from abroad.

(3) The enterprise is located outside the three largest metropolitan areas—Mexico City, Monterrey and Guadalajara (this only applies to industrial facilities).

(4) Imports and exports are kept in balance during the project's first three years.

(5) The investment creates permanent jobs and provides worker training and personnel development programs.

(6) The project employs adequate technology and complies with environmental regulations.

When these conditions are met, no prior authorization is required; it is automatically approved under the new regulations. The firm need only obtain a permit from the Ministry of Foreign Affairs, which authorizes the acquisition of property and enters the investment in the Foreign Investment Registry. Both steps can be done in a matter of weeks.

If the project does not comply with the six conditions or if it would exceed the limits established for classified investment, it requires prior approval by the FIC. The Commission seeks investments that will have extraordinary economic benefits (e.g. enhance export earnings, increase employment and wages, help in the development of less-industrialized regions, or advance national technology and research). The red tape traditionally associated with FIC approval has been reduced. If no reply is forthcoming 45 days after an application has been submitted, it is deemed approved. (Requests by the FIC for further information will prolong the 45-day limit, however.)

The new regulations also permit existing 30-year trusts, which have enabled foreign investors to enter industry and tourism in restricted zones—such as border areas and near the coast—to be extended for another 30 years when they lapse. Nonrenewable 20-year trusts have been set up to allow foreign investment in some sectors (e.g. certain mining areas that previously were off limits to foreign majority control).

Intellectual Property Rights

Mexico's intellectual property regime, long an impediment for foreign investment and technology licensing, has undergone important modifications that should provide protection for technology and trade secrets. The first step toward reforming the rules governing licensing was the publication of new technology transfer regulations on Jan. 9, 1990.

The 1990 regulations modified the 1982 Law on the Control and Registration of Technology Transfers and the Use and Exploitation of Patents and Trademarks. Although under the 1990 rules, all technology contracts had to be government approved and registered, approval was virtually automatic if the contract met one of the following conditions:

(1) Creates new permanent jobs;

(2) Improves the technical skills of employees;

(3) Provides access to new export markets;

(4) Manufactures new products in Mexico that replace imports;

(5) Improves the balance of payments;

(6) Lowers unit production costs;

(7) Develops local suppliers;

(8) Uses nonpolluting technologies; or

(9) Establishes or expands local research and development.

These conditions were extremely lenient and broad, according to local attorneys. If any one condition was met, even if the licensing agreement called for obligations that would have precluded acceptance of registration under the 1982 law, the contract was accepted. Prior to the January 1990 technology transfer regulations, authorities had refused to register agreements containing clauses that: restricted a licensee's exports; limited a licensee's R&D efforts; kept production volumes down or set sales prices; obliged a licensee to buy equipment, tools, parts or raw materials only from certain suppliers; curtailed a licensee's sales freedom; required a confidentiality agreement with a duration greater than the period of the licensing contract.

New intellectual property law
The more significant reform regarding technology transfer is a new law governing intellectual property, passed by Mexico's Congress in June 1991. The legislation, called the Law for the Promotion and Protection of Industrial Property, provides a much broader scope of patent coverage and other protection than existed under previous legislation. It should greatly improve the licensing environment in Mexico, especially with the creation of trade-secret protection, greater limitations on compulsory licensing and immediate protection for a host of products that lacked full patent coverage previously. The new law abrogated the 1982 Law on the Control and Registration of Technology Transfers and its 1990 regulations (discussed in the previous section). Technology transfer contracts no longer need government approval or registration. The following are the important highlights of the new intellectual property law:

Patent term. Patent terms are extended from 14 to 20 years, but will now be counted from the time the application is submitted.

Patentability. Product patent protection under the new law will be available for chemical products, pharmaceuticals, animal foods and agrochemicals, which previously could only receive process patents. Product protection for these items under the old legislation was not scheduled until 1997. Furthermore, vegetable varieties, microorganisms, metal alloys and food and beverages for human consumption, which were not scheduled to be covered as of 1997, will enjoy full patent protection as well.

Inventor's certificates. With the widened scope of protection for products, inventor's certificates—designed to provide some security for unpatentable products—have been eliminated. Inventor's certificates had provided for payments of royalties on unpatentable products. Although these certificates required that third parties pay royalties to the holder, the technology was available to all. In the event that the holder of the certificate refused to permit third-party use, the government could intervene, setting the terms and conditions of the contract. With the elimination of inventor's certificates, the patent holder will be able to control all uses of the patent except as provided for under compulsory licenses (see below).

Exploitation of patent. Under the new law, importation of patented products or products developed by a patented process constitutes exploitation of a patent. This gives foreign companies much greater protection against the risk of compulsory licensing, which may result if the patent holder fails to exploit the patent within three years after it is granted, or within four years following patent application (whichever is longer).

Compulsory licenses. Aside from failure to exploit a patent, the government can institute compulsory licensing in the case of a national emergency or for reasons of national security. Under these conditions, the Commerce Secretariat must decide that without compulsory licensing, production or distribution of basic goods will be impeded, harmed or made more costly. Under the previous law, failure to fully exploit domestic and export markets could result in the application of compulsory licenses.

Industrial designs and utility models. The term for registered industrial designs and models is extended under the new law to 15 years, an increase from the previous seven years. Utility models—tools, instruments and other objects that have undergone minor improvements—are now protected for 10 years. They were not previously recognized under the law.

Trademarks and service marks. The term for trademarks, service marks and commercial names and phrases is extended to 10 years from the previous five-year term, renewable for 10-year periods. The law provides that a simple sworn statement or affidavit attesting to uninterrupted use is needed for renewal, instead of the former requirement that periodic evidence be submitted.

Trade secrets. The new law defines trade secrets as confidential physical information referring to products, production processes, methods of distribution or sale of products or services, which permit a firm or individual to obtain or maintain a competitive or economic advantage.

Remedies and enforcement. Criminal charges, with prison sentences between two and six years can be brought. The new law no longer limits prison sentences for its violations to two to six years, but allows judges to

---

Some Practical Advice

Executives with years of experience in Mexico provide the following tips for firms contemplating new operations in the country:

• **Always seek out professional advice in Mexico as a part of the investment decisionmaking process.** Although the rules and regulations concerning foreign investment have been liberalized considerably and the liberalization process is likely to continue under an FTA, limitations and potential obstacles do exist. A potential local partner may not raise all these issues. To fully appreciate the idiosyncracies of Mexico's regulatory environment, detailed consultation with a professional is a must.

• **Be aware that bribes still exist.** Although bribes are not as common as they were in the 1970s and early 1980s, when the situation was "out of control" according to many observers, they continue to be a part of the business operating environment in Mexico. Despite attempts to modernize the government, companies report that bribes are still requested from a variety of public servants, ranging from plant inspectors to "independent" consultants retained by high-level officials. Although much of the bidding for state companies up for privatization—and for various other concessions—has been clean, there have been reports of requests for sums of money upward of $500,000 to win in certain bidding processes. Some government ministries have a reputation for being amenable to bribes, whereas others, such as the central bank, Banco de México, and the Secretariat of Finance and Public Credit, are considered quite clean.

set the limit instead. In addition, the new legislation explicitly provides aggrieved parties the ability to seek relief for damages and harm suffered through its violation.

Transitory issues. Existing requests for inventor's certificates and process patents for products that could not get patents previously will be convertible into requests for full patent protection during the 12 months following the law's passage, as long as an application or actual patent exists in a country that is a member of the Patent Cooperation Treaty. Under the new legislation, patent protection will be granted in Mexico for 20 years from the date of the original request for an inventor's certificate or process patent.

Firms interested in applying for protection for existing products for the first time in Mexico may do so within the 12 months following the law's passage, provided that (1) an application or actual patent exists in a member country of the Patent Cooperation Treaty and (2) the exploitation of the invention or commercial import of the product in question has not yet begun in Mexico. The patent's term will end in Mexico on the same date it would end in the country where patent protection was originally requested.

Taxation

One of the pillars of Salinas's modernization program has been an overhaul of Mexico's tax system. Government officials have argued that Mexico can never hope for a government that is able to provide services at the level of developed countries without also instituting tax compliance rates similar to those in developed countries. Officials have also recognized, however, that one of the disincentives to compliance is the onerous tax burden borne by the private sector. For years, although taxation did not represent an especially large share of GDP, the burden on foreign-owned companies and major Mexican-owned public enterprises was disproportionately heavy.

The Salinas administration's goal has been to lower the effective rate of taxation while expanding the taxable base. In 1989, the president introduced a major tax reform, which included the acceleration of the implementation of a new 1987 tax law, Title II, two years ahead of schedule. (The chief innovation of Title II was to lower rates while introducing inflation adjustments into the calculation of net taxable income. Effective Jan. 1, 1991, the corporate income tax rate became 35%.) Tax reforms in 1990 and 1991 resulted in additional minor adjustments while eliminating a special tax regime for large sectors of the economy representing more than 16% of GDP.

Tax enforcement

The increased attention paid to enforcement has been of equal importance for companies operating in Mexico. From the time that Mexico
first instituted a modern tax system in 1921, following the Mexican Revolution, until Salinas took office in December 1988, only two cases of
tax evasion were prosecuted by the government.

That situation changed dramatically shortly after Salinas became
president. A rash of audits, prosecutions and subsequent jailings for tax
evasion and fraud during the first two years of his term have significantly increased tax compliance. Audits were up from 1.2% of all taxpayers in 1988 to approximately 10% in 1990. By 1990, the number of
taxpayers had reached nearly three million, up 64% from 1988. Furthermore, Salinas's tax enforcement program has been successful in
raising Mexico's ratio of taxation to GDP from 9.8% in 1989 to an estimated 10.4% in 1990. Increased compliance has permitted the government to lower corporate income tax rates, now set at a maximum of
35%, while raising more revenues from tax collection. Tax revenues,
which account for roughly 40% of the federal government's budgeted
revenues, were estimated to have increased by 8.7% during 1990.

Companies operating in Mexico, however, still complain that effective tax rates are higher than in the US and that yearly adjustments in
the tax code make compliance burdensome. Furthermore, various
groups within the administration often appear to be operating at odds
with one another on tax matters, and the result is a confused tax
regime.

The maquiladora industry has faced this problem most recently.
When a controversial 2% tax on company assets went into effect in
1989, maquiladoras were exempt. According to the government, nearly
three quarters of the tax returns filed by companies in the years preceding the asset tax showed that no tax was due, implying widespread tax
fraud. The new assets tax can be credited against federal income tax
liability and thus does not increase the tax burden of those companies
already complying with the tax code, argue government officials. Its
purpose was to ensure that companies do not escape paying taxes. As
maquiladoras have always been considered cost centers, not profit centers, however, they have generally not had a taxable income to report.
That changed with the December 1990 tax reforms, which now require
maquiladoras to pay a 2% tax on their inventories. Maquiladora operators have argued that the tax runs contrary to the concept of the in-
bond program, and after repeated visits by industry representatives to
the offices of tax authorities, tax officials have promised to rescind the
requirement. The ordeal demonstrates, however, that Salinas's goals of
modernization and deregulation must overcome many obstacles.

Companies may also find that the new tax reforms require additional paperwork and expense. As a result of reforms that went into effect on Jan. 1, 1991, audits by professional accounting firms are now required for all companies with at least 300 employees or annual sales of Ps5 billion (roughly $1.7 million at the April 1991 exchange rate). Penalties for failure to conduct an audit are Ps30–90 million ($10,000–30,000).

Companies should also be aware that, whereas the rule on tax deductions states that only those costs indispensable for the carrying out of a business can be deducted, the actual deductions permitted change each year.

Foreign Exchange and Trade Controls

In November 1991 the government abolished the controlled exchange rate and rescinded the requirement that companies sell foreign exchange earnings to the federal government. (Previously, Mexico had a two-tiered exchange system composed of a controlled and a free rate.) Now that the country has a single rate, all red tape involved in exporting has been eased. The move, which will primarily benefit maquiladora and large exporters, will also generate a growing amount of dollars and other foreign currency held by companies operating in Mexico. (Earlier in 1991, banks were authorized to set up dollar accounts for all companies doing business in the country.)

The free exchange rate applies to all foreign exchange transactions. There are no other exchange controls in Mexico. There are no restrictions on the repatriation of capital.

Following a major devaluation in December 1987, an exchange freeze was applied in March 1988 as part of the heterodox economic stabilization plan known as the Economic Solidarity Pact (PSE) to control inflation. When the stabilization program was renamed the Pact for Economic Stability and Growth (PECE) by the Salinas administration in January 1989, the dollar was subjected to a one-peso-per-day slippage rate. That decline was maintained until the end of May 1990, when the government reduced the slippage to Ps0.8 per day. In November 1990, the rate was cut to Ps0.4 per day, and in November of 1991 to Ps0.2 per day.

Price Controls

Price controls continue to be an important concern for companies doing business in Mexico. The government maintains rigorous controls on a significant number of consumer goods, especially basic foodstuffs and medicines. Moreover, all products and services are subject to the government's anti-inflation economic program in effect since President Salinas entered office.

Price increases for a group of basic "market-basket" products, known as the canasta básica, are set directly by the National Commission for Compliance and Evaluation of the PECE. These products include: corn tortilla, corn dough, corn flour, white bread, wheat flour, soup, pasta, cookies, rice, oatmeal, beef, cooked ham, canned tuna, canned sardines, milk, eggs, vegetable oil and shortening, margarine, beans, canned chilies, tomato sauce, sugar, coffee, salt, chicken concentrate, powdered milk, powdered gelatin, soft drinks, beer, cigarettes, gas stoves, refrigerators, electric irons, blenders, black and white televisions, light bulbs, electric batteries, detergents, soap, bleach, toothpaste, deodorants, shaving blades, notebooks, pens and pencils.

Although officials have sometimes granted price increases, especially when widespread shortages of these products occur, at other times the government has given permission to import products to meet domestic demand while rejecting such price increases. Eggs, meat and sugar have all been imported under special conditions in an attempt to deal with shortages resulting from price controls.

Other products not included in the canasta básica, ranging from insecticides to glass, steel and paper products, are contained in a price surveillance system regulated by the Commerce Secretariat (Secofi). Depending on the product, producers must either register their prices with Secofi or request authorization for price increases. Although traditionally authorities responded to price-increase applications within 60–90 days, since the advent of the PECE, price-increase applications may go unresolved for up to a year. Secofi sometimes grants provisional hikes based on the increased cost of raw materials, packaging and labor. Price increases are usually characterized by the government as a concertación, or consensus agreement, with the industry involved.

Even if a company's product is not included in the canasta básica nor in the list of products monitored by Secofi, the firm is still expected to hold down its prices under the general price freeze recommended by the PECE. The PECE was last extended in November 1991 and is expected to last at least through early 1993. Official pressure and jawboning are used to keep private sector prices in line, although price increases occur and at times.

Companies have reacted to the system of price controls by adopting various strategies. In 1987, prior to the introduction of the PECE's predecessor, the PSE, many companies whose products were not regulated by Secofi raised their prices by large margins out of fear of an impending price freeze. One large consumer goods multinational company that exports most of its production to the US was faced with the anomaly that its products were being sold on the Mexican market at prices 30–40% higher than those charged in the US. "That caused a problem as soon as the market opened to imports, including our own from the US," remarks the company's director general. Some firms that have seen limited price relief since 1987 are nevertheless benefiting from the markups made that year.

Other companies have decided not to locally produce goods subject to price controls, even though such products play a prominent role in their US and international sales. Some businesses have changed the basic makeup or nature of their products in such a way that those products are no longer found on the list of price-controlled goods.

Firms are quick to point out the inconsistency between price controls and Mexico's open border policy. "If we produce a price-controlled product in Mexico, it would be unprofitable because of the price controls. Yet we can now import at any price," comments the director general of one multinational firm located in Mexico. "Why should Mexico prefer imports to local production?"

Labor Environment

Labor is a potentially volatile factor that needs to be carefully managed when doing business in Mexico. At present, the country's traditional labor system is undergoing difficulties, including disputes between competing unions that have often become intermingled with management-labor negotiations. Although the results have occasionally been violent, Mexico will continue to be attractive as a supplier of plentiful and relatively cheap labor for most companies.

Labor unrest is the result of two problems: reduced purchasing power of the average worker's wages and the uncertain political future of Mexico's large labor unions. Although employees in manufacturing have fared slightly better, most have watched their purchasing power decline by more than 40% since 1982. Increases in the minimum wage have consistently failed to keep pace with inflation during recent years, although in 1990, most workers in the manufacturing sector received increases in wages roughly equal to inflation (which reached nearly 30% that year). Compounding the rank and file's anger over lagging wages has been a series of political moves designed to wrest power away from the country's largest and most powerful union, the Confederation of Mexican Workers (CTM), or Confederación de Trabajadores de México, headed by the aging Fidel Velázquez.

Although virtually all major organized labor leaders have publicly supported the Salinas administration, serious conflicts have developed between the president's economic and political reforms and the programs supported by traditional union officials. These conflicts have surfaced and, at times, turned violent. Two of Mexico's most tumultuous strikes during 1990, the Modelo beer brewery strike and the Ford Motors strike at its Cuautitlán plant, both involved attempts by the workers to remove corrupt union leadership along with intense behind-the-scenes maneuvering by various political groups both within and outside the Salinas administration to attempt to take advantage of the situation. Political figures, ranging from Mexico City's mayor to the secretary of labor, have been hard at work to achieve political success in handling labor disputes.

The key players in organized labor include the oldest labor organization, the Regional Workers Confederation of Mexico (CROM), or Confederación Regional Obrera de México, with some 350,000 members from the textile, shoe, garment and maritime industries; the CTM, representing about six million members—a mainstay of the ruling Institutional Revolutionary Party (PRI) and closely tied to the government; and the Revolutionary Confederation of Workers and Peasants (CROC), or Confederación Revolucionaria Obrera y Campesina, which has about 500,000 members and is chiefly made up of unions in the textile, restaurant and shoe industries. All three organizations form part of the Labor Congress or Congreso del Trabajo (CT), and along with other CT-affiliated unions represent about 90% of the organized labor force in the country.

Slightly more than 50% of Mexico's work force is unionized, although unions are even stronger in the industrial sector. Most of the workers belong to one of the nine big national labor federations; only about 20% of union workers belong to single-company unions. Firms can face considerable jurisdictional strife from unions, because each union seeks to get the best working conditions and highest salaries. Federal law requires that collective bargaining agreements be renewed at least every two years. Salaries must be reviewed annually.

Although most companies find labor plentiful and relatively inexpensive in Mexico, lack of industrial maturity can be a problem. In some areas, the fact that work forces are composed chiefly of first-generation factory workers has a negative effect on productivity. Many companies believe their principal operating problem is the serious shortage of skilled labor and management personnel, particularly middle and upper level.

Weighing Wages in Mexico

Firms considering new investment in Mexico often hear conflicting opinions about wage levels. The gap between wages in Mexico and the US has been emphasized by opponents of an FTA, who argue that cheap labor, combined with the advantages of an open border, will result in a massive relocation of companies to Mexico. Labor lobbyists in Washington have presented paystubs of Mexican workers to demonstrate that hourly wages in Mexico are equivalent to only $0.50-0.60. Although the wage differential between the two countries is great, most foreign firms in Mexico have found average worker remuneration five to six times higher than the minimum wage so often cited.

The differences between wages in the US and Mexico, however, go far beyond nominal wage levels. Wages are not calculated on an hourly basis in Mexico, and the amount that appears on the twice-monthly paycheck may represent as little as half of total compensation.

The most comprehensive statistics available on workers' wages in Mexico, and thus the most often cited, track the level of the regional minimum wages. At of the end of 1991, the minimum wage for the Mexico City metropolitan area, all of the state of Baja California and Baja California Sur, Acapulco and major border cities was Ps11,900 ($3.97) per day; Ps11,000 ($3.67) per day for Monterrey, Guadalajara and some other cities; and Ps9,920 ($3.31) per day for the rest of the country.

These minimum wages are dramatically lower than the average wages paid in Mexico's manufacturing sector, however. Even the percentage changes in minimum wages over time are a poor indicator of overall wage trends—at least in the 1990-91 period. Following the steady erosion of salaries in the 1980s, in 1990-91 wages in the manufacturing sector began to increase at a much more rapid pace than did the minimum wage. To produce a more accurate portrait of labor costs in Mexico, BI conducted a survey of companies in Mexico, which revealed that, whereas the minimum wage increased just 18% during 1990 and first-half 1991, most foreign companies granted workers increases just above 30% during the same time period.

Conducted during May and June 1991, BI's survey looked at daily wages provided by companies operating in Mexico City, Puebla and San Luis Potosí. The results are as follows:

(Continued)

Daily Wages, Without Benefits ($)			
	Lowest Wage	Highest Wage	Average Wage
Company A (electrical)	6.66	13.61	8.83
Company B (light manufacturing)	5.35	10.48	8.56
Company C (chemical)	4.59	29.77	8.62
Company D (electronics)	4.97	14.87	6.25
Company E (consumer goods)	8.70	19.30	12.20
Company F (pharmaceutical)	3.96	13.82	9.59
Company G (autoparts)	6.67	13.20	9.83

Citing daily wages is misleading for two reasons, however. First, hourly wages cannot be calculated simply by dividing by eight hours. Workers in Mexico are paid wages for seven-day weeks; the maximum workweek is six days and most companies surveyed have five-day workweeks. The average real workweek in the BI sample consisted of 42.5 hours. Among the surveyed companies, wages ranged from $0.65 to $4.77 per hour, with the average wage ranging from $1.02 to $1.99 per hour. Second, benefits must be added to daily wage figures to obtain an accurate picture of total remuneration. For example, Company D in 1990 paid out nearly 85% over base wages as benefits to workers, thus raising its average hourly compensation (with benefits included) from $1.02 to $1.88.

Each company surveyed added 40-80% in benefits to their payrolls. Most firms provide life insurance, savings funds, a cafeteria where employees may purchase below-cost meals, medical services and monthly coupons (vales despensa) redeemable for food and general merchandise at supermarkets. On average, companies surveyed provided two weeks of vacation time after the second year of employment, a one-month Christmas bonus and an additional eight holidays.

Average Hourly Wages ($)		
	Base Salary	With Benefits
Company A	1.27	2.06
Company B	1.39	2.02
Company C	1.40	2.26
Company D	1.02	1.81
Company E	1.90	2.86
Company F	1.56	2.31
Company G	1.60	2.48

(Continued)

Future of wages

Although wages in Mexico are higher than MNCs might expect, they are still much lower than in the US and Canada. In fact, low pay is causing problems for some companies. Management often complains that wages are too low and government pressure to control inflation by keeping wages down should be eased. Some companies in the Mexico City area report shortages of semiskilled and skilled workers and an average waiting time of up to one month to fill vacant positions.

Many firms argue that at current levels, they simply cannot compete with the informal sector. "It is very hard to find workers at the wages we are paying," comments the director general of an MNC whose plant is located in the industrial zone northwest of Mexico City. "A worker can make more in the informal economy than he can with us."

Increasing productivity: a central concern

MNCs are becoming increasingly concerned about raising quality consciousness among managerial, administrative and factory workers. In addition, the issue of productivity is becoming more important in contract revisions. Although labor organizations accept that productivity must be discussed, workers tend to view it negatively. The following issues are likely to cause disagreement in contract negotiations:

Vacation. Concerned with long worker absences resulting from a great deal of accumulated vacation time, some companies are trying to reduce the time accumulated. Some firms have successfully implemented a vacation premium system: workers accept shorter vacation periods and less vacation accumulation in exchange for a bonus of 25% or more to be received in addition to normal vacation pay.

Job categories and descriptions. The introduction of new technology can help overall productivity, but usually requires rewriting job descriptions and laying off some workers. Unions often oppose new job descriptions, and may require the firm to lay off all workers and make severance payments and then rehire those workers for the new job titles. Some MNCs with contracts containing costly benefits, however, have found that paying severance to all workers and rehiring most of them can be less expensive in the long run, since laid-off workers usually lose all seniority and benefits. The new collective contract need not have more benefits than the current law requires.

Worker training. The drive for greater productivity means that training programs are becoming more necessary. Such programs are generally weak at most firms, however. MNC executives blame this on the current labor law, which considers seniority, not ability, the criterion for promotion. "Until you can promote on the basis of merit and not years worked, companies will have limited interest in really strong training programs," comments one manager.

One company that has implemented a major retraining program for its workers places special emphasis on the plant foremen, who constitute the first layer of management in the plant. "Mexican workers, when properly motivated and trained, can provide the same quality as any worker in the world," explains the company's president. "But you must convince them that this is not just another training program, this involves survival. It is hard to get people to understand that the game has changed."

Wages and benefits

The three-tiered minimum wage is set by the National Minimum Wage Commission, a group made up of representatives of business, labor and government. Minimum wage increases have varied greatly in recent years. In 1990, no minimum wage increase was granted until November 16, when an 18% hike was authorized. As of Jan. 1, 1991, the current minimum wage stands at Ps11,900 (about $4) per day for Mexico City and major border cities; Ps11,000 ($3.65) per day for Monterrey, Guadalajara and other large cities; and Ps9,920 ($3.30) per day for the rest of the country. These are subject to liberal fringe benefits. Actual wages in industry are higher than the legal minimums and increased by 20–30% during 1990 under collective contracts.

The cost of fringe benefits is substantial. Benefits and profit sharing can add more than 70% to base payroll expenses, depending on the salary level of the employee. The most important benefit is profit sharing: All companies are required to distribute 10% of their pretax profits to employees.

The labor law grants seven paid holidays p.a., plus one for Inauguration Day every sixth year. Labor contracts call for another nine to 10 paid holidays. After one year's work, employees are entitled to at least a six-day paid vacation, increased by two days for each of the subsequent three years. As a rule, however, employers grant 15 days under their contracts, and some pay an additional 15-day vacation bonus. (A bonus of 25% of normal pay during the vacation period is mandatory.) A Christmas bonus of 15-days pay is also obligatory and must be paid before December 20. Sick pay is included in only a few contracts, since the National Social Security Institute provides compensation. Where it is included, it can run to 90 days at full pay and 45 more at half pay,

Heading Off Labor Problems

To minimize problems and prevent management-labor disputes from turning into a battleground for political factions fighting for control of Mexico's organized labor movement, companies should keep in mind the following:

• **Improve internal communication.** Before a firm can adequately deal with labor issues, it needs to have a well-developed system of internal communications so that the industrial relations division knows what sales and finance are doing and vice versa. Industrial relations or human resources staff should be viewed as more than just people who cut paychecks or resolve minor personnel problems; they should be viewed as an integral part of the production area.

• **Keep open channels of communication with workers.** The days when a firm could talk with a few union leaders and resolve labor problems are over in Mexico. Today, companies need to keep workers well informed about the company's product, its performance in the market and the company's profit and sales projections. As part of its communications effort, one manufacturing MNC holds quarterly meetings where the firm's director general, finance director and other senior executives visit plants and discuss the company's current condition with the workers.

• **Focus on key employees to help maintain good industrial relations.** Firms should place special attention on the local affiliate and not the leaders of the central union, industrial relations experts recommend. One analyst suggests that companies work closely with the line supervisor. "The supervisor represents the company to the workers more than anyone else. He should be well-prepared and able to explain the concerns of the firm." This is even more important if the line supervisor has a position as one of the internal leaders of the local affiliate.

• **Plan labor strategy in advance.** Firms should clearly define strategies before going to the bargaining table. This requires an in-depth understanding of the labor law. Also, awareness of the conflicts among different unions is crucial. Executives report cases where union leaders warned them that if the company did not make more concessions, the union leadership would be removed and the company would be faced with the uncertainty of dealing with another union. "A company has to decide whether it makes sense to give in on concessions in order to preserve the current labor leadership, or whether it would be better off with a union affiliated with another labor organization. That requires detailed knowledge of the labor sector," says one expert.

depending on the illness. Companies must also contribute a sum equal to 5% of payroll to the National Workers' Housing Institute (Infonavit), established in 1972.

The social security system, administered by the Social Security Institute, provides many other benefits. The cost of social security benefits is shared among employers, employees and the government.

Besides the mandatory fringe benefits, most labor contracts provide for "voluntary" benefits, such as savings plans, life insurance, social and sports activities and lunches. Most large companies also have cafeterias on the premises, which provide below-cost meals to their employees.

Environmental Protection

Companies operating in Mexico can expect to see stricter and more consistent enforcement of existing environmental regulations, as well as passage of more stringent standards in the future. While environmental regulations will not be formally included in the final North American free trade agreement, Mexico's regulatory scheme, at least on the books, is likely to increasingly resemble that of the US.

In January 1991, the US Environmental Protection Agency (EPA) sent an official to Mexico to begin working with Mexican officials to develop a more comprehensive environmental protection regime. Then, in March 1991, President Salinas ordered the closure of the state oil company's (Pemex) Mexico City refinery in order to combat the city's serious pollution problem. The move enabled the government to assert that it had "done its share" in reducing its industrial pollution emissions and paved the way for an aggressive crackdown on industrial plants operating in the Mexico City area.

In the first two weeks of April 1991, the Secretariat of Urban Development and Ecology (Sedue) closed dozens of plants in the Mexico City area. In most cases, the authorities have targeted companies which have failed to comply with previously agreed upon requirements to reduce air contaminating emissions. The campaign's timing—the move coincided with Salinas's visit to the US shortly before Congress was expected to vote on "fast-track" authorization for a trilateral FTA—and its scope are clearly designed to respond to US environmental groups' concerns that Mexico has not done enough to enforce its environmental regulations.

At the time of the plant closing in April, Sedue also instituted a new requirement, obliging companies discovered to be in noncompliance with the regulations to present a bond made payable to the Mexican treasury, equal to the amount of the estimated cost of installing anti-

contaminating equipment. Once the bond is posted, subsequent find-
ings of noncompliance will result in the forfeiture of the amount of the
bond. In addition, a new bond must be posted and penalties may be
applied.

Given the emphasis now being placed on environmental protection
in Mexico, *lawyers and consultants recommend that investors look at Mexico's
environmental regulations as an integral part of considering a Mexican operation.* Mexico, such specialists argue, is cracking down on polluters and is
not willing to promote new foreign investment at the cost of its environment. "Companies should not think that by coming to Mexico they can
escape EPA-type regulations," warns one attorney involved in environmental law. Companies should be aware of the following:

Maquiladora operations are under close scrutiny by the EPA and
Sedue. Routine inspections of in-bond plants by Sedue can be expected,
although the organization lacks sufficient enforcement power because
it has a limited number of plant inspectors. Sedue will often close down
one plant in violation of environmental regulations as an "example" for
other facilities. Firms report, however, that Sedue will work with companies and give them enough time to get plants operating again within
guidelines. New firms are often granted an adjustment period (three to
six months) to acquaint themselves with Mexican regulations.

Most new and existing investments in the manufacturing sector must
prepare an environmental impact statement. Although this list is not
exhaustive, Sedue has been mandated to scrutinize the following categories: federal public works; water works, oil, gas, carbon and general
transportation networks; chemical and petrochemical plants, steel
mills, paper factories, sugar refineries, bottling plants, cement factories,
automotive parts manufacturers, electrical power plants; mining—from
exploration to refining; hazardous waste facilities; federal tourist projects; and forestry in tropical jungles.

Companies with projects that fall into the above categories, but believe that their project will not cause ecological "disequilibrium" or exceed legal pollution limits, may submit a "preventive report" to Sedue.
Otherwise, they must submit one of three types of environmental impact statements: general, intermediary or specific, depending on the
type of project to be undertaken. Compliance with the law among existing companies has been very low, although new investment projects
need to file with Sedue. At present, however, Sedue often does not issue
a definitive operating license.

For companies accustomed to EPA standards in the US or their equivalent in Canada or Western Europe, Mexico's regulations should not be
a burden. The current system does suffer from problems, which have
affected foreign companies:

(1) Despite a comprehensive law, the General Law of Ecological Equilibrium and Environmental Protection (passed in 1988), many technical norms do not exist. This can render compliance with the regulations nearly impossible. Sedue claims that EPA norms will apply for areas in which Mexico has not yet published its own, but some attorneys question the validity of applying EPA norms to Mexican law.

(2) Many areas have yet to be regulated. Firms should be careful to keep up to date on new regulations, i.e. whereas emissions in natural water bodies, including lakes, streams, rivers and the ocean, are all regulated, there are no rules controlling such emissions in the sewer system in urban areas. The lack of clear rules has sometimes prevented foreign investment in sensitive areas, such as the hazardous waste disposal and treatment industry.

Mexico's rules concerning hazardous waste are contained in Chapter 5 of the General Law of Ecological Equilibrium and Environmental Protection. The regulations are based on the "cradle-to-grave" system, which places legal responsibility in perpetuity on the firm that produced the hazardous waste, not just the company hired to dispose of it. Authorization to import hazardous materials will only be granted for treatment, recycling or reuse. The importation of these materials solely for the purpose of final disposal or storage in Mexico is prohibited by law. Hazardous materials brought to Mexico under the maquiladora program must be returned to the country of origin. Although this law has not always been strictly enforced—there are cases of maquiladoras sending such wastes to be disposed of in Mexico—firms can expect to see greater enforcement as environmental concerns augment.

Complying with the regulations
Sedue has broad powers to inspect facilities to verify compliance with the environmental law and regulations. Companies that have failed Sedue inspections have usually been successful in resolving the matter by working with the agency to correct the problem. One firm reported being told by an inspector that it would have to pay a $2,000 bribe to reopen a plant he closed. Instead, the company hired a US engineering firm to prepare a study detailing what new equipment was needed to remedy the problem. After Sedue officials reviewed the results of the study, they permitted the plant to reopen while work was done on the portion of the facility in violation of the Mexican regulations.

Sedue can apply administrative sanctions, including: fines of 20–20,000 times the daily minimum wage in the Federal District; temporary, partial or total closure of a plant; suspension or revocation of environmental impact authorization; and administrative arrest for up to 36 hours. Criminal charges may be brought in certain cases, with violations relating to hazardous wastes treated as the most serious. The possession, importation, exportation or handling of such wastes in a way that "causes or may cause serious injury to public health, ecosystems or their elements" can result in imprisonment from three months to six years and a fine of 1,000–20,000 times the daily minimum wage in the Federal District.

Although many firms have reported that Sedue has traditionally been very lenient with company compliance programs, firms can expect a shift, especially during the period leading up to US congressional approval of an FTA. Sedue is working closely with the US EPA and is likely to take a stricter line on compliance with environmental regulations, particularly in the two most sensitive areas: Mexico City metropolitan and the US-Mexico border.

Credit Conditions

Financial conditions in Mexico have improved considerably in the last few years as a result of a relaxation of credit controls (since 1989) and a progressive lowering of interest rates (since 1990). Today, MNCs can find peso credit readily available at Mexican commercial banks, and many large foreign firms obtain the most preferential interest rates from those banks. In fact, companies report fresh enthusiasm among some Mexican banks in providing medium- and long-term financing, which had virtually disappeared in earlier years.

These changes have caused companies to rethink their financing strategies in Mexico, with some firms considering the use of peso financing for expansion of local operations. Although such financing is still more expensive in real terms than dollar financing, it has become much more attractive since early 1990.

The availability of credit was given a major boost in first-half 1989, when the government reduced required legal reserves of commercial banks to 30%. Prior to these changes, about 90% of all bank resources had been used to finance the federal government. Since then, financing to the private sector has captured slightly more than 90% of all bank credit. Along with the increased supply of credit, companies benefited from a significant drop in interest rates in 1990 and 1991.

Strong relations with at least three commercial banks are recommended. "You are going to have to spend much more time with bank relations here than in some countries," says one finance director. Those most often mentioned as providing good service to MNCs are Banamex,

Bancomer and Banca Serfin—all privatized during 1991–92. (See Chapter 12 for a review of reforms in the financial sector.)

Access to special funds available through government agencies varies, with many programs administered by the national development bank, Nacional Financiera (Nafinsa), now focusing on micro- and small-sized industries. Some programs, however, including export and import credit programs offered by the National Foreign Trade Bank, or Banco Nacional de Comercio Exterior (Bancomext), which had previously been closed to majority foreign-owned firms, were opened again during 1990.

Despite lower-cost peso credit, internally generated financing is still an important concern for financial directors. "I spend much more time in Mexico than I did in the US watching cash flow to make sure cash doesn't freeze up as inventory or receivables for a long period of time," comments the finance director for one manufacturing company. Tighter management of receivables and payables is key to improved liquidity. Chronic slow payment by government offices and state firms in recent years has resulted in some companies putting a percentage cap on sales to the public sector whenever possible. According to MNCs with large government sales, the government's slow payment was a major problem in 1990.

Parallel market and commercial paper

Competition from the parallel market—chiefly casas de bolsa—has led to the elimination of compensating-balance requirements and interest-up-front payments for prime customers. In the past, such charges were often unavoidable, but now larger Mexican banks are usually willing to forgo them—although smaller banks still tend to demand them.

Even though some firms use the parallel, or extrabursátil, financial market as a second source of short-term financing, casas de bolsa and banks are now prohibited from handling extrabursátil commercial paper. The parallel market, which accounted for approximately 60% of total domestic market resources in 1988, was popular with foreign companies with good credit ratings because of its speed and creativity. The government's move to close down the market arose from fear of a large and unregulated credit market.

Since May 1989, the former extrabursátil commercial paper was merged with bursátil (official) commercial paper. Firms that are not listed on Mexico's stock exchange, the Bolsa Mexicana de Valores, may issue the new commercial paper, but it requires detailed disclosure to the national securities and exchange commission prior to authorization. Many companies have shied away from the new paper, and some still use extrabursátil paper despite the difficulties in issuing an instrument that has effectively gone "underground."

Most MNCs in Mexico tend to avoid the stock market as a source of capital. To begin with, commercial paper is expensive because of the need to pay high real interest rates. Also, many firms are discouraged from issuing paper by extensive disclosure requirements.

Dollar financing

Although the cost of peso financing has fallen dramatically—to levels prevalent before the 1982 debt crisis—such financing is still more expensive than dollar financing. In the last two years, firms have begun to look abroad for additional financing. Since the Mexican government reached a debt renegotiation agreement with its commercial bank creditors in 1990, confidence in the strength of the peso has risen. MNCs and local companies that were once afraid of dollar exposure are now taking advantage of the lower rates available in dollar financing. Grupo San Luis, Cemex, La Moderna and Tamsa (all local companies) have begun to locate dollar financing abroad. That, in turn, should help to lower domestic rates.

One new means of obtaining dollar financing is the increasing use of "securitized" bond issues, which are collateralized with future foreign exchange receipts. Mexican private and public companies have been able to successfully launch such issues. Another attempt at dollar financing, but on the domestic market, has been indexed commercial paper, introduced in 1990. Such paper is both bought in pesos and paid out in pesos, but it is tied to the dollar rate and offers lower interest rates as a dollar instrument.

PART III
Sector Profiles

7
Reforms in Agriculture

Greater economic integration among Mexico, the US and Canada will clearly affect each country's agricultural production and related policies. Agriculture, however, is certain to be one of the most difficult sectors to fully incorporate into a North American Free Trade Agreement (FTA). Agricultural policies in Mexico and the US have long been at odds with the free market conditions that are essential for an "open borders" trade policy. Important changes in Mexico's agricultural sector, however, were implemented in early 1992 and will have a significant impact on the attitude of international agribusiness companies toward opportunities in Mexico.

Although Mexican agriculture has traditionally received only limited attention from North American companies involved in agriculture-related business, this situation is changing. In February 1992 Mexico embarked on a major overhaul of the legal and regulatory framework that governs agriculture, which promises to provide foreign and local companies with access to enormous tracts of land and sets the stage for major new investments in the farm sector. Although many opportunities arising from the changes may not materialize before late 1992 or early 1993, companies are already beginning to reexamine their North American operations.

This chapter aims to provide companies with information critical to their planning for future operations in Mexican agriculture, including: a brief overview of the history of Mexico's ambitious agrarian reform program; a review of current production and trade trends; a description of the initial attempts by the Carlos Salinas de Gortari administration to

139

introduce free market reforms to the countryside; a summary of the recent changes in agricultural laws and their consequences; and finally, a look at some of the strategies companies began to adopt in the last few years in anticipation of the legislative changes and investment opportunities that are emerging.

Land Reform

At first glance, Mexico's agricultural sector may not look promising to foreign investors. In recent years, it has been plagued with declining production (output fell steadily as a percentage of GDP, from 15.6% in 1960 to 7.4% in 1989), and much of its best farmland is used to grow grains that can be produced more efficiently in the US. Moreover, until the February 1992 legal modifications, farmland ownership by any corporation, whether foreign or local, was forbidden, and private landholdings were legally restricted in size. Most important, the agricultural sector is home to the ejido, one of the most revered "sacred cows" of the Mexican Revolution of 1910 and the embodiment of agrarian reform. Ejidos—collectively held land parcels that cannot be bought, sold or rented—account for most of the national territory, including a substantial portion of the arable land. With the possible exception of the oil industry (its expropriation occurred after the Mexican Revolution), no other sector of the economy is as closely linked to the current identity of modern "revolutionary" Mexico as are agrarian reform and the ejido.

The Mexican Revolution of 1910 resulted in part from calls for land reform to correct the extreme degree of land concentration in Mexico early in the century. Agrarian reform was a major rallying point for peasants who supported leaders such as revolutionary hero Emiliano Zapata. Zapata's slogan, "Land belongs to he who works it," galvanized poor farmers' support for the revolution, crucial in overthrowing Porfirio Díaz's dictatorship.

Two of the most significant outcomes of the revolution were the Agrarian Reform Act of 1915 and the Constitution of 1917. Together, they provided the government with the right to expropriate large estates and distribute land to peasants. The legal system, despite subsequent changes in the constitution and the Reform Law, still allows the state to regulate and limit property rights, including the expropriation of property. Moreover, the agrarian documents of the beginning of this century are still the basis for current legislation.

One of the key concepts adopted by the Mexican constitution was the ejido. The word ejido was used in medieval Spain to describe communal lands located outside a village. In Mexico, communal landholdings were common prior to the Spanish conquest. The Constitution of 1917 transformed this concept, which has both Spanish and Mexican roots, into an institution of the state. Under agrarian reform, large landholdings could be confiscated, and the government would become the owner. This land would then be distributed to ejido farmers, or ejidatarios, who have the right to enjoy the land but could not obtain ownership. (Ejido land, however, could be passed down to the children of the ejidatario, under the same conditions.) In general, ejido land could not be bought, sold or rented.

Land Redistribution

Despite the broad powers given the Mexican government by the Constitution and the Agrarian Reform Act, actual land redistribution was limited in the years immediately following the revolution. From 1917 to 1933, only 10.7 million hectares (roughly 5% of total farmland in Mexico) were redistributed. The first and most important wave of land redistribution did not occur until the presidency of Gen. Lázaro Cárdenas (1934–40). During his six-year term, Cárdenas redistributed more than 20 million hectares, twice the amount of land handed out prior to his term as president. Analysts argue that his decision to hasten land reform was based on a political objective—to consolidate the support of the peasants for the ruling Party of the Mexican Revolution (PRM), which was renamed the Institutional Revolutionary Party (PRI) in 1946.

In conjunction with his massive land redistribution program, Cárdenas brought various peasant groups together to form the National Peasant Confederation (CNC), which has been an element of the ruling party right up to the present. The CNC has been successful in maintaining relative calm in the countryside and has provided the PRI with an extremely important base of electoral support. Today, the legacy of Cárdenas lives on, as government policymakers face the challenge of reforming Mexico's agricultural system without damaging the strong peasant support for the PRI.

Following the large-scale land distribution carried out by Cárdenas, the percentage of farmland held as ejidos remained fairly stable until the late 1960s. Large landholdings continued to survive and flourish from the 1940s to the 1960s. Private cattle producers were provided with guarantees that their land would not be subject to agrarian reform and confiscated. Large estates, though illegal, were tolerated. Despite legal limits on size, new large private farms (neolatifundias) were formed by combining small landholdings, often placed in the names of relatives or business partners. This practice is commonplace today.

The last major redistribution effort took place in the late 1960s and early 1970s, during the administrations of Gustavo Díaz Ordaz and Luis Echeverría. The land handed out at that time represented more than one third of the total land area distributed in the past. The impressive amount of land distributed during the Echeverría administration, however, belies its importance to farmers. In the majority of cases, the quality of the land made it only marginally suitable for crop production. Almost none of the redistributed land was irrigated, and some analysts claim that less than 10% of the land was suitable for crops.

Since the last great land distribution in the early 1970s, each new president has announced that there was no more land to redistribute; each has subsequently parceled out land to farmers. Although President Salinas said in his first State of the Nation address on Nov. 1, 1989, that the era of massive land redistribution was over, he has redistributed more than 450,000 hectares since taking office.

Today, more than half (53%) of Mexico's national territory (197 million hectares, or 762,000 sq m) is held as ejidos or, in some cases, as communal Indian lands. The amount of land suitable for agricultural production is considerably less than that, however. Arable land is estimated at 35 million hectares or 18% of the total Mexican territory. Estimates vary as to what percentage of Mexico's arable land is held as ejidos, with some analysts claiming that as much as two thirds of all agricultural land falls under the ejido land tenure system.

It is clear from these estimates that ejido tenure accounts for a substantial amount of Mexico's farmland. Compounded by the legal restrictions limiting the size of private landholdings, the result is a severe legal restriction on agricultural landholding in Mexico. Any changes in the laws or regulations governing the ejidos or private property could provide immediate new opportunities for companies interested in agriculture in Mexico.

Although the 1971 Agrarian Reform Law (a revised version of the original 1940 Agrarian Code) states that an ejido should have a minimum size of 10 hectares if it is on irrigated land and 20 hectares if it is on rain-fed land, ejido landholdings are typically much smaller. At present, the average size of a rain-fed ejido parcel is estimated at 6.5 hectares, whereas the average size of an ejido on irrigated land is less than one hectare (0.9 h). Although the average size of a private farm is roughly 70 hectares, nearly three fifths of both ejido and private farms are less than five hectares in area. (The greatest difference between the sizes of ejidos and private farms is seen in the North, where much larger private landholdings and large-scale irrigation projects are found.)

Current Production and Trade

After poor agricultural results in 1988 and 1989, agricultural production rose in 1990, largely because of more favorable climatic conditions. Corn production, which had fallen in recent years from 14.1 million MT in 1985 to 10.9 million MT in 1989, is estimated to have reached 14.6 million MT in the 1990 growing season. Nonetheless, Mexico had to import approximately 3.8 million MT of corn in 1990 to meet the

Table 7-1. Mexico's Agricultural Trade
($ millions)

Principal Exports					
	1986	1987	1988	1989	1990*
Coffee grain	825	492	435	514	236
Frozen shrimp	354	435	371	338	75
Cattle	265	192	203	212	165
Tomatoes	408	200	243	199	396
Vegetables	198	238	269	97	324
Beer	117	216	186	157	76
Processed fruits and vegetables	82	101	114	156	90
Melons	64	88	73	125	76
Sugar	30	79	159	79	—
Orange juice	18	37	72	56	64
Principal Imports					
	1986	1987	1988	1989	1990*
Dry milk	117	135	240	471	304
Corn	166	284	394	441	276
Soybeans	167	220	336	327	78
Sorghum	78	62	138	322	201
Meats	51	45	273	297	129
Other fats	103	44	155	207	139
Oilseeds	147	114	138	149	57
Animal feed	32	18	127	137	39
Hides/skins	54	77	113	93	39
Cattle	66	33	182	87	35

SOURCE: INEGI, Banco de Mexico, BI.
*January to June only.

large national demand. Government officials forecast that corn imports will be down in 1991, whereas other estimates are for at least 1.5 million MT of corn imports for the year.

Overall, grain production reached about 24 million MT in 1990, with corn and beans showing the strongest gains over 1989. Wheat and rice production were down in 1990 from 4.3 million MT and 420,000 MT, respectively, in 1989. Imports of basic grains, including corn, sorghum, beans and wheat, were estimated at more than 8 million MT during 1990.

In recent years, agricultural production has steadily declined as a percentage of GDP, from 15.6% in 1960 to 7.4% in 1989. As a result of favorable climatic conditions, which boosted rain-fed land production (primarily of corn and beans), agricultural production in 1990 as a percentage of GDP rose to an estimated 8%. Agricultural growth has been sporadic in recent decades and grew at rates below the increase in population for most of the 1980s. After contracting by 3.2% in 1988 and by 4.2% in 1989, the farm sector showed positive growth of 3.4% in 1990.

Although production of basic grains increased in 1990, Mexico must still import large amounts of these grains to meet domestic demand. Furthermore, imports of agricultural and processed food products are estimated to have risen in 1990. In 1989, Mexico spent over $4 billion on agricultural and processed food products, up more than $1 billion from 1988, when food imports totaled approximately $3 billion. During

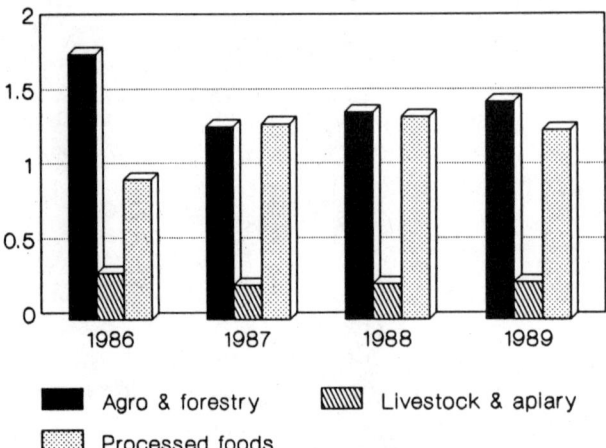

Figure 7-1. Mexico's agricultural trade balance 1986-90 ($ billions). *(Source: INEGI)*

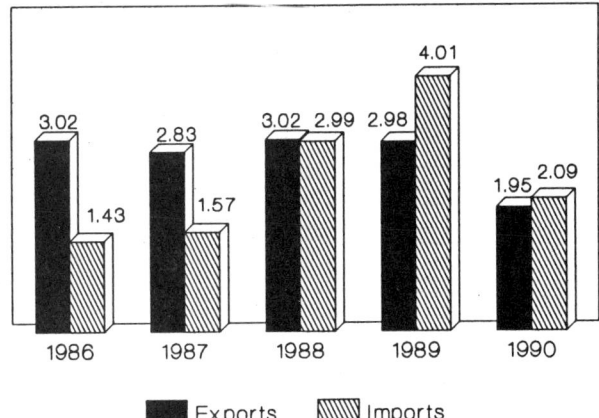

Figure 7-2. Mexico's agricultural export profile, 1986-89 ($ billions). 1990: January–June only. *(Source: INEGI)*

the first six months of 1990, imports of agricultural and processed food products were up by nearly 25%, compared with the first half of 1989.

Mexico's agricultural trade reached approximately $7 billion in 1989 and is estimated to have grown beyond that amount in 1990. The bulk of the trade is with the US, which accounted for nearly $6 billion worth of total trade. The US is both Mexico's leading importer and exporter of agricultural and processed food products. Even if a free trade agreement were not ratified, the US would remain Mexico's most important trading partner in agriculture and processed foods. Mexico's proximity to the US translates into lower-cost, faster transportation of goods. On the other hand, the higher-cost, slower transportation of goods involved in trade with Europe and the Pacific Basin countries will remain important factors limiting these regions' trade with Mexico.

The Salinas Plan: The First Stage

Faced with a declining agricultural sector—in terms of production, investment and infrastructure—the Salinas administration in early 1991 unveiled an agricultural modernization plan called the National Program of the Modernization of the Countryside 1990–94 (Programa Nacional de Modernización del Campo 1990–94). Although it fell short of some of the major reforms then being discussed within the government, the program was an important first step toward modifying agricultural policy.

The document, prepared by the Agriculture and Water Resources Secretariat (Secretaría de Agricultura y Recursos Hidraúlicos) advocated two principal objectives: (1) increase the level of production in the agricultural sector, and (2) raise the standard of living of rural dwellers. To achieve these goals, the plan called for farmers to participate in designing solutions and for "complete respect for the forms of organization and land tenure established in the Constitution."

The plan represented a compromise between some officials within the administration who preferred to do away with the ejidos and those who were fearful that any change could undermine the strong political support and control that the PRI enjoys in the countryside.

The modernization program singled out a series of obstacles that had contributed to the deterioration of the agricultural sector, including:

• A decline in investment, facilities maintenance and research and development;

• Insecurity resulting from the current application of the land tenure system. The prohibition on ownership of ejido land, combined with the various controls on the size of privately held plots, creates a constant fear of confiscation among landholders;

• Excessive government intervention;

• Small size of land parcels held by ejido farmers, which was quite often below the legally prescribed minimum and precluded economies of scale and profitable investment;

• Scarcities of credit, insurance, water, fertilizers, maintenance, seeds and roads; and

• Production distortions caused by price support and subsidy programs, which acted as disincentives to efficient production.

Initial Reforms

To remedy the problems listed above, the Agriculture Secretariat proposed the following reforms:

• Guarantee greater certainty in land tenure;

• Privatize state-owned companies involved in the processing and commercialization of agricultural products;

• Revamp the credit programs of the agricultural bank, Banrural;

• Reduce excessive duties on certain imported inputs;

- Replace generalized subsidies with specific subsidies focused on the region or type of produce; and

- Establish "agroindustrial corridors" to link croplands, processing plants and ports or roads.

Privatization, however, began in 1990 with the sale of parts of the food processing division of Conasupo, the deficit-ridden, government-owned food distribution agency. A large vegetable oil refinery with a 100,000 MT/year capacity, a soybean processing plant with a 330,000 MT/year capacity and a large-scale pasta plant were sold to Anderson-Clayton (a subsidiary of the UK's Unilever). Various sugar mills controlled by the government were sold to local partners of PepsiCo and Coca-Cola (both US) and to a local ice cream company.

Banrural, the rural development bank, eliminated virtually all subsidized credits for the 1990–91 harvest. In December 1990, credits were offered to farmers at Cetes (treasury certificates used as a benchmark for interest rates) plus four to five percentage points. Banrural's 1990 rates prior to the elimination of subsidies were usually Cetes minus one or two points. Still, special assistance exists for a carefully defined group of the poorest farmers through Salinas's antipoverty program, the National Solidarity Program (Pronasol).

Import permits were eliminated for virtually all agricultural products except grains, oilseeds, beans and powdered milk. In 1984, import permits were required for agriculture-related goods totaling 79% of the value of all such imports. By 1989, that percentage had fallen to 43%, although some US producers claim that import permits are still required for about 59% of the value of US agricultural exports to Mexico.

The New Rules of the Game

The February 1992 overhaul of Mexico's agrarian legislation opens a new frontier for agribusiness next door to the US, promising to provide access to hundreds of thousands of acres of land. Word of a possible change in Mexico's ejido land tenure system came during 1990 and 1991, but because of the extremely sensitive nature of land tenure in Mexico, government officials kept mum about the full extent of the new agrarian law until the legislation changing the constitution was introduced in November 1991.

Although Mexico's countryside has long suffered from neglect, lack of finance and inefficiency as agricultural land was divided up into even smaller plots, there was strong opposition from farmer representatives within the ruling PRI party to permit ejido farmers greater freedom.

The farm vote was instrumental in Salinas' narrow and controversial victory in the 1988 presidential elections. And farm organization leaders feared that the reforms would end their political control over ejidatarios who depended on the ruling party for credit and the promise of more land.

However, following the PRI's strong showing the August 1991 midterm elections, Salinas was effectively able to argue that the results were a vote of confidence for his economic liberalization campaign.

End of land reform

The new law essentially ends Mexico's decades-old agrarian reform program. "There is really no more land to give out," says one official. There have been protests in the countryside from communities that were on record as asking for land, but these have been limited. "We expected a much greater risk of social unrest," commented the general director of one agricultural multinational company in Mexico.

Besides halting any new distribution of land, the new law permits ejido landholders to rent their land, form joint ventures, or enter into any other contractual agreement with third parties. While rentals were common before, they were illegal. Investors were therefore unwilling to make major improvements to land that they risked losing because of the illegal nature of the contract.

Now, companies can enter into long-term contracts with ejido farmers, or ejidatarios, with no limits on the amount of land they can control. The ability to control large tracts of land and make improvements on it should greatly boost productivity in Mexico's countryside.

The new law also clears up the cloud of uncertainty surrounding ejido joint ventures, such as the alliance between Gamesa, Mexico's largest cookie and pasta maker, and ejidatarios in northern Mexico (see box in this chapter). Few companies had followed Gamesa's lead because of questions of legality. "We were approached by the government to enter into a long-term leasing arrangement with ejidatarios similar to the Gamesa deal," explains the director general of one food processing company, "but we couldn't take the risk of doing something not within the law. Despite the government's strong promotion of the arrangement, our attorneys told us that it was unconstitutional."

Companies are now looking at the Gamesa venture for ideas on how to structure a deal with farmers. "We no longer have to look for companies to encourage them to invest in the countryside; they are looking for us," says an official at the Secretariat of Agriculture.

Among new projects being developed is an 8,000-hectare eucalyptus tree project in San Luis Potosi, a 50,000-hectare fine wood project in Campeche and a 50,000-hectare export vegetable project in Sonora.

Ownership versus control

The new law also allows companies to own land for the first time since Mexico's revolution early this century. Although foreigners are limited to a 49% share in a landowning operation, special "T" shares corresponding to landholdings will be issued (distinct from a company's normal stock). Hence, a foreign firm could potentially own virtually all of a local company's assets, with the only exception being a 49% limit on the "T" shares.

Still, most executives and analysts argue that land ownership is not the real issue. "Large companies want control of land, not ownership," asserts Ken Shwedel, an agricultural economist. "The new law facilitates that and is much more flexible than I imagined. Companies should look at their operations and reevaluate what role Mexico can play."

Company X started a modest association with small landholders in 1990 to grow and pack vegetables. It is now looking to expand much more rapidly by including alliances with ejidatarios. "Within a year or two we will be able to bring down more sophisticated machinery, once we get the size of our operation up, " says the firm's general director.

Other companies are looking at everything from wheat and corn mills to meat-processing plants, tomato-processing plants and alliances with pig breeders. Questions remain regarding financing, but banks and investment firms are looking at ways to fund agricultural projects. Meanwhile, a new institution, the Agrarian Attorney General's Office, was formed in 1992 and will be in charge of many ejido-company issues.

Company Strategies and Opportunities

Even before Salinas succeeded in changing the laws with the aim of radically transforming the landholding structure in Mexico's countryside, MNCs began actively studying the possibilities of significant reforms. Some firms have already identified niches that could make Mexican agricultural operations very attractive:

(1) **Land rentals.** Some MNC executives in Mexico are studying the possibility of land rental, whereas several companies are already involved in such arrangements. "You don't need to own land to produce efficiently," explains the director general of Company A, "but you do need some level of control." Although rental of land would allow Company A to enter into the production process and have direct control, the company has expressed little interest in becoming directly involved

in farming. Instead, a small landholder or farmer (or another local company) might be contracted by Company A to operate the rented ejidos. In the event of a failure to perform, Company A could try to gain access to the assets of the farmer/producer—not a possible alternative when the only recourse is against the ejidatario. Rentals could help re-activate the flow of financing to ejidos via a third party that has control over the land and is creditworthy.

(2) **Financing.** For some companies, the first step may involve fund-ing agricultural operations. Company B is cautious about getting in-volved in a land rental. However, the firm would be willing to help fi-nance a joint venture between a national organization and a group of ejidatarios if a long-term supply of products could be guaranteed. The company currently avoids all dealings with ejidos, preferring to source from small landholders, advancing funds and materials in return for a contractual promise backed by promissory notes.

(3) **Large-scale sourcing.** Company C is considering Mexico as a sourcing site for its core-business requirements worldwide. Much of the land suitable for growing the products Company C requires, however, is either held as ejidos or in small landholdings, neither of which are via-ble for efficient production. "There are some crops that do not require large tracts of land, but in our case we need to be able to control large areas," explains the firm's director for international/global sourcing. "In order to be cost efficient, we have to build a large packing plant, and that requires a lot of production to keep it going." The firm may join with a Mexican partner that could provide labor or rent land from ejidatarios now that changes have been made in the agrarian law.

Key Attractions

The advantages of doing business in Mexico for food processors and other agriculture-related companies are numerous: proximity to the US market, which translates into reduced transportation costs; a better win-ter climate for various types of winter produce; attractive land for tropi-cal agriculture; synergies with the local market, where acceptance of lower-quality production complements demand for higher-quality items in the US; and low labor costs, which make production with a high labor component—from vegetable cutting to fresh produce production—more attractive. With the prospect of virtually no duties for US-Mexican trade under an FTA, and possible changes in agrarian laws, Mexico is likely to play an increasingly important role in the US's food industry.

The most optimistic companies are those firms studying sugar cane, mangos, strawberries, raspberries, papaya, oranges, orange juice and pulp, bananas, pineapples and other tropical fruits, avocados, frozen vegetables, asparagus, mushrooms and carrots. Animal slaughtering operations as well as processed foods from poultry, pork and beef have also been highlighted as attractive investment areas.

Investment in Mexico already exists in some product areas, such as frozen vegetables. Bird's Eye, Green Giant and Campbells (all US) have operations in Mexico involving processing for the US market. Bird's Eye imports seeds, fertilizers and equipment from the US, nurtures small plants in its greenhouses and then turns the plants over to local farmers, who grow and harvest them. The company then freezes the produce and sends it in large boxes to the US, where it is repackaged into smaller boxes and readied for supermarket delivery. Some firms have transferred other steps of the production process to Mexico, including vegetable cutting operations.

Other areas of opportunity, particularly in tropical agriculture, remain virtually unexplored. Because of the need for large tracts of land for economies of scale in tropical fruits (much more land is needed for pineapples, for example, than for broccoli), until now, Mexico's restrictions on ejido land use and size of private landholdings have limited investment in this area. With the changes described in this chapter now in place, plantation-style production could become an important new source of tropical fruits for companies. Long-term leases of ejido land would permit investors to control sufficiently large tracts for a long enough period of time to make necessary investments in land improvements, i.e. the planting of trees, to produce efficiently and recoup initial costs.

Prospects for Basic Grains

In general, companies do not see many opportunities in Mexico for production of basic grains. According to the director of agricultural production for a leading US agricultural firm, "Mexico will have a hard time producing wheat and corn at costs competitive with the US, given Mexico's land. "Increased access to technology would help some to increase volume, but the costs involved in production in Mexico will always be higher because of inadequate soil and climate."

Still, opportunities to export corn to Mexico are likely to remain restricted by calls for self-sufficiency. Despite the economic costs, many analysts believe that the political price of an open borders policy in corn would be excessive because of its central role as a subsistence crop for most of Mexico's peasants. Even though the government seems willing to allow free trade in most other grains, corn and beans will probably continue to be highly controlled.

Better prospects for export to Mexico exist in soybeans, wheat and sorghum—grains that Mexico will probably import in greater quantities in the coming years, especially under a more competitive environment brought on by a free trade agreement. Unlike the US, where wheat is grown on marginal rain-fed areas, in Mexico some of the best agricultural land is dedicated to wheat cultivation—especially in the irrigated zones of the North. For instance, in a more competitive environment, much of the land in the Bajio (a rich farmland area of Mexico that is currently being used to produce wheat with high yields) would most likely be switched over to greater value-added and more labor-intensive crops such as fruits and vegetables, sectors in which Mexico has a comparative advantage vis-à-vis the US.

Some MNCs operating in Mexico, however, argue that any changes must be gradual. An executive at one company admits that Mexican grain production is not competitive with US output in terms of price per metric ton. This means that producers in the poultry, pork, cattle and dairy industries are faced with expensive ingredients for animal feed. If the market in grains remains protected, other productive sectors will become uncompetitive. The executive argues that a rapid opening of the borders in the area of grains will not be sufficient to save much of Mexico's poultry and pork industry. Grains and feeds from the US will be more expensive in Mexico, as a result of transportation costs—thus, pigs and chickens can be fed less expensively in the US than in Mexico. Even though transportation expenses would increase the price of US-sourced chicken and pork in Mexico, the additional amount would be lower than the cost increase associated with transporting grain. "Mexican producers can be as efficient as their US counterparts and still run the risk of being uncompetitive because of high costs in animal feed and grain production in Mexico," explains the director general of one firm.

Models for Investment in the Countryside: Ejido Joint Ventures

In the last few years, the Agriculture Secretariat has been busy promoting investment in the countryside. Among the major projects, Gamesa has received most of the publicity. Another project involving chicken raising, however, also serves as a model of how companies can design their agricultural strategies.

(Continued)

Growing Beans and Wheat for PepsiCo's Mexican Sub

Gamesa, Mexico's largest cookie and pasta maker, was acquired in October 1990 by PepsiCo Inc (US) through Sabritas, its wholly owned Mexican snack food subsidiary. The purchase solidifies PepsiCo's leading role in the estimated $1 billion Mexican snack food market by bringing together a company that produces salty snacks (Sabritas) with a firm that produces sweet snacks (Gamesa). Months before its acquisition, however, Gamesa had attracted local attention for other reasons: It had become a pioneer in a joint venture between the private sector and ejidatarios.

The initial goal of the project is to raise beans and wheat on 5,000 hectares of land in northern Mexico, much of which is ejido land. Because private companies cannot directly manage ejidos, a complicated structure was set up to permit Gamesa to associate with the ejidatarios. Gamesa set up a subsidiary, Promotora Agropecuária Gamesa, which then entered into a trust (Fideicomiso Vaquerias), with Dicamex, a nonprofit organization that oversees the ejido production. State and federal government agencies, as well as the ejidatarios, were also made partners in the venture.

This scheme effectively separates the firm from direct management of the project and avoids direct employer-employee relationship with the farmers. Through the trust, Gamesa supplied them with tractors and seed and helped complete an irrigation system within the 5,000 hectare area. (The federal government stepped in to provide the firm with foreign debt-conversion rights outside of the normal swap program, because the irrigation work constituted infrastructure improvements.) In return, the farmers agreed to a 12-year association with Gamesa, renewable annually.

Although the new farming methods will require less than 25% of the 400 ejidatarios to work the land, they will all receive a guaranteed minimum profit equal to 8% of the crop's gross sales. In addition to this "profit sharing," the 80–100 farmers who actually work on the land will receive wages.

The project permits Gamesa to source agricultural products from an efficient production unit that would not otherwise have existed. In addition to the benefits of a reliable supply from a nearby source, Gamesa will be able to recoup its initial investment by taking a share of the venture's profits. Although the arrangement may very much resemble a rental of ejido property with the subsequent contracting

(Continued)

of a portion of the farmers to work the land, government lawyers claim that it is completely legal. Instead of receiving rent, the farmers get a share of the profits from a joint venture.

Ejido Sourcing for Chickens

Although Gamesa has received widespread publicity for its innovative "partnership" with ejidatarios, government officials have been hard at work on another project involving ejido land and private capital. As with the Gamesa deal, officials have been providing the private investors with advice, financing leads and logistical support. Unlike Gamesa, no special swap financing was necessary to sweeten the deal. Instead, sources close to the venture believe that the prospects for profitability are strong enough to make the arrangement attractive without special subsidies.

In 1989, a strategic alliance involving C. Itoh (Japan), Provemex (Mexico), Tyson Foods (US) and Banamex, a Mexican bank, was set up to manufacture chicken products for sale in the Asian market. C. Itoh wanted to diversify its sourcing base for chicken yakitori, a popular Asian food item, which had become costly to produce in Japan because of the large labor component involved. Provemex was looking for ways to expand its Mexican business—raising and slaughtering chickens—to include other production processes, such as chicken deboning for chicken products. Tyson Foods sought new markets for surplus dark chicken meat, which is in less demand in the US than white breast meat.

Tyson ships chicken legs to a Mexican maquiladora which, with the technical assistance of C. Itoh and financing from Banamex, is able to process the chicken as yakitori. The chicken product is then sold to a trading company for marketing in Asia.

After its setup, the maquiladora's production exceeded 750,000 chickens per month, and was expected to reach two million per month by late 1990. The processing plant exceeded productivity rates in the US and Japan, not only in labor costs, but also in chickens processed per man-hour. The venture was so successful that C. Itoh increased supplies from Mexico eightfold. In response, Provemex expanded its sourcing of chicken in Mexico for both its export and domestic businesses.

Although Provemex is already involved in domestic raising of chickens for local end-users, including the fast-food restaurants

(Continued)

Kentucky Fried Chicken and McDonald's, it needed to substantially increase its domestic production. To increase its local supplies, Trasgo, a wholly owned subsidiary of Provemex, is now setting up an alliance with ejidos that government officials hope will be a model for other companies planning to become involved in Mexican agriculture.

The advantage of working with ejidos relates to space limitations for raising chickens. Unlike the production of some items with very large economies of scale, chicken raising is usually confined to a maximum of 48,000–100,000 chickens per area. These limitations are designed to protect the operation in the event of an outbreak of disease. By dividing the raising areas into smaller units and separating each unit by a significant distance, the risk of losses resulting from disease is reduced.

Given the need to spread out the chicken-raising areas, Trasgo believed that working with various ejidos would be an effective way to manage the project and limit the costs associated with supervision of labor. By entering into an alliance with the ejido farmers and giving them a percentage of profits, Trasgo hopes to provide important incentives for local farmers to produce more efficiently.

Trasgo will provide the ejidatarios with chicks, technical assistance on care and feed at cost, plus a charge representing financing costs associated with setting up the operation. The ejidatarios will then raise the chickens and return those that are grown to Trasgo after nine weeks, in return for payment. After Trasgo completes payment on a 10-year loan, the ejidatarios will no longer be charged for additional financing. The payment scheme is set up so that more productive farmers (measured in terms of the chicken mortality rate and feed conversion to pounds of meat) will be compensated with greater discounts in the cost of inputs. Construction of the chicken farms began in early 1991. The project is expected to increase production by 2.4 million chickens per month, eventually reaching 4.4 million chickens per month, close to 14% of current national production.

More Projects on the Way

Besides the Gamesa and Trasgo projects, other firms are studying similar type ventures with ejidatarios. Tropicana (US), in a joint venture with Procigo (Mexico), is looking at a project that would involve

(Continued)

growing oranges on ejido land in Northern Veracruz. Evans Food (US) is studying slaughtering operations in Mexico. Other leading US food companies are investigating fresh fruit, frozen vegetables and semiprocessed agricultural goods projects that would involve co-ordination or management of ejido resources. In most cases, a joint venture or alliance with a Mexican partner is being set up to legally deal with ejidatarios.

8

The Automotive Industry

No industry is as critical to Mexican economic revitalization or to the international competitiveness of US manufacturing as the automotive industry. President Salinas has singled out this sector as the most important to Mexico's plans to establish itself as a serious manufacturing competitor on the global stage and a chief rival to East Asia's famed "Tigers" of the 1980s—South Korea, Taiwan, Singapore and Hong Kong—the countries that set performance and growth standards for all other newly industrialized countries (NICs). In reaction to intensified competition from Japanese vehicles in North America, US motor vehicle manufacturers and parts producers have also identified Mexico as their latest and most dynamic production site among the NICs.

Until recently, Mexico has been a limited export platform for the US and Canadian markets, while domestic production has been hindered by extensive government regulation and, in the 1980s, by severe recession. Because of these negative business conditions, Mexico has emerged only recently as an important and possibly key player in the international automotive industry. The ratification of a free trade agreement (FTA) between the US and Canada in January 1989, however, along with the parallel regionalization in the European Community (EC) and Pacific Basin, has lent a new urgency to integrating Mexico further with the US and Canadian economies. As integration progresses over the next few years, Mexico's status as a budding world-class producer will be enhanced.

Whatever the outcome of FTA talks, it is certain that foreign investment in Mexican automotive plants, as well as trade in vehicles and parts, will grow rapidly in the 1990s. This chapter examines these prospects, first summarizing major legislation and events that have shaped the development of the industry and prepared it for its role as a global competitor.

Automotive Decrees of 1962–83

The first automotive decree, commonly referred to simply as the Integration Decree, was announced on Sept. 1, 1962, but not actually implemented until March 1, 1965. Ironically, the presidential decree was crafted by the secretary of commerce and industrial development, Raúl Salinas Lozano, the father of Mexico's current president. Envisioned during a period when intense nationalistic sentiment heavily influenced government policies, the first presidential decree regulating the automotive industry raised issues that remain the subject of controversy today, e.g. local-content percentages, foreign equity participation, trade balances and employment.

In 1962, Mexico's automotive sector was a fledgling industry that lacked a strategic plan. Only 67,000 vehicles were produced that year by 10 companies operating in the country, whereas another seven firms simply imported passenger cars manufactured elsewhere. Scarcely 15–20% of the parts contained in vehicles assembled in Mexico were sourced locally. Under these circumstances, the automotive industry generated large trade deficits. Individual manufacturers found it difficult to earn profits, since economies of scale could be achieved only when 150,000 vehicles were produced per manufacturer, per line, along with five different models. With just 10 manufacturers producing 67,000 units with multiple lines, Mexico's industry could not operate profitably.

The 1962 Decree

The Integration Decree was issued during a period in which Mexican decisionmakers focused almost exclusively on the development of the domestic market and sources of employment. The government provided a protected environment for Mexican manufacturers, particularly in new, potentially high-growth industries, such as motor vehicles and autoparts. Initially, export production at internationally competitive quality standards or prices was not an issue.

To meet the explicitly political objectives of the government and to protect the industry, the 1962 decree embodied classic import-substitution regulations intended to stimulate domestic production:

• Sixty percent of the parts/components contained in vehicles put together in Mexico had to be sourced locally (measured in direct cost terms).

• All finished motors and other critical parts like transmissions, shock absorbers and drive shafts were required to be produced in Mexico, i.e. could not be imported.

• All completely knocked-down or semi-knocked-down kits from which cars were manufactured (normally containing a maximum of 20% local content) were prohibited from being imported, as were all fully assembled vehicles.

• Government price controls and production quotas were established.

The motor vehicle manufacturing plants—which were mostly foreign owned at the time and are entirely foreign owned today—complained about the Mexican government's policies and felt discriminated against in favor of local producers of autoparts. After two decades, however, the results brought about by the changes in import regulations have, for the most part, been positive. As indicated in Table 8-1, both vehicles sales and automotive employment skyrocketed, sales increased at a rate of approximately 32% p.a., and employment rose at 69% p.a.

Under the tutelage of the government, the Mexican automotive industry was sheltered from international competition in the autoparts sector. The vehicle manufacturers were required not only to source 60% of their parts from local suppliers, but were also expressly pre-

Table 8-1. Mexican Vehicle Sales and Employment: 1962–82
(000's of unit sales and individuals)

	1982	1972	1962	% Change 1982/1962 (yearly)
Domestic Vehicles	466.7	233.4	65.2	31.9
Export Vehicles	15.8	2.2	—	—
Total Vehicles	482.5	235.6	65.2	31.9
Employment (Vehicles and Parts)	119.0	30.0	8.0	69.4

SOURCE: Mexican Automotive Manufacturers Association (*Asociación Mexicana de la Industria Automotriz*—AMIA).

vented from vertical integration. This meant that the autoparts suppliers were, by definition, majority Mexican-owned enterprises. Two additional decrees (passed in 1972 and 1977) stipulated that the maximum foreign participation allowed in the supplier sector was 40%. The added legislation spurred the development of an automotive industry that was divided clearly between foreign-owned vehicle producers and domestically owned suppliers, two distinct groups with different interests.

In the years following the implementation of the government's decrees, the automotive industry prospered. Since the sector was very vulnerable to cyclical changes in demand, however, the administration created added protection during periods of recession by increasing price controls and limiting the number of lines that any single manufacturer could produce. When the economy resumed growth, the government tended to loosen its controls. Despite its early successes in generating employment and sales, however, the automotive industry was unable to reduce its foreign trade deficit, which burgeoned to unprecedented levels. During the industry's boom years of 1978–81, the automotive trade deficit reached $2.3 billion. Although the government had tried earlier to stimulate exports in order to reverse this negative trend, its efforts were undermined by an expanding Mexican market that rendered export promotion unattractive.

All of this changed abruptly in 1983, with the incontrovertible evidence that the country's economic crisis could not be overcome quickly. Under these circumstances, the Mexican regulatory framework was recast and import substitution scuttled. The 1983 Automotive Decree sounded the alarm that in an anemic domestic market, the only hope for the industry was export production, initially aimed at the rapidly expanding US market.

The 1983 Decree

In 1983, vehicle sales reached their lowest level in a decade, following four consecutive years of explosive growth that had turned the Mexican industry into the fastest growing in Latin America. Given the rapid expansion of the Mexican market from 1977-81, the automotive industry focused virtually all its attention on domestic demand. The decline in oil prices in the early 1980s and the economic crisis of 1982–83, however, forced the government to rethink its automotive policy. When vehicle sales in 1983 barely accounted for 50% of 1981's figures, the new Miguel de la Madrid administration concluded that the automotive sector needed to be restructured. The industry's new objectives were embodied in the 1983 decree, The most important provisions of which were as follows:

• Local content was defined in stricter terms so that it was calculated using a cost-of-parts formula rather than by direct costs.

• Under the new calculation, minimal content for cars was set at 50% for 1984 (to rise to 60% in 1987), whereas ratios for trucks and buses were higher (model year basis).

• Passenger car manufacturers were restricted to producing only one line in 1986 and 1987 after being permitted to offer three in 1984.

• Exceptions to both the local-content formula and permissible lines were granted if car manufacturers *exported* at least 80% of their production.

• If an automaker complied with the export provision, then local-content requirements were to be half the normal rate, i.e. 30% for cars produced *and* exported in model year 1987, and an additional line would be permitted (expressly for export).

This new decree was clearly intended to attract foreign investment devoted to export production, although ostensibly it was to rationalize manufacturing. The economies of scale that could make it a reality, however, were out of the question in a country in which total automobile production was scarcely 300,000 units in 1983. From the vantage point of scale, each manufacturer would be required to produce about 150,000 vehicles per line to achieve global standards. With five major producers each manufacturing one line, this would mean the market would need to be two or three times larger than Mexico's 1983 domestic market or it would have to be redefined to include the rest of North America, particularly the US.

Economies of scale and exports
Given this strategy, it was possible to envision economies of scale, but only for a specific manufacturer—perhaps only for one line devoted exclusively to exports. Ford (US) emerged as the one company prepared to produce a line of subcompact vehicles, the Mercury Tracer, designed by its joint venture partner, Mazda (Japan), and exported to the US and Canada. In early 1984, Ford announced it was investing $500 million to build a new export plant in Hermosillo, Sonora, with a capacity to produce 130,000 cars p.a. Although Ford's actual exports through 1989 only approached half that figure, the problem was the high cost of imported parts from Japan, rather than the quality of the Mexican-assembled vehicle and its acceptance by sophisticated US consumers. Subsequently, Ford expanded the plant to a capacity of 170,000 units in 1989–90, with 75% of its parts US-sourced. In doing so, it established a

Table 8-2. Mexican Vehicle Sales/Domestic and Export: 1981–89
(000's units)

	1989	1988	1987	1981
Domestic	445.87	341.92	247.96	571.01
Export	196.00	173.15	163.07	14.43
Total	641.86	515.07	411.04	585.44
% Domestic	69.5	66.1	60.3	97.5
% Export	30.5	33.9	39.7	2.5

SOURCE: AMIA.

new trend and standard of Mexican production that executives at Nissan (Japan) and Volkswagen (Germany) would emulate. Mexico, through these efforts, would become a center of subcompact export production for North America.

In order for the industry to reach its export potential, however, the major motor vehicle and autoparts producers had to change their production strategies and demonstrate to the Mexican government that further liberalization of the automotive regulations would benefit the country's trade balance, foreign investment position and consumers' satisfaction, as well as domestic employment. All of these requirements were proven to the government and private industry's satisfaction during the period from 1983–89, when the automotive sector became the leading manufacturing source of foreign exchange.

Exports and Automotive Industry Restructuring

By 1987, it was evident that the decision to liberalize the rules governing vehicle production in Mexico and to focus on exports had paved the way for a turnaround in the depressed industry. 1987 was critical because it was the first year that Ford began to benefit from its investment in Hermosillo. Although domestic sales that year were the lowest in 15 years—9.1% lower than in 1983—the rapid growth in export sales more than offset the downturn. Overall vehicle sales for the year were 39.2% higher than four years earlier. The dramatic impact of exports on total vehicle sales for 1987–89 is summarized in Table 8-2, along with the contrasting figures for 1981, when exports were unimportant.

Since 1987, exports have accounted for about one out of every three vehicle sales. By 1989, the US "Big Three" automobile manufacturers—

Ford, Chrysler and General Motors—were responsible for exporting about 75% of all Mexican vehicles. At the beginning of the decade, these firms did not even participate in export marketing. Their success has encouraged other foreign manufacturers to do the same, because export sales have redefined the basis for success in the Mexican automotive industry. If export sales are combined with domestic market sales for 1989, the leaders were

(1) Chrysler, with a 25.1% share of total sales of 641,862 vehicles;

(2) Ford, with a 19.8% share of total vehicle sales;

(3) Nissan, with a participation of 18.8%;

(4) General Motors, with a 17.5% participation in the total market; and

(5) Volkswagen, with a 17% share in total sales.

These conclusions provide firms monitoring the sector with strong evidence that the ability to export was critical to the success of the new automotive industry in Mexico. Exporting enabled Chrysler and Ford to surpass Nissan, which, in 1981, was the leader in Mexico in both domestic and total overall sales. There is every indication that the trend toward increased exports and achieving international standards for the automotive sector will grow even stronger, as both Nissan and Volkswagen follow Ford's example in initiating large new investments in Mexico.

Export Boom: Vehicles, Autoparts and Maquiladoras

The export drive has had a dramatic effect on the automotive trade balance, which is comprised of three major product categories: vehicles, motors and other types of autoparts. A fourth important category, maquiladora (maquila) exports, are treated separately, as service rather than merchandise exports. In 1981, the Mexican automotive sector produced a $2.3 billion deficit, but eight years later, in 1989, thanks to the export boom, a $1.7 billion surplus was achieved.

At first, the reversal of the automotive deficit, which began in 1983, was initiated by explosive growth in motor exports by the vehicle manufacturers. The increased investment required to obtain much greater installed capacity and higher-quality standards was made possible through the de la Madrid administration's relaxing of local-content rules and other incentives. The results were immediate and inspiring, as motor exports skyrocketed from barely $200 million in 1982 to more than $1 billion in 1985 and nearly $1.4 billion in 1989.

Since the price of these motors is about $1,000 per unit, some $1.4 billion were exported in 1989—or seven times more than in 1982, before the new automotive legislation.

Although autoparts exports in general, and motors in particular, grew strongly in the mid-1980s (1983–87), that role subsequently has been reversed for vehicle exports, as can be seen from Table 8-3.

From 1985–89, vehicle exports soared from about $141 million to $1.57 billion, for an average yearly growth rate of 278%. The share of vehicles in total automotive exports increased from 9.1% to 41.3% during 1985–89.

Autoparts other than motors also grew rapidly. From 1985–89, exports of these diverse products increased at an average yearly rate of approximately 33%. These exports are especially critical to Mexicans since they are produced mostly by majority Mexican-owned companies, as opposed to the foreign-owned vehicle and motor manufacturers. Although there are probably 350 Mexican autoparts companies, only a fraction actively participate in exporting. A few years ago, the 10 largest companies accounted for two thirds of all parts exports and, although no comparable figures are available for today's market, interviews with specialists indicate that the situation has not changed.

In spite of the fact that the autoparts manufacturers are Mexican

Table 8-3. 1985-89 Automotive Exports: Autoparts,
Vehicles and Maquiladora
($ billions)

	1989	1988	1987	1986	1985
Automotive Exports (merchandise account)	3.79	3.51	3.30	2.27	1.55
Autoparts	2.23	2.02	1.97	1.72	1.41
—motors	1.37	1.37	1.29	1.15	1.04
—others	.86	.65	.68	.57	.37
Vehicles	1.57	1.49	1.33	.55	.14
Automotive Maquila Exports (services account)	.73	.60	.38	.31	.33
Total Exports	4.52	4.11	3.68	2.58	1.88
% Maquila	16.2%	14.6%	11.5%	12.0%	17.6%
Auto Trade Balance (merchandise only)	1.68	1.42	2.01	1.48	.59

NOTE: Maquila exports include only the value added in Mexican production.

SOURCE: Banco de México; AMIA; Secretariat of Commerce and Industry (Secofi).

firms, as decreed by law, the most efficient either have foreign joint venture partners or are linked to foreign firms through licensing agreements or other technology arrangements. It is this connection that has enabled Mexican companies to compete in international markets.

Some of the largest Mexican autoparts companies with leading export programs are listed below along with the products they export.

(1) Cifunsa SA de CV: Bearing covers, monoblocks and transmission blocks;

(2) Rassini SA de CV: Automotive springs;

(3) Spicer SA de CV y Subs: Transmissions;

(4) Nemak SA: Aluminum motor heads;

(5) Central de Industrias SA de CV: Automotive seats;

(6) Industria Automotriz SA: Truck cabins/body stampings;

(7) Moto Diesel Mexicana SA de CV: Machined pieces (diesel engines);

(8) Metalsa SA de CV y Subs: Chassis, motor mounts, stamped parts;

(9) Electro Optica SA de CV: Directional signals/lights, mirrors; and

(10) Super Diesel SA: Axles and brakes.

Although this list is not exhaustive, it illustrates the variety of products manufactured in Mexico for export, primarily for the US market. Such Mexican suppliers will continue to play an important role in future free trade areas with the US.

Autos and maquilas

Another source of automotive export development has been the mostly US-owned maquiladoras. The importance of these border facilities can hardly be overstated. They provided the first evidence to the de la Madrid administration that foreign-owned production plants could help extricate Mexico from its debt crisis without challenging or undermining the country's sovereignty. Although the maquilas had existed for almost two decades, it took the prolonged recession of the 1980s to convince the government that if they were to produce significant exports, companies could not be hampered by the Mexicanization laws, which required a firm manufacturing in Mexico to be at least 51% Mexican-owned. Given this restriction, the maquiladoras, which are devoted exclusively to export, proved to be the most successful way to attract foreign investment and state-of-the-art production facilities (see Chapter 11 on the maquiladora industry).

As Table 8-3 shows, automotive exports from Mexican maquiladoras increased at a rate of 30% p.a. from 1985–89. During that period, such exports mushroomed in dollar terms, from $370 million in 1985 to $730 million in 1989. If maquiladora exports—which are measured purely as value added and are reflected in the services account of the balance of payments—were included in the merchandise trade account, the 1989 automotive trade surplus would grow by 30%, to approximately $2.41 billion.

Competitiveness and the 1989 Automotive Decree

Two powerful and far-reaching results of the 1983–89 export boom have been the integration of Mexican automotive production into the larger North American industrial arena and the passage of the 1989 Automotive Decree. The decree further liberalized conditions for operating in the sector, with a goal of rationalizing Mexican production and making it more competitive in the global marketplace.

The tightening relations between Mexico and US manufacturers are revealed by the fact that in 1989, 83% of the vehicles exported from Mexico were destined for the US market. Mexico accounted for 13% of all US autoparts imports (third behind Japan and Canada) and was also the third-leading trading partner of the US (again, only preceded in importance by Japan and Canada). At the end of 1989, Mexican automotive employment totaled a robust 263.9 million workers, more than twice the 113.9 million employees characterizing the industry, including the maquiladora sector, in 1983.

The 1989 Automotive Decree, which was issued on Dec. 11, 1989, followed more than a year of negotiations among the leading interest groups—vehicle and motor manufacturers, the Mexican autoparts industry and the government. The decree liberalized the conditions under which the current vehicle manufacturers operate in Mexico, while protecting them, at least initially, from new foreign competitors. It also protects the Mexican autoparts suppliers by continuing to enforce minimal content requirements and the Mexican national interest through mechanisms that guarantee automotive trade surpluses. The following specific provisions liberalize regulations for motor vehicle manufacturers operating in Mexico:

• Automakers are allowed to import cars or trucks (for the first time in 30 years).

• Vehicle manufacturers may choose to produce as many different models in Mexico as they like, unencumbered by government restrictions.

• Vehicle manufacturers may freely select their autoparts suppliers, which can be either Mexican or foreign.

• Calculation of local content will no longer be tied to cost-of-parts or materials imports, but will instead be defined on the basis of national value added, determined by subtracting imports from total domestic and foreign sales.

In addition, financial mechanisms are being made available to foreign autoparts suppliers, through which they can control their Mexican operations instead of being relegated to 40% minority ownership.

To counterbalance these new benefits, the decree puts in place the following four critical provisions—explicitly designed to protect the current players in the industry:

• The total number of vehicles imported into Mexico may not exceed 15% of domestic sales (Mexican) during the 1991 and 1992 model years, for each manufacturer. The figure will be raised to 20% for the 1993 and 1994 model years.

• For every $1 value of new cars imported, the manufacturer must export $2.5 for the 1991 model year, $2 for the 1992 and 1993 model years and $1.75 for the 1994 model year.

• Overall, the vehicle manufacturers must maintain a positive trade balance in order to be permitted the above import privileges.

• At least 36% of a vehicle's content must be sourced domestically from the Mexican autoparts industry, down from the previous 50–60% local-content requirement.

One other explicit constraint in the decree prohibits the import of any subcompact car until 1993. This provision was included to compensate Nissan and Volkswagen, the only two current subcompact producers, for their large investments in Mexico.

The 1989 decree was designed as part of a delicate balancing act. Although it provides for a novel degree of openness, the decree also retains strong controls, thereby revealing that neither the government nor the industry representatives are prepared to open the market entirely. In theory, it would appear that further growth could be hampered as easily as stimulated by such a contradiction. The major industry players have responded positively, however, and developments during the first nine months of 1990 gave every indication that the Mexican automotive industry is destined to play an important role in North American industry and in any future free trade pact between the US and Mexico.

1990 Mexican Automotive Developments (January-September)

• **Ford** completed its plant expansion in Hermosillo in April, which increased its capacity from 130,000 to 170,000 units p.a. Through September, Ford exported 88,604 Tracers/Escorts to the US and Canada—33.6% more than during the comparable January-September 1989 period. The standards of production at Hermosillo rank among the best in the world, and all vehicles produced there are for export. Ford is Mexico's export leader, with a 35% share in car exports in 1990.

• **Chrysler** remained the overall leader with 53,845 vehicle exports, 17,724 of which were pickup trucks; the total was 11% lower than the results for the first nine months of 1989.

• **Volkswagen** announced a five-year, $950 million investment, aimed at doubling production and focusing on exports. During the first nine months of 1990, Volkswagen exported 32,282 automobiles (ranking second after Ford), but 103.7% more than it exported during the same period in 1989. Volkswagen exports Golfs and Jettas to the US.

• **Nissan** announced a six-year, $1 billion investment to construct a new plant in Aguascalientes, and to modernize other existing facilities. A major objective of the expansion is export development, with a goal of 100,000 units p.a. in exports by the end of Salinas's term in 1994. These vehicles will be destined for Japan, Latin America and the US.

• **Mercedes Benz (Daimler)** announced a $400 million investment to increase to 80% its stake in Famsa, a local firm, and to modernize facilities with an eye to developing an export line to the US.

• Ford became the first producer to import vehicles, numbering 7,200 as of August, under a June 8, 1990, revision of the auto decree.

• **Ford** announced it will invest $700 million in its automotive motor plant in Chihuahua beginning in mid-1991. The plant produces two liter, four-cylinder motors for the Topaz and Tempo car models. Ford estimates that the plant expansion will nearly double production capacity, from 280,000 motors to approximately 500,000 p.a.

(Continued)

> • **Overall domestic sales** in Mexico for the first nine months of 1990 increased 21.2% over 1989's figures, to 385,391 vehicles. Export sales for the same period grew by 15.5% over 1989's sales to 187,026—a record level.
>
> • **Total Mexican sales** (domestic and export vehicles) set a new record of 572,417 units, 19.2% higher than during the first nine months of 1989.
>
> • **Merger, acquisition and joint venture** activity in the autoparts industry proceeded at an accelerated pace.

The Automotive Industry Under a Free Trade Pact

During 1990, rising exports and considerable investment activity continued to characterize the automotive industry (see box). These developments, along with the growth during the preceding three years, have been scrutinized by automotive executives and more recently, have become of major interest to the presidents of both Mexico and the US. It is clear that the automobile sector is setting the trend in making Mexican industry globally competitive and, as such, is serving as a model for other industries preparing to compete in a North American free trading area.

Increased attention is being given to the automotive sector's future under an FTA. This is not simply good fortune, however; it is linked to larger global events in the automotive industry and beyond. These include the elimination of internal trade barriers among members of the EC by 1992, as well as the opening up of the Eastern European market. Although US motor vehicle manufacturers, specifically Ford and General Motors, account for almost 25% of sales in the lucrative and expanding EC market, they have had much less success in a second burgeoning regional market, East Asia, led by Japan and the rapidly developing NICs (South Korea, Thailand, Malaysia and Taiwan).

Given the growing trend toward regionalization, as well as the sweeping efforts of automotive manufacturers to globalize their production and marketing operations, Mexico has become a natural choice for US vehicle producers who wish to participate in a market with vast growth potential in the coming decades. What makes Mexico advantageous is not primarily its cheap labor. Far more important are its proximity to the US and its market potential. If Mexico signs an FTA with the US and Canada, the free trade area will number about 360 million inhabitants, even larger than the EC. Under an FTA, Mexico would be likely to further liberalize remaining barriers to US trade and investment, including export performance requirements, local-content rules and import restrictions. Industry experts envision the following benefits emerging from North American market integration:

• **Greater opportunities to supply the Mexican market with US products.** US vehicle manufacturers and autoparts producers will benefit from the Mexican consumer's growing appetite for "imported" vehicles and parts, which will be further whetted by the elimination of Mexico's 20% tariff on imported vehicles. The specific area that will be most dynamic in dollar terms is autoparts trade. By the end of 1989, Mexico ranked second with a 19% share of all US autoparts exports, outranked only by Canada, with a 53% share. No other country came close, since the third place leader was Japan, with a scant 4%. Still more important was the fact that Mexico's share had increased by 50% in four years, from a 13% share in 1985, whereas Canada's share declined 25% during the same period, from 71% in 1985. Under an FTA, these exports would be stimulated further as Mexico is increasingly selected to be the entry-level vehicle producer for the North American region. Parts suppliers will naturally follow the vehicle producers to their facilities in Mexico.

• **Growth in sales to the US market by the Mexican subsidiaries of North American vehicle manufacturers.** About 230,000 units were exported in 1990. This figure could easily double by 1995, to 425,000–500,000 units. At the same time, sales of domestic vehicles could increase to more than 800,000 in 1995, or about twice 1989's figure.

With growth of US imports of vehicles and parts from Mexico likely to continue, the US automotive trade balance with Mexico will worsen. In 1989, this balance produced a $907 million deficit in autoparts, up from $566 million in 1985. The impact of this deficit is ameliorated, however, by the fact that the US content of these imports is approximately 40%, whereas comparable imports from Japan contain less than 2% US content, as measured by the US Trade Commission's 1988 figures.

• **Restructuring and an upgrading of the production technology of less efficient Mexican auto plants.** With liberalization of Mexican investment restrictions and performance requirements in the sector, the "Big Three" US manufacturers could restructure their operations for greater efficiency and integration with the US operations. This could lead to an increase in model specialization and overall output and would improve their competitive position relative to Japanese firms.

• **Transfer of production facilities to Mexico by foreign competitors.** Perhaps the largest potential opportunity for automobile manufacturers under an FTA would be the transfer of plants to Mexico for the production of entry-level vehicles. As of 1989, almost one million cars and small pickup trucks manufactured in Japan, South Korea, Brazil and Yugoslavia were sold in the US. Although it would be optimistic to assume that production of all these vehicles will ultimately be transferred to Mexico, it is likely that a major portion of the manufacturing operations will be, because Mexico provides production quality and cost advantages that other existing sites do not.

Many foreign producers, particularly Asian, already have a US Big Three affiliate or joint venture partner that manufactures in Mexico. Daewoo Motors and Kia Motors (both South Korea), which make the Pontiac LeMans for General Motors (GM) and Festiva for Ford, respectively, sold about 115,000 vehicles in the US in 1989, whereas General Motors's other affiliate, Isuzu (Japan), registered sales of an additional 75,000 cars in the US under the GM Geo and Isuzu names. Ford's Japanese partner, Mazda, builds its 323 model on the same platform as the Tracer (in Hermosillo) and sold 61,000 in 1989. Finally, Chrysler's Japanese partner, Mitsubishi, sold another 62,000 pickups in the US in 1989 under both the Mitsubishi and Chrysler names. The Asian affiliates of these companies, which account for 312,000 units worth of sales, would be prime candidates for transfer to Mexico, as would production of the 38,000 Volkswagen Foxes currently manufactured in Brazil.

• **Greater emphasis by new manufacturers on serving the Mexican market.** Since the Mexican market represents major growth potential, it is likely that new manufacturers will focus more production on serving that market.

• **Improved product quality.** From the Mexican consumer's perspective, the developments listed above will enable Mexicans to obtain the largest variety of vehicles ever, made with state-of-the-art rather than obsolescent technology. The existence of modern plants and the newly established rights of manufacturers to select their own suppliers will also lower the price of vehicles and parts. The signing of an FTA should accelerate these trends.

Other Side of the Coin: Some Potential Problems

Regionalization, lean production techniques and geographical proximity are the obvious competitive advantages that Mexico has to offer automotive manufacturers seeking a larger share in the growing North

American market. Mexico's relatively cheap labor will continue to make it a critical offshore source for labor-intensive autoparts production.

Despite these advantages, however, there are some important obstacles to further automotive integration and some problems to be resolved. Most of the difficulties revolve around labor-related issues and local content. The United Auto Workers union (UAW) opposes any FTA between the US and Mexico, since the union views potential job gains in Mexico as losses to its US membership. Industry executives argue, however, that the vast number of new jobs generated in Mexico by vehicle manufacturers are likely to be created by companies from East Asia rather than the US.

Another problem is US Corporate Average Fuel Efficiency (CAFE) standards, which require automakers to produce vehicles that average 27.5 miles per gallon, as well as divide vehicles into domestic and import categories. The domestic fleet consists of those vehicles comprised of at least 75% US-Canadian content or value, and the imports consist of those containing less than 75%. Both fleets are subject to the same fuel-efficiency requirements.

The distinction between domestic and imported vehicles arose because the UAW wanted to inhibit the ability of US manufacturers to either import small cars from, or move small-car production to, low-cost foreign production sites. Because US car manufacturers concentrate the production of large cars at domestic sites, they must also retain some local small-car facilities to achieve the required fuel-efficiency average for the fleet.

If the small cars manufactured in Mexico were considered domestically produced under an FTA, US manufacturers would find it easier to meet the fuel-efficiency standards. This would have important strategic implications, as it would permit companies to rearrange the mix of vehicles in terms of what is produced offshore and what is manufactured in the US. It would allow them to move a larger share of small-car production to Mexico—shifting it from production sites in the US or Asia—at substantial cost savings.

At the same time, however, the CAFE standards cannot prevent foreign, particularly Asian, car manufacturers from transferring additional production to Mexico in order to improve access to the US market. If they do so, then conflict is likely in the US Congress, since manufacturers in East Asia traditionally utilize only minimal US content. Complaints that Asian producers are trying to "enter through the back door" are certain to be raised if vehicles assembled in Mexico are considered part of the US domestic fleet. To correct such a conflict, local-content classifications would have to be negotiated.

A third problem with the FTA is the so-called Chicken Tax, a 25% tariff on all light trucks and two-door utility vehicles. At present, this tariff is being used against Japanese producers. Both CAFE and the tariff will provide still another forum for trade conflict between the US and Japan and, to a lesser extent, South Korea, because of the enormous trade deficits that the US has with these East Asian countries.

Another important problem—this time for the Mexicans—is that an FTA will further expose the weakness of the heavily protected domestic autoparts industry. Already, the more powerful companies are increasing their foreign affiliations. For smaller firms without such affiliations, with technology that is decades out of date, there is trouble ahead. For them, consolidation is probably the best choice.

Phasing in an FTA may take several years and, provided companies have time to resolve many of the previously discussed problems, the potential advantages appear to greatly outweigh the disadvantages for the automotive sector. Mexico is likely soon to supplant South Korea as the US's leading vehicle supplier among the NICs. Both the North American automotive industry and US and Mexican consumers will benefit.

Case Example

A Glimpse of the Future with Ford

Ford has set the standard for some of the most dynamic automotive developments in Mexico. With the reopening in the first half of 1990 of its Hermosillo plant, which has a newly enlarged production capacity of 170,000 vehicles, Ford positioned itself to be the leading exporter of passenger cars manufactured in Mexico. Although the plant was only open for about eight months during that year, it enabled Ford to export 88,604 Tracers and Escorts to the US and Canada, permitting the company to lead the industry by capturing 35% of Mexican car exports for 1990.

The significance of Ford's achievement cannot be measured in numbers alone. Both the Tracers and Escorts have been selected by car enthusiast magazines such as Car and Driver for their top quality. This recognition has enhanced Mexico's image as a global manufacturing site and has produced a demonstration effect for other car manufacturers. Nissan (Japan), for example, is increasing investment in its Mexico facilities, especially in its Aguascalientes plant, and is planning a major export drive to Japan and North, Central and South America. Volkswagen (Germany) is following Ford's lead as well, by dramatically increasing its export capacity.

Ford's achievement in Hermosillo is also notable because it is an example of a successful global alliance with a Japanese competitor. In partnership with Ford, Mazda designed the small cars exported from Hermosillo. Many US customers have purchased Escorts and Tracers, at least in part, because they admire the Mazda association and are aware of the high-quality vehicles being produced in Mexico by the alliance.

Sourcing engines

If Ford's example in passenger cars has shown that small, top-quality entry-level vehicles can be manufactured in Mexico, then the firm's more recent announcement that it will also source engines in Mexico provides a further glimpse of the future. In January 1991, Ford announced that it was closing its Chihuahua engine plant for refurbishing. When the plant reopens in 1993, it will be capable of producing 500,000 four-cylinder engines for export to the US and Canada. This production will represent 20% of Ford's North American engines. Although other automobile manufacturers, such as General Motors, have also exported engines from Mexico, they have yet to allocate as large a percentage of their production to Mexico as Ford.

Ford's export leadership has been anchored by huge investments in Mexico that have totaled about $2.8 billion over the past decade. Although these outlays have been utilized for domestic production as well, the bulk has been devoted to export operations. The same is true for the $1 billion Nissan and Volkswagen investments.

The Ford example illustrates how Mexico will become increasingly integrated into the manufacturing and marketing operations of the world's leading automotive manufacturers for small cars, engines and parts. For Ford, Mexico will continue to be the sole global source for the Tracer (Lincoln-Mercury division), whereas production of the Escort will occur in Mexico and Wayne, Michigan (Ford division). Of the approximately 500,000 Mercury Tracers and Ford Escorts to be manufactured annually, Mexico will provide about one-third.

The power of Ford's example as a pioneer in the integration of the North American automotive industry is attested to by the fact that it is being emulated by other international automotive firms. A North American FTA will only further support this trend.

9

The Opening in Petrochemicals

Financial necessity and intensifying global competition have forced a new wave of openings for private investment in Mexico's petrochemical sector over the last few years, as Petróleos Mexicanos (Pemex), the cash-strapped state oil conglomerate, races to consolidate Mexico's position as a major producer and exporter. Although hydrocarbon exploration and development remain off limits for private investors, Pemex has ceded its formerly sacrosanct monopoly over certain petrochemical products in a move to accelerate its drive for growth and new markets. Foreign investors are expected to be among the chief beneficiaries in what is essentially part of a broader privatization process under way in recent years.

What Mexico Offers

Mexico could be the best place in the world for a petrochemical industry. In addition to holding what are estimated to be the world's largest hydrocarbon reserves, it is adjacent to the huge and affluent US market, which is 250 million strong. Once a North American free trade agreement (FTA) is finalized, Mexico will have even easier access to the US market as well as to Canada, which has a population of 25 million. Mexico is also near South America, with its 304 million inhabitants. Its own domestic market—82 million, with more than half under the age of 30—is growing at a 2.1% annual rate. Although the minimum wage in Mexico is only about 12,000 pesos—or approximately $4—per day, the standard of living and the buying power of consumers are expected to rise over the next several years.

Mexico is, in fact, closer to the US West Coast market than is the US's own petrochemical industry (which is largely concentrated on the US Eastern Seaboard). Mexico has Atlantic and Pacific coastlines, which provide easy shipping routes to Asia and Europe. It already takes advantage of its Gulf coast through steady trade in hydrocarbon products with US Gulf coast companies. Furthermore, Mexico has skilled labor and a petrochemical industry tradition. The sector's scientists, workers, products and safety record get high marks from US executives. Inexpensive labor is also available, although this is not as critical for the chemical industry as it is for other sectors, since, with only 90,000 workers, the industry is not a significant employer. Mexico also has a stable government that actively encourages foreign investment. According to government officials, every international petrochemical company has expressed interest in setting up a Mexico-based operation.

What, then, are Mexico's drawbacks as a potential hub of the petrochemical industry? Because of a shortage of investment capital, available raw materials cannot be fully accessed. Pemex's extensive bureaucracy is said to retard industry growth, although executives claim that creation of a petrochemical division has made the giant oil monopoly more responsive to the needs of the petrochemical industry, which accounts for only 7% of its business.

Mexico also lacks adequate infrastructure—its roads, railways, pipelines, ports and communications all need development. With interest rates near 30% at the beginning of 1991, the cost of capital is high. This is insignificant for foreigners bringing money from abroad for plants and equipment, but it makes investments by Mexicans extremely costly, and at times impossible. Meanwhile, the waning of government subsidies, as well as the greater opening to foreign capital, is a boon to foreign investors but is causing local producers to scramble to compete, not only among themselves but in the world market.

The Sanctity of Oil

The effects of the brief 1991 Persian Gulf on US-Mexico energy policies may be felt well into the future. Instability in the Middle East has underscored Mexico's status as the US's closest and most stable source of crude oil. Though the US would like to see an opening in Mexico's oil sector, the fate of Petróleos Mexicanos (Pemex), the

(Continued)

state-owned oil monopoly, will almost certainly be excluded from free trade negotiations. This issue is more likely to be confined to private talks between the two countries' administrations.

Pemex is the largest company in Mexico, with 1989 sales exceeding the total sales of the 15 next largest companies in the country (including General Motors, Teléfonos de México, Ford Motor Co, Volkswagen, Mexicana de Aviación, Celanese Mexicana, Nestlé, IBM and American Express). Furthermore, it is also the largest single source of foreign exchange to Mexico. In 1990, Pemex's crude oil exports brought in approximately $9 billion worth of foreign currency.

Most important, Pemex is one of Mexico's "sacred cows." The company was founded following Gen. Lázaro Cárdenas's decree to nationalize US and British oil companies in 1938, one of the major events in the history of Mexico. The oil expropriation is not only symbolic of Mexico's sovereignty, but also generated a significant amount of the funds required to finance Mexico's industrial development during much of this century.

The importance—both symbolic and real—of oil in Mexico acts to limit the government's ability to implement policies to open the oil industry to foreign participation. Nonetheless, President Carlos Salinas de Gortari has taken steps to permit the entry of foreign capital in some areas. By reclassifying a group of primary petrochemicals as secondary, Salinas permitted private (and limited foreign) participation in the production of petrochemicals, traditionally reserved for the state (see box on pages 186–188). The most important future changes are likely to be in oil exploration. Although Pemex produces petrochemicals, the firm sees itself primarily as an oil company and has focused most of its attention on oil exploration and recovery.

Risk vs service contracts

The first signs that Mexico was reconsidering the role of foreign capital in the oil sector came in November 1990. During a two-day summit between Salinas and US President George Bush, US Treasury Secretary Nicholas Brady announced that a $1.5 billion loan from the US Eximbank would be available to finance exploration and drilling. The loan proceeds will be limited to contracts between Pemex and US firms. The US media immediately characterized the loan as a historic opening, although Pemex officials were quick to respond that service contracts with US firms were nothing new.

The Eximbank financing, which by March 1991 was still being designed, could involve guarantees for loans from commercial banks

(Continued)

for as much as $6 billion. The loan itself has raised little debate in Mexico. Though it does not give US oil companies what they want, i.e. risk contracts, it shows that greater US participation in oil exploration can take place without a major political debate, as long as US companies are seen as merely providing services to Pemex. Unlike a service contract, in which the private party's compensation is determined in advance at a fixed amount, a risk contract provides that compensation be determined by the amount of oil discovered and that it may be set in percentage terms rather than as a fixed amount. Salinas has insisted that risk contracts in oil exploration are prohibited by the Mexican Constitution.

Some critics argue that funding for service contracts is merely a prelude to granting of risk contracts, despite Salinas's repeated denials. Others contend that, insofar as foreign governments are willing to finance Pemex's expansion, it is less likely to be forced to offer foreign oil firms equity participation or risk contracts. Some industry observers believe that once foreign companies are involved in exploration, albeit under a service contract arrangement, it will be much easier for the government to contemplate a modified form of a risk contract. Given the Salinas administration's propensity to use trusts and other mechanisms to permit greater foreign participation in other sectors as a means of sidestepping nationalistic laws, such a tactic cannot be ruled out.

What's next?

Predictions regarding risk contracts are very difficult to support. The following points should be considered, however:

- **Once foreign firms are involved in exploration as part of a service contract, further opportunities may evolve.** Indeed, if some type of risk contract were permitted, it would probably be designed to resemble a service arrangement, thereby avoiding the legal prohibition on risk contracts.

- **The administration will do all it can to prevent foreign participation in the oil sector from becoming a political issue.** The topic will not be included in free trade talks or become a major political initiative. Recent demotions and staff changes in the administration, including the dismissal of the undersecretary of energy, reflect Salinas's desire to keep the oil issue out of the local media. Comments by the dismissed official were used by a local newspaper in late

(Continued)

January 1991 to support claims of mounting US pressure on Mexico to increase sales of crude oil to the US.

• **US pressure in the trade negotiations will be felt, however, with regard to petrochemicals.** At present, certain basic petrochemicals are reserved for the state, whereas foreign participation in secondary petrochemicals is limited to 40%. The US will push for a further reduction in the number of petrochemicals classified as basic and for the elimination of the 40% ceiling on foreign equity in investments in secondary petrochemical production.

• **Much of the Salinas administration's attention to oil policy will focus on limiting the effects on investor confidence of sudden changes in the price of crude.** Since the Persian Gulf war in 1991, government officials have tried to downplay the impact of events in the Middle East on Mexico's economy. At the same time, they have created a special contingency fund and are using hedging mechanisms like the futures market to assure investors that Mexico will not be harmed by volatile oil markets and a potential drop in oil prices in later years.

Challenges Under an FTA

Industry executives expect an FTA with the US and Canada to have a negative effect on Mexico's petrochemical industry initially. Although these executives generally favor such an accord, they view the industry as extremely vulnerable to stiff competition from US imports. Consequently, they are asking that a gradual opening of the market be negotiated, with a five- to six-year phase-in period to give the sector the opportunity to adjust.

Mexico's petrochemical industry is small compared with that of the US, which is not only 20 times larger than Mexico's, but is also the largest in the world and benefits from both economies of scale and the most advanced technology. The petrochemical industry is a capital-intensive one in which labor cost—one of Mexico's comparative advantages—matters little. To be able to compete with the US, Mexican producers would need time to modernize and increase the scale of their operations. Although the industry has been gaining in productivity and became increasingly export oriented in 1980–89, quick growth is not foreseen, and few such plants are expected to come on stream in the next few years.

The industry is being squeezed hard by costs: On the one hand, Mexican companies pay a high price for funds within Mexico and, because Pemex can no longer meet domestic demand for many products, firms must purchase them elsewhere at high world prices. At the same time, a domestic price-control program restricts the amount of money Mexican companies can charge for their final products within Mexico. With the domestic inflation rate exceeding the rate of devaluation of the peso, exporters have also been squeezed.

Furthermore, Mexican companies are worried about the effects of the US recession on their businesses. They expect the recession to hurt their exports to the US, and they anticipate facing more competition within Mexico as US producers seek new markets for their own products. Concern already exists that petrochemical products, e.g. polypropylene, are being dumped in Mexico. One executive says it would be easy for US firms to ship 5% of their products in Mexico, destroying Mexican producers. If Mexican companies dumped 5%—or even 100%—of their products in the US, however, it would hardly dent the industry.

DMT/PTA: A Free Trade Opportunity

Mexico could boast a fully-integrated textile industry based on petrochemicals. Instead, the Mexican-sourced raw materials for such a sector travel around the world for processing, returning to North America in the form of finished products. Under a free trade accord, the textile industry should become an attractive area of opportunity.

Petrocel, a unit of Grupo Industrial Alfa SA, is the world's second-largest exporter of DMT and PTA (dimethyl terephthalate and terephthalic acid), from which polyester is made, with annual exports of $200 million, or about 20% of the world market.

To make DMT and PTA, Monterrey-based Petrocel buys paraxylene and methanol from Pemex, and what Pemex cannot supply, Petrocel buys mainly from large oil companies in the US.

Petrocel sells DMT and PTA to Taiwan, Thailand and South Korea, where it is turned into polyester yarn or polyester film. The film, for video- and audiotapes, is made in a technology- and capital-intensive process, then exported worldwide. In the much more labor-intensive textile manufacturing process, however, the yarn is shipped to Hong Kong or Malaysia to be knitted or woven into fabric. In some cases, the fabric is cut there and sewn into garments; in others, it is shipped to Honduras for cutting and sewing. From there it is shipped to the US, to be sold to the world's richest consumer market.

Provided an adequate transition period is negotiated, enabling the local industry to overcome some of its problems, local executives expect several benefits to come from an FTA. These include an expansion of the domestic market, opportunities for increased local exports to the US and an enhanced competitive position for the North American petrochemical industry vis-à-vis producers worldwide. By improving Mexico's image abroad and consolidating many of the reforms under way in Mexico over the last few years, an FTA could also bring foreign investment to the sector, freeing critical investment capital at Pemex (enabling it to focus its resources on oil development and building related infrastructure) and helping alleviate bottlenecks in the supply of basic feedstocks to the domestic industry. Moreover, an FTA could stimulate labor-intensive industries that depend on petrochemicals for their products and can take advantage of Mexico's wealth of labor.

The Role of Pemex

Mexico's petrochemical industry revolves around Pemex, which has proven hydrocarbon reserves totaling 66.8 billion bbl and estimated reserves believed to exceed Saudi Arabia's, making Mexico the fifth-largest oil producer in the world. Operating at 91% of capacity, the firm produces 2.6 million bpd, as well as 3.6 billion cu ft per day of natural gas. It exports 1.4 million bpd, with 56% of oil exports p.a. ($4 billion) going to the US. The state oil company serves as Mexico's cash cow, contributing 30% of the nation's $201 billion gross national product and accounting for 35% of its total tax revenues.

Under Mexican law, only Pemex may produce basic petrochemicals, which are defined as those resulting from the first transformation from petroleum. Production at Pemex is insufficient to meet domestic demand or to boost export levels, however. Pemex-produced petrochemicals—with prices sometimes 50% below those of the world market—are first choice for Mexican purchasers, but are insufficient to meet their needs. Consequently, local buyers are forced to import a portion of their requirements. Competition to meet that "leftover" demand is fierce, with the world's largest oil companies fighting for market share. Natural gas and basic petrochemical feedstocks are already being imported, as is gasoline. Pemex itself estimates that if it does not boost output, the nation will be importing oil by 1997. To avoid this, the company estimates that it needs $6 billion over the next five years for maintenance, exploration and development, refining and petrochemical operations.

The world's seventh-largest producer of basic and secondary petrochemicals, Pemex is integrated with 109 complexes, employing 27,600 workers. Operating at 91% of capacity in 1989, its petrochemical facili-

Petrochemical Industry: Vital Statistics

Mexico is the 15th-largest petrochemical producer in the world, with 3% of worldwide production capacity. Its petrochemical industry contributed $9 billion, or 2.6% of the nation's GDP in 1989. With plant utilization at 89% of capacity, total production was 20.47 million MT, worth $6.51 billion. Exports totaled 1.69 million MT and were valued at $958 million, whereas imports amounted to 1.67 million MT and were estimated at $1.56 billion, resulting in an industry trade deficit of $606 million. Sales growth averages 7–8% p.a. Of the industry's $16.3 billion in assets, $8.54 billion belongs to Pemex; the remaining $7.76 billion belongs to private industry. The petrochemical sector employs 90,000 people, supplies goods to 42 economic sectors and demands goods and services from 31 other sectors.

The industry produces basic and intermediate products, synthetic resins, synthetic fibers, synthetic rubber, adhesives, lubricants and additives.

Pemex's product line

Pemex produces 17 basic petrochemical products: ammonia, benzene, butadiene, ethane, ethylene, heptane, hexane, methanol, n-paraffins, pentanes, dodecylbenzene, propylene tetramer, carbon-black feedstock, toluene, ortoxylene, paraxylene and xylene.

It also produces 17 secondary products: acetaldehyde, acetic anhydride, acrylonitrile, cumene, cyclohexane, ethylene dichloride, ethylbenzene, ethylene oxide, hydrogen cyanide, isopropyl alcohol, low-density polyethylene, high-density polyethylene, styrene and vinyl chloride monomer.

In 1990, the firm imported the following petrochemical products: propylene, acetonitrile and natural gas. It exported ammonia, monoethylene glycol, high-density polyethylene, styrene, acrylonitrile, liquefied petroleum gas (LPG), butanes and penthanes.

Current Pemex investments

The firm's current investments total $8.54 billion, with $7.07 billion in basic operations, $1.29 billion in secondary operations and $168 million in "unruled" operations. Private investment totals $7.76 billion, with $4.1 billion invested in secondary operations and $3.66 billion in unruled operations.

ties produced 16.8 million MT, up 9.2% from the previous year. It imported 55,498 MT, up 61% from 1988, with its largest import (39,632 MT), the gasoline additive MTBE, used to oxygenate gasoline to reduce pollution. Petrochemical exports fell 13% in 1989, to 450,398 MT, as exports of ammonia fell 43%, polyethylene wax exports fell 14% and exports of high-density polyethylene and ethylene dichloride were suspended.

Regaining Control of Pemex

The Carlos Salinas de Gortari administration, recognizing that labor problems at Pemex were inhibiting the industry's efficiency and would represent an obstacle to new investment, moved in early 1989 to regain control of the state oil company.

Following a shootout between union loyalists and police forces, the government ousted Joaquín Hernández Galicia, known as La Quina, the kingpin of the Petroleum Workers Union for 28 years. La Quina was jailed and replaced with Sebastián Guzmán Cabrera, a union leader amenable to government plans to boost profitability. Such plans, however, meant cutting costs, curbing the runaway corruption that had become synonymous with Pemex, trimming the power of the union and, in general, taking steps to improve efficiency.

Pemex CEO Francisco Rojas estimated that the labor contract signed in July 1989 would save the company $1 billion through 1990. Thirty thousand jobs were eliminated in the year after the contract was signed, leaving a still huge work force of 140,000. Through the contract, the union ceded its right to assign 40% of Pemex's outside contracts (an enormous source of kickbacks to union leaders) and gave up its 2% commission on maintenance contracts. It retained its 2% commission on construction contracts, however, and union members received benefits and wage gains amounting to 22%.

To enhance profitability and efficiency, the company is decentralizing through creation of divisions to handle international marketing, including spot market sales (through Mexicanos Comercial Internacional); regional joint ventures (through Mexpetrol); exploration and development; and refining operations.

In addition, the New York-based consulting firm McKinsey & Co was hired to study the cost of producing each product at Pemex plants. This should help Pemex restructure its pricing policy and should prove indispensable to private investors evaluating petrochemical opportunities.

Pemex's biggest complex, La Cangrejera, located in Veracruz, incorporates 24 petrochemical plants and has annual capacity of 4.2 million MT, making it the fourth-largest facility in the world. Among the other major complexes are Pajaritos, Cosoleacaque and Minatitlán, also in Veracruz; Cactus, in Chiapas; and Ciudad Madero, in Tamaulipas.

Pemex complexes are being built on the coast, near offshore oil and gas drilling centers and at or near import and export terminals. Older plants are located inland, however, since Pemex-owned and other petrochemical plants were not initially built for exports. The planning rationale was: the closer to Mexico City—the largest population center—the better.

Then, in 1979, Mexico began to export crude oil and, in 1982, petrochemicals. In the same year, to facilitate exports, the government began offering incentives to companies building installations on the coast. Meanwhile, Pemex was selling its products fob at their destination; clients all over the country paid the same freight charges. The government's strategy was to develop the country by helping to expand industry; now, its policy is to curtail subsidies. For example, Pemex currently prices products fob at its own installations; customers pay for transportation. Petrochemical entrepreneurs initially built their plants close to their homes. At present (since they must absorb transportation costs) they are building coastal plants closer to their sources of supply and convenient for ocean transport.

Investing in the Industry

Investment capital in Mexico is in short supply. Thus, the country is looking for funds for Pemex from local and foreign private industry and foreign governments. Since December 1988, when President Carlos Salinas de Gortari took office, the administration has devised avenues through which capital infusions can be made. Also, in March 1990, Salinas returned from Japan with a loan commitment of $790 million to improve air quality, including $775 million to improve oil refinery operations. In late November 1990, the US promised Mexico a $1.6 billion Eximbank credit to be used to buy US oil services and equipment.

A crucial step was taken in August 1989, to boost profitability and resolve Pemex's inability to supply basic feedstocks to the petrochemical industry. At that time, the government reclassified petrochemicals according to their strategic importance—in essence partially privatizing petrochemical production. Pemex reduced the number of so-called basic petrochemicals it had been authorized to supply, either by producing or importing them itself, from 34 to 20. The government's list of "secondary" petrochemicals was increased to 66. This move is important because relaxation of foreign investment laws in May 1989 permits 100% foreign ownership of secondary petrochemical projects, provided such ownership is established through trusts or with the approval of the National Petrochemical Commission and the National Foreign Investment Commission. Otherwise, only 40% foreign ownership of secondary projects is allowed. Plants to produce chemicals on either list may be owned by anyone. International executives active in the chemical and secondary petrochemical sectors say they would not be surprised to see the 20 remaining basic petrochemicals whittled down even further in the near future.

In a complementary move, Pemex unveiled two project-financing programs designed to boost output. The first, the Advanced Payment plan, is designed for projects under construction that have been delayed by a shortage of funds. Under the plan, investment groups pay Pemex for petrochemical products they will receive in the future. These monies will be used to complete the delayed construction of petrochemical plants, with clients then receiving a fixed volume of products annually, until the product value is sufficient to cover the prepaid amount plus interest.

Under the second plan, known as the Build-Lease-Transfer program, bids are opened on new development projects. Pemex, however, chooses the technology, engineering and construction standards and supervises construction of the plants. The state oil firm also operates the facility and leases it with the option to buy. The lease is paid through a long-term chemical-product supply contract.

The two programs are innovative and could go a long way toward solving problems of capacity and supply, and they have evoked some interest. Two Build-Lease-Transfer projects—involving acetaldehyde for Celanese Mexicana SA in one instance and acrylonitrile for Cydsa SA in another—were scheduled to begin production by January 1991, whereas the preliminary agreement for a third—a $400 million aromatics complex near Monterrey—has been signed by multiple parties, including Grupo Industrial Alfa SA's Petrocel and Temex units, Idesa's Sosa unit, Celanese, Grupo Primex SA, Mitsui Corp and Banca Serfin. Pemex wants to build a $500 million plant in Dos Bocas, Tabasco, to produce ethylene and derivatives, including vinylchloride and polyethylene. Some chemical company executives, however, are not happy with the programs, saying that their firms should not be in the financial engineering or in the construction business but ought to concentrate on what they know best: producing chemicals. They say their lack of autonomy in the programs is a problem, as is negotiating pricing and interest rates.

In a further step to encourage investment in the industry, the process for project approval has been streamlined. Under new rules, petrochemical joint venture applications are automatically cleared by the

Mexican Petrochemical Commission after 45 working days, unless the commission challenges them. The proposal then advances to the National Foreign Investment Commission. If not challenged by this agency within 45 business days, the proposal is automatically authorized. Previously, this process could drag on indefinitely.

Some government and industry officials believe current incentives are sufficient to draw the required investment, and time alone is what is now needed to disseminate information throughout the world about the opportunities available in Mexico's petrochemical industry. Others, however, say the programs do not provide enough benefits for Mexican or foreign investors and that the government will have to put more chips on the bargaining table. These could include: reducing its overseeing of plants constructed under the Build-Lease-Transfer program, further liberalizing its petrochemical classifications to allow entry of more private investment and perhaps even easing the ban on foreign participation in hydrocarbon exploration and development, which have been a source of nationalistic pride since the oil fields were expropriated from foreign hands in 1938.

Petrochemical Classifications

In August 1989, Mexico's government reclassified basic petrochemicals in an effort to open the sector to private investors and help avoid shortages. The new classifications are:

Basic Petrochemicals

Under the Constitution, only the state can produce the following 20 chemicals. What the state cannot produce, companies may import.

Ammonia	Methyl Tert-Amyl Ether
Benzene	Methyl Tert-Butyl Ether
Butadiene	N-Paraffins
Carbon-Black Feedstock	Ortoxylene
Dodecylbenzene	Paroxylene
Ethane	Pentanes
Ethylene	Propylene
Heptane	Propylene Tetramer
Hexane	Toluene
Methanol	Xylenes

(Continued)

Secondary Petrochemicals

Projects to produce these 66 substances can be 40% foreign owned or 100% Mexican owned. With government approval, foreign firms can boost ownership to 100% through nonrenewable trusts.

ABS	Formaldehyde
Acetaldehyde*	Hydrogen Cyanide
Acetic Acid	Internal Olefins
Acetic Anhydride	Isobutyraldehyde
Acetone	Isoprene
Acetone Cyanohydrin	Isopropyl Alcohol*
Acetonitrile*	Maleic Anhydride
Acetylene	Methyl Amines
Acrylene	Methyl Methacrylate
Acrylic Acid	N-Butyl Alcohol
Acrylonitrile*	Nitrobenzene
Alpha Olefins	Nitrotoluene
Ammonium Nitrate	Oxo Alcohols
Ammonium Phosphate	Paraformaldehyde
Ammonium Sulphate	Pentaerythritol
Aniline	Phatalic Anhydride
Butyraldehyde	Phenol
Caprolactam	Polybutadiene
Chlorobenzenes	Polybutane
Chloromethanes	H.D. Polyethylene*
Chloroprene	L.D. Polyethylene*
Cumene*	L.L.D. Polyethylene*
Cyclohexane	Polypropylene*
Cyclohexanone	Propylene Oxide
Dimethylterephthalate	Styrene*
Ethanolamines	SAN
Ethyl Chloride	SBR
2 Ethyl Hexyl Alcohol	Terephtalic Acid
Ethylamines	Tert-Butyl Alcohol
Ethylbenzene*	Urea
Ethylene Dichloride*	Vinyl Acetate
Ethylene-Propylene Copolymer	Vinyl Chloride*
Ethylene-Propylene Elastomers	
Ethylene Oxide*	

*Products reclassified in August 1989 as secondary rather than primary petro-chemicals.

(Continued)

Secondary Petrochemical Producers

Mexico's secondary petrochemical industry comprises 28 businesses, which operate 32 production plants. Capacity at end-1989 totaled 1.94 million MT/year, up 13% from the previous year, whereas output rose 4.9%, to 1.42 million MT. In 1989, imports rose 232% from the previous year, to 55,173 MT, with the main imports ethylene glycol, 2-ethyl hexanol and acetic acid. Exports totaled 41,605 MT, down from the preceding year, and consisted mainly of DMT, TPA and ethylene glycol.

In addition to Pemex, the companies operating in this sector include: Adhesivos SA, Becco Industrial SA, Catalisis SA, Celanese Mexicana SA, Derivados Maleicos SA, Fenoquimia SA, Formoquimia SA, Glicoles Mexicanos SA, Grupo Primex SA, Industriales Cydsa Bayer SA, Industriales Químicas Delgar SA, Industriales Químicas del Pacífico SA, Industrias Derivadas del Etileno SA, Industrias Monfel SA, Industrias Químicas Priha Guadiana SA, Industrias Resistol SA (Grupo Irsa), Nalcomex SA, Némesis SA, Novaquím SA, Petrocel SA (Grupo Industrial Alfa), Petroderivados SA, Polioles SA (Alfa), Productos Químicos Borden de México SA, Química Avangar SA, Síntesis Orgánicas SA, Soquimex SA, Tereftalatos Mexicanos SA (Temex, an Alfa unit) and Univex SA.

Current Investment and Goals

As of end-1990, investment in secondary petrochemicals totaled $9.2 billion, with 80% ($7.35 billion) domestic and 20% ($1.87 billion) foreign, according to the National Petrochemical Commission. (This pertains to plants and equipment, not office space or workers.)

Pemex investments totaled $8.54 billion, with $7.07 billion in basic petrochemical operations, $1.29 billion in secondary operations and $168 million in "unruled" operations. Private investment totaled $7.76 billion, with $4.1 billion in secondary and $3.66 billion in unruled operations.

The petrochemical commission seeks $7 billion in investment over the next five years to bolster the industry. It wants $2.5 billion designated for investment in basic petrochemical operations and $4.5 billion in secondary and unruled operations. The commission has estimated a 1990 trade deficit in basic and secondary petrochemicals of at least $600 million and says that if investment targets are not met, $7.9 billion will be needed through 1995 to import petrochemical products for the domestic market. If the investment is made, the commission estimates a trade surplus of $5.3 billion.

According to the commission, essential to this strategy are a methanol plant, to produce 825,000 MT/year; two aromatics complexes, each to produce 350,000 MT/year (of benzene, toluene and paroxylene); one naphtha-cracking complex and one gas-cracking complex, to produce a total of 1.72 million MT/year of propylene, ethylene and butadiene.

Infrastructure and Transportation Problems

Pemex owns and operates about 60,000 km of hydrocarbon-related pipelines, of which 13,166 km transport natural gas, 5,142 km carry crude oil and 1,414 km convey petrochemicals. By law, only Pemex can own and operate hydrocarbon-related pipelines.

Pipelines and barges are the most practical way to get chemicals from place to place. In the absence of a good system of pipelines or a river network, however, inland petrochemical plants must depend on highways and the railroad. Highways are an expensive and perilous conduit for chemicals. Primex, Cydsa and Polimeros use them to transport highly dangerous vinyl chloride monomer, for example. Executives agree, however, that because of problems with the railroad, too many chemicals are transported by road. In Mexico, 80% of chemicals are moved by road, in contrast to the US, where 90% of chemicals are transported by rail.

Mexico's railway system is antiquated, dating from the 1890s. Schedules are not precise, bottlenecks are frequent, the line network is inadequate and the track and car sizes are not capable of handling today's freight. Container cars, the industry ideal, cannot be accommodated by Mexico's railcars. In the south, trains run on narrower-than-normal tracks. Only the state can legally own and operate the system. Some private firms, including Ford Motor Co (US) in Hermosillo, have built spurs to connect their plants to the national track network.

Coastal ports are inadequate but under development, with petrochemical companies building their own wharfs and holding tanks. They receive no federal tax breaks for improving this infrastructure. Executives say container shipping should be used to speed handling, but that appropriate cranes, lifts and freight beds are not available.

Storage is also a problem. Total storage capacity is only about 5% of production capacity, a factor that often creates bottlenecks.

Companies find they must invest in electrical-power infrastructure (erecting poles and lines) without compensation from the government, because electrical power is reserved for state ownership. Electrical outages and uneven current constitute a potential problem that could result in ruined chemical batches, so plants have back-up electrical sources.

Telephone communication is problematic throughout Mexico, so large petrochemical companies have satellite hookups. A fiber-optic system is available in Mexico City for certain businesses, mainly banks and brokerage firms; other key businesses, including major chemical companies, have installed—or are installing—centrex systems.

Investment Opportunities

Good prospects exist today for entering Mexico's petrochemical market, and opportunities will increase with time as the economy opens further and the free trade accord with the US and Canada is formalized.

The most obvious opportunities lie in supplying the substances for which Pemex cannot meet current demand, the most basic of which is natural gas. Another is the building of plants to supply products presently manufactured by Mexican industry. Foreigners, with their lower-cost funds, could do this more cost effectively than Mexicans. Maquiladora plants are an option being employed for petrochemical production by DuPont (US), ICI (UK), BASF and Bayer (both Germany), among others. Still, only 1.3% of Mexico's in-bond plants are involved in production of petrochemicals. One drawback for building such operations in the petrochemical sector is that a good deal of output is currently consumed within Mexico; under the rules governing maquiladoras, at least 50% of production must be exported.

Other indirect opportunities also exist. Throughout the country, a basic need is strengthening infrastructure, which includes not only railroad systems, roads and ports, but also telephone and other telecommunication systems, computer systems, systems of automation and all the services and programs related to them. Fresh programs are needed for Mexico's system of accounting, for example. Financial services need to become automated. Agencies that provide temporary office workers are also essential. Executives say that services provided to Mexican firms by multinational companies—in the fields of law, accounting and auditing—often are not of satisfactory quality.

Every company cites the need for better education. Some (e.g. Grupo Irsa and Novum) have established a system of industry-related scholarships for employee training. Both firms are controlled by Mexico City-based Desc, the Sociedad de Fomento Industrial SA.

Downstream industries—textiles, plastics, packaging—are considered excellent investment opportunities. In many cases, materials sent out of the country to be processed—and imported as final products—could be processed in Mexico and exported as final products.

Checklist: Handling Relations With Pemex

Pemex officials recommend:

• DEAL with company employees in a friendly, not adversarial, way.

• BE open minded. Respect the fact that Pemex employees are quite knowledgeable.

• BE patient. Everything works at Pemex, but at its own speed. It's profoundly bureaucratic, but it functions. A non-Mexican company might want to hire someone—perhaps a former Pemex employee—to deal specifically with Pemex.

• BE direct and honest in what you are saying, in what you can offer and cannot offer.

• BE realistic about supply and delivery deadlines. Be aware, however, that Pemex officials are sometimes unrealistically optimistic about such deadlines and try either to pin them down or adjust your production planning accordingly.

• STATE proposals clearly, and follow them up. Understand that Pemex officials have many concerns competing for their time and they will not necessarily follow up on your proposal. To get a commitment in writing, officials say you might have to repeatedly go to their office and stand over them.

• BE persistent.

• GO to the appropriate official level. Your cause may be as lost if you take it to the general director as if you take it to the entry guard.

• YOU can complain; you can speak freely; there's real dialogue now between Pemex and its clients.

Pemex clients recommend:

• NEVER talk about Pemex, even to company officials. Complaining about Pemex could cost you your contract.

• DON'T expect Pemex officials to come to you. Whether they're buying from you or selling to you, you go to them, and you speak with them at their convenience.

• DON'T expect red-carpet treatment, even if you're a major client.

• COME to the bargaining table with proposals, not problems.

• LISTEN to Pemex's needs, and do everything within your power to provide what is needed.

Petrochemical
Company Profiles

Because of the high-technology, capital-intensive nature of the petrochemical industry, many foreign companies have gained entry into the
sector in Mexico through agreements based on the transfer of technology to, or through forming joint ventures with, local firms. This section
contains profiles of several of the major petrochemical companies in
Mexico. These reviews include overviews of their growth strategies and
of their cooperative ventures with multinational corporations.

Grupo Industrial Alfa

Grupo Industrial Alfa SA's petrochemical business accounted for 35%
of the corporation's 1989 revenue of about $2 billion, up from 28% in
1988. Exports for the business totaled about $317 million, of which
$231 million were direct exports, making the firm Mexico's leading ex-
porter of petrochemical products.

Operating profit for the business declined 26% in 1989, reflecting
the effects of Mexico's domestic price restraints, but accounted for 39%
of the corporation's total, up from 33% in 1988. In addition to petrochemicals, the industrial giant has operations in steel, food and products as diverse as cardboard, rugs, industrial machinery and aluminum
parts.

Of the firms within Alfa's petrochemical business, Akra Fibras
Químicas makes nylon and polyester fibers and is in a technology partnership with Akzo NV (Netherlands). Akra Nylon de México makes
nylon, polyester fibers and lycra and has a technology agreement with
DuPont (US). Petrocel, which produces raw materials for polyester, has
a technology accord with Hercules (US); Temex, which also manufactures raw materials for polyester, has technology contracts with Pemex
and Amoco (US); Polioles, which makes urethanes, polyester raw materials, polystyrenes, solvents and specialty chemicals, has a technology accord with BASF (Germany); Indelpro, which produces polypropylene
resins, has a technology agreement with Himont (US). The last production company, Selther, makes mattresses and polyurethane foam. Another firm in the group, Copeq, promotes global trade between firms
within and outside Alfa. Sales volume rose 30% in 1989, with import
growth exceeding export growth and product mix shifting toward
value-added manufactured goods.

Through its Petrocel and Temex units, Alfa is involved in the largest
planned Pemex turnkey project to date. The $400 million aromatics
complex near Monterrey will ensure the two companies a supply of benzene, toluene and paroxylene.

Polioles, operating at 50% of capacity in 1988, now operates at full capacity. The company is 57% owned by Alfa, 3% owned by a private Mexican investor and 40% owned by BASF's Wyandotte unit. The firm's strategy is to look for niches; it currently is seeking out customers in the $200,000 range, which it believes would be difficult for a Texas company, for example, to service in the Mexican market. The firm feels that its strength lies in service orientation, knowledge of the customer and diversity of its product line. To accommodate lesser customers, the company might ship in smaller amounts and with greater frequency, set up a tank within the customer's operation, "because he's short on money" or help customers adjust their machines to work better with Polioles products. A priority for the company is cost cutting. It is reducing overhead and fixed costs, reviewing yield and productivity. "We're very close to world standards," says a top officer.

Polioles imports all the propylene oxide it uses, about $10 million p.a. The substance is produced in the US by Dow Chemical and Arco and in Europe by Royal Dutch Shell and Dow. The firm buys 80% of the styrene it uses from Pemex and imports the rest, and buys 80% of the ethylene oxide it could use from Pemex and does without the rest, because the substance is too dangerous to import. The company also occasionally imports butanol as well as specialty chemicals—catalyzers and additives for expandable polystyrene.

Celanese Mexicana

Celanese Mexicana SA de CV, with $700 million in sales in 1989, is the largest petrochemical company in Mexico, after Pemex. It manufactures and markets chemical fibers, plastics, specialty products and flexible films. In 1989, profit was severely hurt by the downward trend of international petrochemical prices and, because of the domestic price-limiting economic pact, the inability to pass on to customers the increased prices for main feedstocks. Sales in 1989 totaled 464,192 MT, with 19% going to exports. Capacity grew 10%, to 1.1 million MT/year.

Celanese plans to invest $700 million through 1995, in part to diversify products for export and the local market. According to one official, it is premature to discuss a US-Mexico FTA, but the company believes its wisest course in meeting global competition is to improve efficiency through better employee training, raising overall quality, better servicing of clients' needs, maintaining high standards of plant safety and addressing ecological concerns. The firm is purchasing technology from the Japanese and other foreign sources.

Celanese was the first US petrochemical firm to enter Mexico after the 1939 expropriation of foreign oil holdings. It invested in textiles in

1944, perceiving opportunities in the manufacture of rayon and acetate fibers and attracted by the country's labor force and market. Celanese Corp—now Hoechst Celanese Corp—reduced its holding in the company to 40% in the 1960s. For years, exports were marginal. In 1979, however, Celanese Mexicana altered its strategy to make exports a priority, designating 25–30% of its output for export, a strategy it says positioned it to survive the economic crisis of the 1980s. To boost exports, sales representative offices were established in 1989 in Brussels, São Paulo, Guatemala and New York; Celmex Marketing Co, headquartered in Dallas, Texas, was already in existence.

The fibers division operates 14 plants for the production of cellulosic fibers, nylon and polyester for textile and industrial markets. Capacity totals 250,000 MT/year, with captive consumption of 72,000 MT and sales of 178,000 MT into the market.

In 1989 the Univex SA unit, Mexico's only producer of caprolactam, boosted capacity by 50%, to 75,000 MT/year. Major raw materials used by the company are ammonium and cyclohexane, supplied by Fertilizantes Mexicanos SA (Fertimex—the state fertilizer producer) and Pemex.

HCPP Mexicana

HCPP Mexicana SA (Hoechst Celmex Performance Products) was incorporated in 1989 to penetrate the market for engineering resins and high-performance petrochemicals. Celanese Mexicana holds 40% of the unit, Hoechst Celanese Corp controls 40% and Química Hoechst de Mexico SA, 20%. The unit's products are: Nylon 6, a natural and modified polymer; Impet, a modified polyester; Celcon, an acetal copolymer; Celanex, a polybutylene terephthalate; Riteflex, a thermoplastic elastomer; Vectra, a liquid crystal polymer; and Durel, a polyarylate.

The chemicals division has 25 plants at seven sites, with total capacity of 728,000 MT/year. Sales fell 18% in 1989, as exports plunged because of a drop in global prices. Domestic sales were flat despite a drop in 2-ethyl hexanol and butanol; and vinyl acetate, esters and acetone sales increased. Sales rose in product groups such as monomers and amines, reflecting the strong paint market; solvents, boosted by auto industry demand; intermediates; plasticizers; water soluble polymers, produced through its Derivados Macroquímicos unit; and resins, produced through its Resinas de México SA unit.

In one of the Pemex turnkey operations, Celanese has built a plant to produce 75,000 MT/year of vinyl acetate monomer, using acetic acid and ethylene as raw materials. The plant was scheduled to start up in early 1991. A facility to produce 30,000 MT of acrylic acid is planned, and new plants were established to produce diketene and arylides, which are used as bases for dyes and pigments.

The Packaging Materials Group operates six plants with total capacity of 43,000 MT/year, of which 31,000 MT are sold. Sales rose 9%, with plants running at 83% of capacity to produce flexible packaging, i.e. cellophane, bioriented polypropylene and polyethylene film; rigid packaging, including polyester bottle grade resin, traded under the name "Tercel," and preforms for bottles; and cellulose casings, traded under the name "Celpack."

Novum

Novum SA, a unit of the industrial giant Sociedad de Fomento Industrial SA de CV (Desc), is a holding company in Mexico City with businesses in the petrochemical, pharmochemical, agrochemical, aviculture and food sectors. Sales for 1989 rose 18%, to about $220 million, with petrochemicals representing about 40% of total sales.

Novum's petrochemical sector makes products for the rubber, tire, paint and waterproofing industries as well as the industrial/chemical sector. In a realignment of Desc units, it recently acquired Mexico's third-largest poultry producer, Univasa. Through that acquisition and the much more significant purchase of its only local rival producer of synthetic rubber and carbon black, Ules Mexicanos, it doubled in size in 1990. Novum was formed in a 1986 restructuring of Desc operations.

Novum's strategy is to incorporate itself into a global system. In this way, the company aims to gain competitive advantages in technology, market familiarity and domination and differentiated product lines. Part of its plan is diversification, which would help it to offset business cycles in the sectors in which it operates. To boost exports, the firm has set up marketing offices in the US and Europe.

Through Novum's Negro de Humo Negromex unit, Mexico is the world's fourth largest producer of carbon black. Annual sales of the rubber strengthener total $70 million, with 50% exported, mainly to Europe and the US; some is exported to Latin America, and some to Asia. Novum's partnership with Cabot Corp (US), which is the world's largest producer of carbon black and owns 40% of Novum's operations, gives the company access to the most advanced technology related to the product.

Synthetic rubber accounts for $180 million of Novum's sales, produced through its Industrias Negromex unit. Although the firm would be interested in finding a partner in this field, it currently develops its own technology. Novum has the highest number of researchers with doctorates in rubber research in Mexico and continuously updates their training. According to Novum, any partner would have to be a technological leader; conforming with corporate policy, the company would maintain majority interest in any such partnership.

Major imports include butadiene and styrene monomer, vinyl chloride, paroxylene and ortoxylene. Novum has had to defer expansion of synthetic rubber operations because of problems obtaining butadiene supplies. What Pemex cannot supply, Novum buys from Europe and the US.

Novum's pharmaceutical sector supplies government outlets through bidding contests. Its aim is volume sales at lower prices, and its antibiotic production is entirely integrated; for other pharmaceuticals, it formulates the products from imported raw materials.

10
The Computer Industry in the 1990s

Mexico's computer industry is poised for explosive growth in the 1990s, largely because of its critical role in President Salinas's modernization plan. Computers are essential to Mexico's future since they will provide competitive advantages to every important industrial and service sector—especially those becoming further integrated into the North American and global strategies of multinational companies. Salinas has targeted these industries (automotive, telecommunications, financial services and tourism) for liberalization.

The opening of these sectors is being accomplished through presidential decrees that free foreign companies to manage their Mexican subsidiaries by greatly reducing the government control that has inhibited the integration of Mexico into most firms' broader strategies. The edict regulating the computer industry, announced on April 3, 1990, set the stage for Mexico to figure prominently in the marketing and manufacturing plans of large global companies and smaller Mexican firms. According to US government figures, Mexican computer, peripheral equipment and software sales in 1990 were about $1.1 billion and are projected to rise an average of 20% p.a. in 1991 and 1992. In fact, industry experts believe that growth in certain areas could quintuple in the 1990s.

Before the latest decree, computer production was tightly controlled by the government, which sought to stimulate development of a domestic industry. This policy, however, kept foreign firms from achieving economies of scale that would allow Mexican consumers to buy state-of-the-art equipment at globally competitive prices. The 1990 mandate altered the situation dramatically. This chapter will briefly describe the rules that previously regulated the industry, analyze the significance of the 1990 decree and its impact on the future development of the industry and review the strategies of select players in the market.

"Draft" Decrees of 1981 and 1987

Before 1990, Mexico did not have an official computer ruling. Instead, the industry was governed by two "draft" decrees prepared in 1981 and 1987, respectively. Over time, these drafts were administered as though they had the full force of other presidential mandates.

Before the first edict was passed, all computers were imported into Mexico. To encourage domestic investment in the industry, the 1981 decree stipulated that all firms intending to supply the Mexican market were required to set up local manufacturing facilities. This regulation was the same as that passed in the first Automotive Decree of 1962; local production under a regime of import substitution had come to the computer sector.

Under the mandate, all new computer firms were required to be established as Mexican, i.e. with at least 51% Mexican capital. Each manufacturer, however, had to reach a separate agreement with the government concerning local content, investment and operations. As a result, there were no uniform standards under which the decree was administered.

For example, although the production of microcomputers was reserved for Mexican companies, in April 1985, the government decided to allow IBM to construct a plant that would be a wholly owned subsidiary. This reversal of policy was precipitated by the country's worsening economy and by IBM's commitment to increase its Mexican investment in the proposed plant from $6.6 million to $91 million over a five-year period. Mexican institutional customers and private sector consumers benefited because IBM began to provide the market with state-of-the-art technology, a major improvement over the obsolete products offered by other manufacturers. The IBM decision set an important precedent for Mexico: It increased the competitive climate as "Big Blue" surged to leadership in the expanding microcomputer market.

Manufacturers of mainframes and minicomputers could also be 100% foreign owned if the firms agreed to utilize high percentages of domestic content in their final products. (The recommended levels varied from product to product.) Ultimately, the incorporation of Mexican inputs proved very difficult because, at the time, most Mexican suppliers were incapable of furnishing the high-quality materials required by foreign firms. In addition, compliance with the computer mandate was particularly troublesome, since the government's local integration formula was complicated and ambiguous.

The 1987 computer decree (even more strict than the previous one) aggravated the local-content issue. It required that foreign manufacturers of minicomputers use at least 30% Mexican content in 1987 and 40% in 1989. When these levels could not be met, the government agreed to return to the less stringent requirements of the 1981 decree. MNCs, in effect, were granted import quotas as a percentage of their Mexican domestic production. These quotas were applied every two years and permitted both producers and distributors to import a reduced percentage over a six-year period. For the first two years, the manufacturers were entitled to import four times as much as they produced in Mexico; twice as much during the second two years; and an equal amount during the final two.

Throughout the time during which the 1981 and 1987 edicts were in force, the government closely regulated the industry. In addition to imposing local content requirements, import permits and limitations on foreign capital, the administration regulated products that could be imported. Although the decrees did not enable MNCs to operate as efficiently as they would have liked, the government interpreted the regulations in a flexible enough manner to allow the industry to expand very rapidly from 1982–89. As shown by Table 10-1, microcomputer sales showed the greatest increase.

Despite the inefficiencies of the two decrees, the industry grew at a spectacular rate. This was all the more remarkable since most of the

Table 10-1. Microcomputer, Minicomputer and Mainframe Computer Sales and Market Shares, 1981 and 1989

($ millions)

	1989*		1981	
	Sales	% of Market	Sales	% of Market
Micros	360	60	26	20
Minis	150	25	91	71
Mainframes	90	15	12	9
TOTAL	600	100	129	100

SOURCES: US International Trade Commission, US Commerce Department.

*1989 market share reflects mid-1990 figures

domestic economy slumbered through the country's prolonged recession. Growth statistics show the following factors:

• Growth for microcomputers, minicomputers and mainframes averaged 52.2% p.a.

• Microcomputers grew fastest, averaging 183.5% increases p.a. from 1982–89.

• Mainframe sales placed second, averaging 92.9% growth p.a. in the same period.

• Minicomputer sales grew at the slowest rate, at 9.3% p.a. during the period.

As impressive as domestic performance seemed, growth in export sales was even more dramatic. In 1982, computer exports amounted to just $2.8 million. By 1989, IBM alone exported $380 million, as it delivered on its 1985 agreement with the government to ship leading microcomputers abroad. The production of microcomputers for export also enabled IBM to justify imports of crucial mainframe components for the Mexican market.

IBM's ability to produce computers within world-class standards provided an example for other leading MNCs that wanted to export. Hewlett-Packard followed the example and by 1989 was able to ship more than $63 million overseas for sale in global markets. In 1989, computer firms in Mexico exported $740 million in computers and peripherals to the US, while importing only $563 million, for a trade surplus of $177 million.

Although the original computer mandates fostered the early success of MNCs like IBM and Hewlett-Packard, it became increasingly clear that a loosening of operating conditions would be necessary to stimulate further growth in both the domestic and export markets. As the economy became increasingly open, however, it was essential to distinguish between new investors and the older players who had established their plants under the former decrees. The older players would have to be granted some form of protection against the new entrants, particularly in the area of imports.

The 1990 Computer Decree

The April 3, 1990, Computer Decree addressed the issue of loosening controls on the computer market, just as Mexico was intensifying its efforts to get free trade talks going with the US and pressing forward with other sectoral decrees to open the economy to foreign investment. By early 1990, Salinas had restored the country to a strong growth trajectory. Mexico was becoming more attractive to computer firms as a booming domestic market and an important export base that could produce world-class products at very competitive prices.

The 1990 decree had three key objectives:

(1) To increase the competitiveness of the computer industry;

(2) To enhance the competitiveness of those industries that rely on computers to achieve superior performance; and

(3) To offer Mexican consumers the widest possible variety of state-of-the-art computer hardware and software at internationally competitive prices.

To achieve these goals and promote greater investment and sales, the decree altered the tariff structure for computer products and offered fiscal incentives to those companies operating in Mexico so they could better prepare to confront new competition. The mandate eliminated cumbersome import permits for all computer products (except used machines) and allowed foreign MNCs to supply the Mexican market solely through exports for the first time in a decade. Each of these changes is examined in the following pages.

Liberalizing computer operating rules
By rescinding the requirement that computer companies had to establish domestic plants if they wanted to market their products in Mexico, the government opened up sales possibilities for new entrants at a fraction of the cost expended by firms that had invested in Mexican production facilities under the old rules. Obviously, companies exporting products such as microcomputers to Mexico's burgeoning market also faced a much lower financial risk, since exports may be easily expanded and contracted as market conditions warrant.

Although such a change was advantageous to firms not manufacturing in Mexico, it also benefited those companies producing there by enabling them to rationalize their production of computers, peripherals, parts and software. Since the April 3, 1990, decree eliminated the need for manufacturers to maintain production facilities in Mexico, established MNCs are now free to abandon the manufacture of any unprofitable product. These companies are at a disadvantage, however, to the extent that they may have invested in unprofitable ventures purely to comply with government regulations. To compensate for this, the government offered these manufacturers powerful fiscal incentives.

Fiscal incentives

The following incentives are to remain in force until March 31, 1993:

• MNCs operating under the former decrees may import up to 80% of the value added to their Mexican production and investments in manufacturing facilities (stock) duty free.

• These same companies may import up to 200% of their investments in technology, including software development programs, also duty free.

These incentives are intended not only to compensate foreign computer manufacturers, but also to reward Mexican firms, and to encourage them to develop more competitive products for global markets. The decree, however, requires new entrants to pay tariffs on all computer products and parts imported into Mexico and, in some cases, raises the previous tariff rates to protect existing firms.

Tariffs

Although the trend under Salinas has been to aggressively reduce tariffs to stimulate trade and investment, computers are something of an exception. In two critical categories, finished computers and peripherals (e.g. monitors, printers ar.d keyboards), tariffs have been doubled. For most other products, the tariff level has been cut or left intact.

Table 10-2. New Computer Tariffs and Import Requirements vs Old

Product	Tariff		Requirements	
	Before	Now	Before	Now
Computers	10%	20%	Import permit	None for new; permit for used equipment
Monitors, printers, keyboards; other peripherals	10%	20%	Import permit	None for new; permit for used equipment
Memory units	10%	10%	Import permit	None for new; permit for used equipment
Banking peripherals	20%	10%	Free	None
Modems	15%	15%	Import permit	None
Electronic cards	15%	15%	Free	None
Parts, except electronic cards	10%	5%	Free	None

SOURCE: *Expansión*; Servicios de Estrategia en Electrónica SA de CV.

Overall, the new decree divided related products into three distinct groups and assigned tariff rates to each of these categories. They are finished computers (20%), most parts and components (10%) and scarce inputs (5%). Table 10-02 provides a sample of typical products and their appropriate tariff rates under the new edict, compared with the applicable rates under the former decrees, as well as government requirements.

Competitive Implications

The established computer companies in Mexico have responded favorably to the 1990 regulations. They believe the increased tariff rates for finished computers and monitors, keyboards, printers and other peripherals will enable them to confront a new generation of competitors, particularly firms at the low end of the market, which will initially only export into Mexico, without establishing production facilities.

Although the April 3, 1990, decree appears very protective, it is significantly less so than other recent edicts, such as the Automotive Decree (see Chapter 8). This decree only grants companies with plants in Mexico the right to import cars. In addition, it explicitly prohibits any firm from importing subcompacts (i.e. low-end vehicles) until 1993. By comparison, the computer mandate should foster a swift opening of the Mexican market.

The more important question is how the computer decree will ultimately affect the industry in Mexico. The following implications are immediately apparent:

• **Competition will increase dramatically.** This will be especially true in the microcomputer sector, as new East Asian manufacturers mount aggressive export promotion drives. Although the primary focus of the new products will be on price, increased quality, variety and service will be critical as well.

• **Competitive battles will be won through the effective implementation of corporate strategy.** Each firm will need to identify those segments of the market that offer the best opportunities. It then must respond swiftly to customers' needs by providing more efficient products and services than its competitors. Corporate strategy will increasingly focus on corporate, rather than individual, customers.

• **Brand image and customer satisfaction will be more important in a market inundated with new offerings.** Differentiating among similar products will be one key to success.

To shed light on possible changes in competitive tactics under the new decree, the following sections provide examples from distinct computer-related product sectors of the ways companies have begun to organize their strategies.

Microcomputer Competition:
An Illustration

Microcomputer sales comprised about 60% of the local computer market in 1990. The market-share leaders in microcomputers are, in order of rank, IBM, Hewlett-Packard and Printaform (a local firm). These microcomputers are priced at $2,000–12,000. They include vastly different machines distinguished by price, function (power) and prestige (brand).

One way to illustrate the effect of the computer mandate on competition among microcomputer producers is to differentiate the products in a table that measures price and brand offerings in Mexico, before and after the new decree, as depicted below:

	Less Prestigious	More Prestigious
Lower End: BEFORE	Differentiation/low prices.	Differentiation/medium prices.
Lower End: AFTER	Very wide offering/ primarily kits from Taiwan.	Limited offering/absence of some brands.
Upper End: BEFORE	Differentiation/high prices.	Differentiation/high prices.
Upper End: AFTER	Diversified offering, but limited demand in a price-sensitive market.	Incomplete offering/ absence of some very important brands.

As the table shows, there will be intense price pressure at both the low and high ends of the microcomputer market. The most prestigious international producers (e.g. IBM and Hewlett-Packard) must focus on upgrading products and services and offering powerful workstations or networks to corporate clients. A growing advantage could be in the breadth and sophistication of the way the systems are packaged, i.e. the degree to which the products actually help business customers solve their most pressing problems. Total price and value will contain a critically important service factor that will be measured in terms of product availability, reliability and effectiveness, as well as customer satisfaction. Software sales will also make more of a difference as manufacturers struggle to establish hardware standards that will enable a wider spectrum of customers to utilize their software regardless of the brand of computer they own.

At the lower end, price will become still more important as some top East Asian brands, like South Korea's Leading Edge, attempt to gain a foothold in the market. Their strategy could be similar to that in the US. They will offer very high-quality/performance machines that are IBM compatible and carry a relatively low price. In addition, some high-cost Mexican component producers may be driven out of business by more efficient foreigners.

Corporate Approaches:
IBM and Hewlett-Packard

As important as the price/performance/brand matrix is, in the long run a company's success will be determined by the effectiveness with which each individual firm cultivates and continues to satisfy its largest and most profitable customers. Careful planning and marketing are critical.

The manufacturing sector in Mexico accounts for approximately 30% of the computer market. The automotive industry has been the most important industry in this sector. Both IBM and Hewlett-Packard, two of the sector's most powerful leaders, have targeted different manufacturing companies. They offer slightly different product lines, however. Whereas IBM has focused on marketing mainframes, mini-computers and microcomputers, Hewlett-Packard has concentrated on selling minicomputers, microcomputers and peripherals, especially laser-jet printers.

Both of these US firms are convinced that software and consulting services will become more significant to the industry. Hewlett-Packard has gone so far as to incorporate this belief in its trademarked communications message to industry, "Your partner in competition." The company believes it is not selling only hardware or software to its clients, but also advantages that this firm can use against its competitors. Manufacturing clients account for about 40% of Hewlett-Packard's Mexican business. Its major manufacturing projects focus on manufacturing operations, management and automation. The firm is a leader in automotive robotics.

Hewlett-Packard's machines and consulting advice are also used for financial and accounting management. Leading customers include companies in financial services, telecommunications and trade. The computer company has at least 40 industry consultants who work to meet the needs of its leading corporate clients. Hewlett-Packard's sales in Mexico totaled slightly more than $135 million in 1990 and are projected to nearly double by 1994, reaching $250 million. Perhaps the most impressive of the firm's achievements has been its growth rate of over 40% for the past few years—about three times the industry average.

IBM's marketing profile has been even more driven by the manufacturing sector, which (including the automotive industry) accounted for more than 50% of its client base in 1990. Nevertheless, distribution enterprises (29% of client base) and retailers (16%) also provided Big Blue with profitable business opportunities. The company's Mexican sales were comprised as follows: mainframes, 25%; minicomputers, 30%; microcomputers, 30%; and software, 15%. Precedents established in the US and conversations with company executives indicate that consulting services and development of software will be growing businesses for IBM in Mexico.

Keys to success

Computer companies at the top end of the market, such as IBM and Hewlett-Packard, should ultimately achieve greater success in the 1990s by allying themselves closely with and selling to the most powerful sectors of the Mexican economy: automotive, telecommunications, financial services and petrochemicals. These newly deregulated industries are struggling to become more competitive as they emerge from decades of inefficient operations and government control. Since these sectors are dependent on foreign capital and technology to achieve their objectives, they will also rely on foreign-owned computer firms to assist them in gaining competitive advantages as Mexico integrates further with the other North American and international markets.

The opportunities for Mexican companies are also enormous. Analysts predict that by 1993, Mexican-owned firms will export $400 million worth of computer equipment. Computer services exports are expected to grow as well.

In 1990, total Mexican sales of computers and peripherals amounted to $1.14 billion, as opposed to $0.29 billion in 1981, when the first computer decree went into effect. Growth has averaged almost 37% p.a. This trend will persist in the 1990s, and increases in specific areas may be even greater.

The challenge for the largest companies will be to integrate Mexico into other global strategies. The new computer industry regulations have already made it possible for corporations like IBM and Hewlett-Packard to initiate these steps as they prepare for the new competitive environment (see Hewlett-Packard case study on next page). The leading firms will concentrate their efforts on selling a combination of service and performance, particularly to corporate customers. For the

Mexican consumer, lower prices resulting from increased competition will be the greatest benefit, as they will be able to purchase top-quality products at internationally competitive prices.

With the affiliates of US companies such as IBM and Hewlett-Packard already exporting large amounts from Mexico—reaching almost $500 million in 1990—it is clear that globalization is well under way. A trilateral free trade agreement with Canada and the US will only accelerate this process.

Case Example

Planning for Integration: Hewlett-Packard's Regional Initiatives

Executives of Hewlett-Packard de México are confident that a North American free trade agreement (FTA) will benefit the company's already booming business. Bolstered by an aggressive sales and development strategy, as well as integration of local production into an overall corporate planning framework, the MNC affiliate is coming off the best year (1990) in its history and expects an FTA to fuel further expansion.

Hewlett-Packard representatives claim that expansion under Mexico's nine-year old Computer Industry Development Program has given the firm a competitive edge. The government program required computer manufacturers to maintain high levels of exports and local sourcing. Exports from the company's two Guadalajara plants had to compete internationally with products from subsidiaries in other countries—making quality a must for Mexican managers. "We were already operating in a global trade environment," says the Mexico subsidiary's Business Development Director Salvador Quirarte.

Mexico as global sourcing site

A broad opening of the computer industry in 1990 under the new Computer Decree has allowed the MNC to redirect its Mexico strategy, bringing local activities further in line with overall corporate planning.

As part of this process, the company is converting its Guadalajara manufacturing facilities from what was formerly high-overhead, low-volume production geared primarily for the domestic market. The firm's former minicomputer plant is bing transformed into the exclusive Hewlett-Packard producer of a line of impact printers to be exported around the world. According to Quirarte, "If our facilities here didn't fit into the company's overall strategy, there wouldn't be any reason to manufacture in Mexico."

The 1990 opening eliminated import permits for computers and parts and created incentives that allow for duty-free imports. "We had our doubts about how the opening was going to affect us. But 1990 turned out to be the best year we've had in Mexico," says Quirarte. "The fact is, the opening put us in a situation that, in market terms, looks a lot like what the FTA will be. We don't anticipate any shock from the FTA."

FTA expectations

Hewlett-Packard has been a strong supporter of the FTA concept, with parent company CEO John Young lobbying actively for the treaty through the Business Roundtable, a US lobbying group. The firm has set up a three-country task force—composed of representatives from its US, Canada and Mexico offices—to analyze the potential effects of an FTA on the company's business. The company is also participating in a study sponsored by Mexico's National Electronics Industry Association.

Hewlett-Packard expects economic growth in Mexico under the FTA to increase the demand for company products and services. A continued opening of the computer sector will also raise the number of products available, giving potential clients more choice. "The FTA will clarify the rules of the game," says Quirarte. "We hope it will eliminate the restrictions that limit us in terms of foreign investment and industrial development."

Still, company studies have identified the following areas of concern for the upcoming FTA negotiations:

Patent and industrial secrets protection. A new intellectual property law should meet most of the industry's concerns in this area (see Chapter 6). Approval of that law was viewed as a show of good will in anticipation of formal FTA negotiations.

Clear antidumping rules. The company is hoping for greater clarity in the rules governing antidumping and the importation of used equipment and products for resale.

Rules of origin. According to Quirarte, "Rules of origin should mark a middle ground, fostering domestic manufacturing and local sourcing without putting a damper on competitiveness."

Adapting organizational structure

The company has undertaken a far-reaching corporate reorganization to coincide with the consolidation of regional markets. It includes steps that will soon bring North American operations under one roof.

Hewlett-Packard Intercontinental, the parent company's corporate division that currently coordinates operations outside the US and Europe, has created a new regional subdivision, know as Hewlett-Packard Americas. Under the new scheme, all activities in the US, Canada and Mexico will soon report to a single office and eventually, all Latin American operations will be included.

As the first step toward the gradual integration of this macroregion, former Latin America Regional General Manager Manuel Díaz was made sales director of the fledgling Americas Division in January 1989. New Latin America General Manager Rui da Costa notes that the corporate integration will take place with or without an FTA. "We're now looking at things in terms of regional markets," he says.

Mexican managers expect the new Americas division to give them better access to corporate resources and to problem-solving capacity. They also stress the impact on client support services. "US clients who have operations here want to deal with one Hewlett-Packard, not a separate one in each country," Quirarte says, adding that customers will find security in the company's new organization.

Hewlett-Packard went through a similar process last year, when it consolidated supervision of operations in Japan, the Far East, Australia and Asia into a new Asia-Pacific Region within Hewlett-Packard Intercontinental. Eventually, the intercontinental division will be phased out, and the company will be organized into three separate divisions: Americas, Europe and Asia-Pacific.

Hemispheric initiatives

Da Costa predicts a North American FTA will serve as a catalyst for other Latin American countries to move forward with similar regional trade initiatives, including US President George Bush's Enterprise for the Americas Initiative, the Andean bloc and the Southern Cone Common Market. He believes that, "In the long run, the movement is toward creation of a hemispheric agreement." Hewlett-Packard expects to benefit from hemispheric integration, supplying high-technology products vital for the competitiveness of firms and governments.

Besides the company's operations in Mexico, where it maintains two factories for the manufacture of personal computers and impact printers, Hewlett-Packard has an agreement with Edisa (a Brazilian firm) involving technology transfer and import sales. The MNC has its own sales offices in Argentina and Venezuela and contracts sales representatives in most other countries. Although the firm is still waiting for other Latin American markets to mature, da Costa believes that the most likely candidates for future company expansion are Colombia and Chile.

Latin American sales equaled 4% of total corporate sales in 1990, or approximately $539 million. Hewlett-Packard de México's sales have increased by an average of 33% p.a. since 1982. 1990 was the best year ever for the Mexico subsidiary, with a 42% growth in sales. First-quarter 1991 sales showed continued solid growth.

Hewlett-Packard de México is constructing a new $8 million office building in Mexico City. The rapidly expanding subsidiary will eventually occupy both the new site and its current offices.

11

The Maquiladora Industry

Mexico's maquiladora, or in-bond, industry has evolved into a vital off-shore production option for US-based companies undergoing intense competitive pressure in their home markets. The availability of low-cost labor for generally low-skill assembly work is not the only source of the maquiladoras's attractiveness, but it is the chief draw for MNCs seeking cost-efficient production in a low-risk environment.

Although the rest of the Mexican economy languished for most of the 1980s, it was exports in general, and the maquiladoras in particular, that pointed the way toward the economic liberalization of the 1990s and the free trade agreement (FTA) talks with the US and Canada. The maquiladoras, which assemble mostly US-manufactured components for reexport to the US, have been around since 1965, but it was not until the beginning of Mexico's protracted economic crisis in 1982–83 that the country's political and economic decisionmakers acknowledged the crucial role of the maquiladoras in helping integrate Mexico as a competitive player into the global economy.

This chapter reviews the evolution of the in-bond industry in Mexico, its importance to the country's economic recovery in the last several years and how its role may be modified under a North American FTA.

Maquiladoras: Exception to the Rule

Before the economic crisis of the 1980s, Mexico's strong GDP growth (which peaked at 8% p.a. during 1978–81) was based almost entirely on an import-substitution model that emphasized protection of domestic manufacturers from foreign producers through the maintenance of high tariffs and special import licenses. Foreign participation in Mexican operations was limited to a maximum of 49%. By severely curtailing foreign operations, Mexico adopted an inward-looking, nationalistic trade policy. Although this approach stimulated growth and raised domestic employment levels, it reduced the competitiveness of Mexico's industry in the global market.

This policy was feasible as long as the price of oil continued to increase in world markets and capital poured into Mexico in the form of bank loans, with creditors believing oil was the best form of collateral. Once international oil prices began to plunge, however, and Mexico announced its inability to meet foreign debt obligations in August 1982, a new economic development model was adopted. At this point, the liberalizing of trade and foreign investment became a priority, with the aim of spurring growth through exports and boosting Mexico's ability to compete in increasingly global markets. In many respects, the maquiladoras' success became a prototype for the new economic model.

From 1965 to the Present

Maquiladoras have their origin in Mexico's Border Industrialization Program, established in 1965 to encourage industrial development and employment along the 2,000-mile US-Mexico border. Under this program, officials offered tariff concessions to export operations along a 20-km stretch of the border. Later, the program was expanded to include all of Mexico. Today, it is known as the maquiladora program.

Legally, politically and economically, the maquiladoras are treated differently from other business enterprises in Mexico. Maquiladoras are an exception in terms of ownership, marketing strategy and their level of international competitiveness. Unlike most other enterprises in Mexico, maquiladoras are primarily 100% wholly owned subsidiaries of US companies. They combine state-of-the-art technology with relatively cheap labor rates in Mexico to enhance their efficiency and competitiveness in international markets, particularly the US and Canada. The maquiladoras are also exceptional in that they are required by law to export two thirds of their total production. This restriction has the obvious objective of protecting Mexican manufacturers. From a legal standpoint, the maquiladoras are regulated by special decrees, the most recent of which was published on Dec. 21, 1989.

Viewed historically, the maquiladoras have been an anomaly. Although the rest of Mexican industry sputtered throughout most of the 1980s, averaging less than 1% growth p.a. in real terms from 1982–89, the maquiladoras grew at explosive rates during the same period. The reasons are evident: Whereas the import-substitution model guided the behavior of majority-owned Mexican companies in a highly protected market, maquiladoras were required to export their output to the world's most competitive markets. Hence, their manufacturing operations had to be allowed to function under a set of specialized, liberal rules, which were codified in the maquiladora decrees. In addition, repeated devaluations of the peso made Mexican wage rates increasingly competitive in US-dollar terms. These special conditions have fueled the industry's expansion (today there are some 1,600 maquiladoras) and have generated enormous benefits for Mexico: They have enabled the sector to become the second leading earner of foreign exchange, after petroleum exports, as well as to significantly raise employment, attract greater foreign investment and perhaps most important, to forge closer and substantially greater economic ties with the US.

From the US's vantage point, the maquiladoras have provided an effective means of response to the intensification of global competition in the US marketplace, especially in automotives and electronics, which have experienced increasing price competition from low-cost East Asian producers. By producing in low-cost maquiladora plants on the US-Mexico border, US manufacturers have been able to survive and prosper under this stiffer competition. Even Asian producers—particularly the Japanese—have in recent years increased their own presence in Mexico's in-bond industry in order to cut production costs and enhance their own competitive position in the US market.

Measuring Maquiladora Exports and Imports

When analyzing the impact of maquiladoras on Mexico's economy, it is important to understand the different methods of recording maquiladora performance (statistics) used by Mexican and US government sources. The most significant difference in the recording of maquiladora statistics is that the Mexicans consider exports from the in-bond plants to be services. These are entered net of imports, as value added, in the Mexican balance of payments. Value added is comprised primarily of wages, salaries and benefits; raw materials and packaging; miscellaneous expenses; and profit. In the US, however, US imports from the maquiladoras are recorded as merchandise imports and are not limited to net figures. In fact, the US International Trade Commission (USITC) and Department of Commerce (DOC) distinguish between US content (duty free) and non-US content (dutiable) for tariff purposes and record the gross figure.

US imports from the maquiladoras are listed under tariff provis-

---

(Continued)

ions 9802.00.60 and 9802.00.80 of the Harmonized Tariff System (HTS); these special provisions were formerly known as 806.30 and 807.00 of the Tariff Schedules of the US (TSUS). Under the HTS, as under the TSUS, manufacturers that assemble or process US components abroad for reexport to the US are subject to duties that are levied effectively only on that portion of the product's value that is added abroad, *not* on the product's final value. Since approximately 50% of the value added to goods in Mexico is labor, the maquiladoras have furnished US manufacturers with a cost-effective means of producing intensely price-competitive goods.

Although it appears logical to expect that the dutiable portion of US imports under HTS 9802.00.60 and 9802.00.80 would correspond to the value-added figures on the Mexican books, this is not the case. The Mexican government authorities—the National Institute of Statistics, Geography and Informatics (INEGI), the Secretariat of Programming and Budget (SPP) and the Secretariat of Commerce and Industrial Development (Secofi)—do not disaggregate their figures by individual country.

Question of third-country content
In addition, the products that are assembled by maquiladoras frequently contain components that were manufactured neither in Mexico nor in the US, but in some third country, such as Taiwan or Japan. The product content from this third country is not recorded by the Mexican authorities because the value was not added in Mexico, but it is counted by US customs officials since the content or value was present in the product at the time it was imported from Mexico. These discrepancies between Mexican and US data have existed throughout the 25-year history of the maquiladora program, and they continue to widen. It is generally asserted by industry experts that the Mexican figures are understated.

Final differences in the data involve the time lag between the Mexican and US sources and the frequency of reporting. The Mexican data contain more detail and are available on a monthly basis, but are released after a five- or six-month time lag. For instance, in January 1991, Mexican figures were available through July 1990. Official US sources have access to only tentative aggregate figures for all of 1988 and 1989, at the product level.

In spite of these differences, it is possible to measure the performance of the maquiladora industry fairly accurately by focusing on growth in terms of value added, employment, trade and new plant start-ups. Because of the premium of timeliness, the Mexican data are emphasized in this report, supplemented by US statistics.

Regulation:
The Maquiladora Decrees

Prior to 1983, maquiladoras were tolerated rather than actively encouraged. They were considered by Mexican officials to be foreign entities that had no vital role in nationalistic development. The special regulations governing the industry's operations stipulated that 100% of production had to be exported, and the excess of administrative paperwork made it difficult for foreign operators to function efficiently.

Moreover, until the beginning of the steep devaluations of the peso in 1982, the cost of Mexican labor was relatively expensive compared with that of other lesser-developed countries—e.g. South Korea, Taiwan, Hong Kong and Singapore, the four East Asian "tigers." As Table 11-1 indicates, the hourly cost of labor for a Mexican production worker, including benefits in 1981, was 42% higher than for a worker in South Korea; 36% higher than a Taiwanese worker; and 18% more than a production worker in Hong Kong. Because of these significant wage differentials, it was hardly surprising that US semiconductor companies and textile firms that initially had maquiladora operations in Mexico transferred these plants to East Asia in the 1970s.

1981 was a watershed year for Mexico. It marked the zenith of domestic development, while revealing Mexico's vulnerability to foreign wage competition among other lesser-developed countries. It also exposed the country's vulnerability to abrupt changes in global oil prices. Policymakers began to realize that this situation could potentially imperil future growth unless the economy were restructured and made more competitive in global markets, implying a shift away from exclusive concentration on domestic markets. Although 1981 was a year of record domestic growth (8%), it was quickly followed by an economic crisis in

Table 11-1. Mexican vs East Asian Wages for Production Workers
(benefits included; $ per hour)

	1983	1981	Change 1981/1983
Mexico (maquilas)	1.03	1.85	(44.3%)
South Korea	1.23	1.08	12.2%
Taiwan	1.27	1.18	5.5%
Hong Kong	1.52	1.51	0.7%
Singapore	2.21	1.79	23.5%

SOURCE: US Department of Labor.

1983, a year of steep peso devaluations and severe economic contraction (negative 4%).

At the same time, peso devaluation and the shift in relative exchange rates globally enhanced the competitiveness of Mexican labor vis-à-vis Asia and stimulated a boom in the maquiladora sector. As Table 11-1 illustrates, the hourly wage for a Mexican production worker declined from $1.85 in 1981 to $1.03 in 1983 (a 44% drop), which was 115% lower than a comparable worker in Singapore, 16% lower than a South Korean counterpart, 19% less than a Taiwanese worker and 32% below the wage of a production worker in Hong Kong.

The 1983 Maquiladora Decree

As significant as the peso devaluations were, there would have been no rapid growth in the in-bond industry without changes in government attitudes, as reflected in the maquiladora decrees. Before 1983, in-bond plants were required to export all their production. The 1983 Maquiladora Decree (Aug. 15, 1983) sought to change this.

In this decree, the Mexican government made it permissible for maquiladoras to sell up to 20% of their production on the domestic market. The ruling contained so many restrictive clauses, however, that as of April 1988, scarcely more than a dozen firms had received government approval for such sales. The restrictive conditions included one that made approval contingent on whether the Secretariat of Commerce and Industrial Development (Secofi) believed the production of national manufacturers was sufficient to satisfy demand or whether the articles manufactured by the maquiladoras were different enough from those of domestic suppliers. If a maquiladora were to receive authorization, it was to be granted for one year only and could be rescinded at any time. Given these limitations, the 1983 decree represented only a tentative first step, a political testing of the waters to gauge the reactions of Mexican and US businesspeople and politicians to an opening in the sector. As such, this decree was a precursor to the 1989 decree, which simplified implementation procedures and allowed for up to one third of maquila production to be sold on the domestic market. For such an important change to be implemented, however, it was necessary for top Mexican officials to promote bold new trade and investment policies.

A critical step toward implementing a new and more liberal economic policy occurred in August 1986, when Mexico became a signatory to the General Agreement on Tariffs and Trade (GATT), initiating broad tariff reductions that, by 1990, would bring tariffs to a maximum rate of 20%, from a previous maximum rate of 100%. More important, Mexico's entrance into GATT meant that for the first time, the country announced its intention to radically liberalize its economic system through modernization measures that were embodied in international agreements. Almost overnight, Mexico replaced its import-substitution regime with policies designed to increase its manufacturing prowess and competitiveness in global markets. Key to these new policies were export development and promotion, and it was in this context that active promotion of the maquiladoras began.

In 1986, as in 1983, Mexico again experienced a severe economic crunch, in which GDP declined by 4%. It was not until 1989 that GDP achieved the levels that it had reached in 1981 and 1982. Given this stagnation in the domestic market, exports became the chief means of stimulating growth, foreign exchange earnings and employment. By December 1989, President Salinas had initiated many new decrees aimed at achieving these objectives, as well as attracting additional foreign investment. One of the most important of the new initiatives was the 1989 Maquiladora Decree.

The 1989 Maquiladora Decree

The 1989 decree stated explicitly that a key objective was the integration of the maquiladora sector with the national economy. Incentives were provided to achieve this goal. Integration with the domestic economy had two important meanings: the right for maquiladoras to sell their products on the Mexican market and the incorporation of local inputs and raw materials (Mexican) in the assembly process. Clearly, the maquiladora operators have been more interested in selling their products in Mexico because of their competitive advantages over national producers, whereas the Mexicans have been interested in supplying the plants with higher percentages of local materials, since historically only about 1.7% of these inputs have been Mexico-sourced. To allow the assembly plants the right to sell in Mexico without either restrictions or a quid pro quo would have hurt the domestic suppliers. On the other hand, requiring the maquiladora operators to increase their levels of integration involved the risk of losing competitiveness, since local suppliers often could not meet the global quality standards or delivery demands of the maquiladoras.

Mexican officials confronted this conflict by offering powerful tax incentives to maquiladora operators who cultivated Mexican suppliers and increased local content. The most important change in the 1989 Maquiladora Decree is that it permits the plants to sell up to one third of their production in Mexico without the restrictions that existed under the previous decree. Maquiladoras may now qualify for domestic sales merely by maintaining a positive foreign currency account. In practice, this means that the total value of maquiladora imports must be less than the amount of foreign exchange expended on operating costs in Mexico—such as wages, rent and supplies.

Technically, the decree states that the maquiladoras are entitled to sell the equivalent of up to 50% of their preceding year's export sales on the domestic market. In other words, if a maquiladora's 1990 exports totaled $100, then it would be eligible to sell $50 domestically in 1991. From this perspective, the domestic sales would represent one third of current production, valued at $150. Normally, the duties on these domestic sales would be applied to foreign content only, but the rate at which the duty is applied is the one applicable to the finished product. If a maquiladora opted to increase national content to levels specified by the government, however, then the duties on the domestic sales would be applied at rates applicable to the components integrated into the final products, rather than on the final products themselves. Of course, the tariff rates for components are substantially lower. In order to qualify for these lower rates, the Mexican government has stipulated that the maquiladoras must achieve 2% integration during the first year, 3% in the second year and 4% in subsequent years.

Although these changes do not amount to a complete deregulation of the industry, they do indicate a growing willingness on the part of Mexican officials to reduce restrictions on foreign enterprises. Because the changes are so recent, it is not possible to evaluate their long-term effect, although after examining the performance of the maquiladoras during 1983–90, a tentative judgment is provided.

Maquiladora Performance (1983–90)

The maquiladoras have outperformed all other major export categories since 1983. Mexican officials measure maquiladora performance largely in terms of value-added exports (foreign exchange earnings), employment generation and integration with the marketing and manufacturing strategies of companies selling their products in the US. During 1983–90, Mexico began to restructure its economy by focusing on the export sector in order to capture scarce foreign exchange. These changes are reflected more dramatically in maquiladora exports than in any other area.

Value Added: Mexican Data

The superior achievement of the maquiladoras can best be appreciated when value-added exports, which are recorded in the service account, are compared with merchandise exports (see Table 11-2 on page 221). By distinguishing between these two types of exports, as the Mexicans do, it is possible to illustrate their very different growth rates and to pinpoint the precise industries and products that are fueling maquiladora expansion. Overall, exports are a key indicator of a country's ability to compete internationally, with manufacturing exports being the most critical index. For Mexico and other lesser-developed countries, manufacturing exports are especially significant because, unlike traditional commodity exports, they capture much higher prices in international markets (long term) as a result of their greater value added. Virtually all in-bond exports consist of manufactured products.

In 1983, the first year of the economic crisis, Mexico's exports were dominated by crude petroleum, which came to 66.3% of total merchandise exports. The crucial manufacturing sector accounted for only 20.5% of total exports, indicating that Mexican products were overpriced and uncompetitive in global markets. Part of the problem was the substantially higher cost of Mexican labor relative to countries in East Asia. More important, Mexico's long-protected enterprises were undercapitalized and utilized outdated technology.

Six years later, after a series of currency devaluations (in 1982–83 and 1986–87) foreign direct investment in Mexico surged, particularly among companies that sought to enhance export capacities. In 1983, foreign direct investment amounted to $461 million; four years later, in 1987, it skyrocketed more than fivefold to $3.25 billion, as the Mexican government actively courted foreign investors. One of the incentives offered was a debt-swap program that entitled corporations to purchase

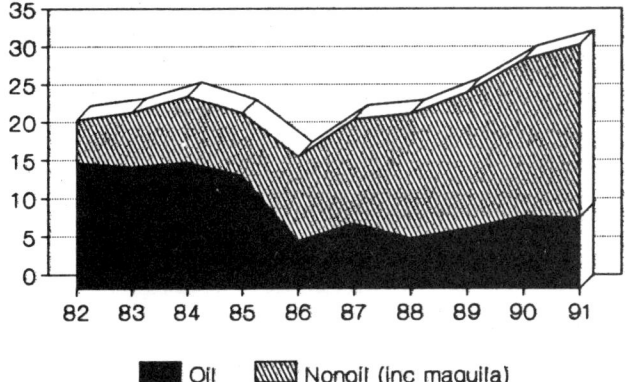

Figure 11-1. Export profile—oil vs nonoil ($ billions). 1991 figures are forecasts. *(Source: Banco de México)*

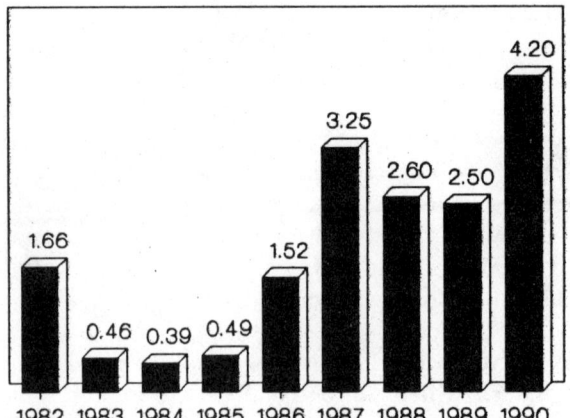

Figure 11-2. Foreign direct investment ($ billions). 1990 data
is estimated. *(Source: Banco de México)*

Mexican debt at deeply discounted prices and to "swap" it for pesos to
make domestic investments. A significant percentage of the swaps was
used by maquiladoras. The positive effect of the devaluations and swap
incentives appeared almost immediately as a boom in merchandise and
maquiladora export accounts.

In 1983, companies with direct foreign investment in Mexico exported $1.67 billion and produced a surplus in the commercial balance
of $225 million. In 1987, barely four years later, these same firms ex-
ported $6.83 billion while registering a surplus of $1.89 billion in the
merchandise balance. The results were also very impressive when
judged by the structure of exports. By 1987, 44.4% of merchandise exports were manufactured goods, for an increase of 117% over 1983.
Crude oil accounted for only 34.8% of the exports, as opposed to 66.3%
in 1983. By end-1989, it was clear that the restructuring of exports was
continuing, as manufactured items represented 55% of exports, and
crude oil made up only 32%.

As impressive as these merchandise export figures are they exclude
the maquiladoras, whose rate of growth outperformed manufactured
exports in the merchandise account. Maquiladora performance as measured by value added is illustrated in Table 11-2, where it is compared
with merchandise exports in general and manufactured exports in particular during the 1983–90 period.

From 1983–89, maquiladora exports (value added) increased at a
rate of 55.9% p.a., whereas merchandise exports grew at about half that
rate, or 28.9% p.a. More significant, since maquiladora exports are net

Table 11-2. Maquiladora Exports vs Merchandise Exports, 1983-90
($ billions)

	1990	1989	1987	1985	1983
Total Merchandise Exports	26.36	22.76	20.66	21.66	22.31
Manufactured Exports	NA	12.53	9.91	4.98	4.58
Maquiladora Exports	3.57	3.05	1.60	1.27	0.82
As % of Manufactured Exports	NA	24.4%	16.1%	25.5%	7.9%

SOURCE: Banco de México, INEGI.

of imports, they produced approximately 66% more surplus in 1989 than merchandise exports ($3.05 billion vs $1.89 billion).

It is even more revealing to identify those industries responsible for producing the largest number of value-added exports. Although there are 11 manufacturing categories, only two, electric and electronics and transportation equipment, have dominated maquiladora exports during 1983–90. Throughout the first seven months of 1990, these two sectors accounted for nearly two thirds of maquiladora value-added

Table 11-3. Value-Added Maquila Exports in Electric and Electronics, Transportation Equipment and Textiles and Apparel Sectors vs Total Maquiladora Exports (11 sectors), 1983-90
($ billions)

	1990*	1989	1987	1985	1983	Avg. Annual % Change 1990–83
Electric and Electronics	1.37	1.24	0.68	0.57	0.41	33.4%
Transportation Equipment	0.87	0.73	0.38	0.33	0.17	58.8%
Textiles and Apparel	0.20	0.18	0.10	0.09	0.06	33.3%
Total of 3 Sectors Above	2.44	2.15	1.16	0.99	0.64	40.2%
Total All Maquila Sectors	3.57	3.05	1.60	1.27	0.82	47.9%

*Total 1990 figures for the leading sectors are estimated based on average monthly statistics through July 1990. The total for all 10 sectors is the actual figure for all of 1990, however.

SOURCE: INEGI.

Table 11-4. Value-Added Maquila Exports in Electric and Electronics, Equipment and Textiles and Apparel Sectors vs Total Maquiladora Exports (11 sectors), 1983–90
(% of total)

	1990*	1989	1987	1985	1983	Avg. Annual % Change 1990–83
Electric and Electronics	38.4	40.7	42.4	44.7	50.0	(1.7%)
Transportation Equipment	24.4	23.8	24.0	26.1	21.0	0.5%
Textiles and Apparel	5.6	6.0	6.3	6.9	7.6	(0.3%)
% of 3 Above Sectors	68.4	70.5	72.7	77.6	78.6	(1.5%)
Total % All Maquila Sectors	100.0	100.0	100.0	100.0	100.0	—

*1990 figures for the individual sectors are the average of monthly figures through July.
SOURCE: INEGI.

exports (62.8%). Table 11-3 illustrates the total value of the 11 maquiladora categories and the dominant contributions of the three leading sectors, in dollar terms, whereas Table 11-4 shows the contribution of these leading sectors in percentage terms. Textiles and apparel, currently the third-ranked category, has placed a distant third throughout the period; its inclusion, however, highlights the superior performance of the electric and electronics and transportation equipment sectors.

Differentiation and Shifts in Market Share

A comparison of Tables 11-3 and 11-4 indicates the continued leadership of Mexico's two most important in-bond sectors, but reveals the emergence of transportation equipment as the most critical exporter, in terms of growth in both dollar amount and market share. It was the only leading sector to increase by these two important indicators during 1983–90.

In dollar terms, transportation exports grew 25% faster than those of electric and electronics and textiles and apparel. Yet, in absolute dollar value, electric and electronics exports for 1990 still surpassed the transportation equipment sector by about $0.5 billion and remained the leader in this category, a position it has held for the last seven years.

Table 11-3 also discloses that the annual growth rate of sectors not among the top three foreign exchange earners had an aggregate average of 13.6%, or less than one quarter of transportation and equipment's blazing 58.8% rate, and a little more than one third of electric and electronics' and textile and apparel's second and third top rates. These differential rates of growth indicate that although maquiladora operators are diversifying their manufacturing activities, they are making much smaller capital investments outside of the leading sectors. Still, Table 11-4 shows that in percentage terms, the top three sectors accounted for 10.2% less of the total maquiladora exports in 1990 than they did in 1983 (78.6% vs 68.4%, respectively). This reduction amounted to average declines of 1.5% p.a., which in turn translated into growth of 1.5% p.a. in the eight nonleading sectors. The most important of these sectors was "other," which more than doubled its participation, to 14%. This category is, of course, a catch all for different industries. Two other relatively fast-growing sectors included furniture and other wood and metal products and chemicals.

Finally, despite the overall decline of share of exports for the top three Mexican economic sectors, they continue to represent 68.4% of

Is Maquiladora Production for You?

As a general rule of thumb, the following criteria are helpful in identifying the types of industries that benefit most from maquiladora production in Mexico:

• Proven high growth in other offshore production environments;

• Prior success in Mexico;

• High labor-input ratio;

• High wage rates for equivalent jobs in the US;

• Availability of supplies, management personnel and production facilities in planned plant location;

• Bulky products with high transport costs;

• Products of high value, with substantial inventory carrying costs;

• Favorable US duty treatment and eligibility for Mexican import incentives; and

• Potential use of cost-competitive Mexican raw materials or components, if available.

the total. Even if the leading electric and electronics and textiles and apparel industries continue to lose market share, as they have during 1983–90, it is critical to emphasize that these declines have been registered in an unprecedented boom period. As a result, their dollar investments have soared and are likely to continue growing briskly.

Against this background, the achievement of the transportation equipment sector appears especially impressive. Although the market share of electric and electronics lost almost 12%, and textiles and apparel declined 2%, transportation equipment's participation increased by almost 3.5% in the seven-year period under examination. This leadership in export growth will widen further in the future as the Big Three US automobile manufacturers increasingly integrate Mexican operations into their North American marketing plans (see Chapter 8 on the automotive sector).

US Imports From Mexico Under HTS 9802.00.80 (US Data)

Data on US imports under HTS 9802.00.60 and 9802.00.80 are widely used as key indicators of Mexican maquiladora development. Of the two tariff regimes, the latter accounts for more than 99% of maquiladora imports from Mexico; therefore, it is the specific regime examined here.

Data available from the USITC (as of January 1991) not only confirm the conclusions derived from analysis of available data from Mexico, but also provide an additional international perspective. The USITC's statistics reveal that Mexico and its maquiladora plants are the third leading foreign source of imported products under HTS 9802.00.80, trailing only Canada and Japan, which are the two chief suppliers of US components assembled abroad for reexport to the US. Total imports under HTS 9802.00.80 in 1989, amounted to the following dollar amounts and percentages from the three leading countries:

Canada: $25.7 billion (35.2% of world total)

Japan: $16.8 billion (23.1% of world total)

Mexico: $11.8 billion (16.1% of world total)

More significant still than these aggregate figures, which include both dutiable and duty-free content, is the fact that 51% of HTS imports from Mexico were made up of US content (duty free), as opposed to only 2% from Japan and 33% from Canada. The vastly greater US content in the imports from Mexico results because they are supplied by subsidiaries of US companies, whereas those from Japan are not. The growing use of HTS 9802.00.80 by US subsidiaries in Mexico is illustrated in Table 11-5.

Leading the way in HTS 9802.00.80 product categories from Mexico in 1989 were motor vehicles and autoparts, electrical conductors and television receivers and parts. These products correspond with the transportation equipment and electric and electronic categories in the Mexican data. Perhaps an even more important indicator of the competitive advantage that HTS 9802.00.80 affords the maquiladoras of US firms is that 44% of all 1989 imports from Mexico utilized this tariff provision. If the petrochemical, steel and agricultural imports are subtracted from the overall import totals, however, then an astounding 78% of the remaining $14.5 billion entered US customs under 9802.00.80. This included 95% of all television apparatus and parts, 93% of motor vehicles, 88% of electrical articles and 78% of motor vehicle parts imported from the maquiladoras under the special foreign assembly provision. These products belong to precisely those industries that are subjected to the most intense price competition in the US market.

Two observations about these products and their manufacturers should be noted. First, in the case of television apparatus and parts, the major beneficiaries of HTS 9802.00.80 are the US subsidiaries of Japanese, not US, companies. In fact, the Japanese investment in this type of maquiladora operation, which is concentrated primarily in the Tijuana, Baja California area, was considerable enough in 1989 to enable Mexico to supply 20% of all color television sets sold in the US. In other words, HTS 9802.00.80 can also be used by subsidiaries of foreign companies to gain competitive advantages. Since Japan has learned how to exploit this leverage, while simultaneously producing enormous trade surpluses with the US, it is certain that during the free trade negotiations among Mexico, Canada and the US, the Japanese trade and minimal US content problems will be a major focus. After all, the primary objec-

Table 11-5. US Imports From Mexico Under
HTS 9802.00.80, 1986-89

($ billions)

	1989	1986	% Yearly Change 1989/1986
Duty Free (US content)	6.0	3.3	27.2%
Dutiable (Foreign content)	5.8	3.1	29.0%
Total	11.8	6.4	28.1%

SOURCE: USITC, USDOC.

tive of a free trade pact with Mexico is *not* to provide the Japanese with more effective and cheaper ways to increase their penetration of the US market.

In addition, it is important to note that the automotive industry is relying more than ever on electronic devices that add considerable value to increasingly sophisticated vehicles. As a result, there is a crossover between the transportation equipment and electric and electronic sectors. For example, tape decks and electrical conductors for wiring harnesses, along with specially designed lighting and electrical alarm systems, are indicative of the growing overlap between these two leading in-bond sectors. It is certain that transportation equipment manufacturers will become even more significant customers of the electric and electronics industry.

Using Tariff Concessions to Competitive Advantage

Firms contemplating an industrial operation in Mexico aimed at exporting to the US should have intimate knowledge of the US Harmonized Tariff Systems Items 9802.00.60 and 9802.00.80 (formerly known as Tariff Schedule Items 806.30 and 807.00). They represent the most important tariff incentives for firms that produce outside the US customs area but use US-sourced parts and materials, a practice often referred to as "outward processing." US duties on 9802.00.60 and 9802.00.80 qualified products are levied only on the amount of value added outside the US. Unlike the Generalized System of Preferences, these incentives do not carry local content or substantial transformation requirements.

Item 9802.00.60 allows metal products (except those made of precious metals) that have been manufactured in the US to be further processed offshore and reimported into the US, with duties levied only on the value of foreign processing.

Item 9802.00.80 allows US-sourced fabricated components that are assembled outside the country to be imported into the US, with duties assessed only on the amount of foreign value added. It is this incentive that is most significant to the maquiladora industry.

Firms using these schemes to enhance global competitiveness fall into the following categories:

• **US-owned firms that have shifted their labor-intensive assembly to lower-wage countries as a means of cutting production costs.**

(Continued)

Maquiladoras fall into this category. An example is the offshore assembly of several hundred US-originated components into heat exchangers.

• **US firms that locate production operations offshore for other than wage-cost reasons.** Such companies may want to penetrate the host market—which may only be possible by local manufacturing—while servicing the US market under the most beneficial tariff conditions.

• **Non-US companies using US components in their assembly operations.** Like their US counterparts operating overseas, such firms may choose US-made components because of price, quality, supplier reliability or because there is no local alternative. Pressure of one form or another to "buy American" may also enter into the equation. When high tariffs would otherwise make sales of such products to the US prohibitive, duty savings offered by 9802.00.80 may be crucial.

• **International firms with metal processing operations.** The lion's share of 9802.00.60 operations is accounted for by Japanese companies purchasing waste aluminum cans in the US, shipping them back to Japan for processing into rolled sheet aluminum and reshipping them into the US market, where they are resold to US can manufacturers.

Other programs

Canada, the European Community (EC) and Japan have their own versions of the US's preferential tariff program:

Canada has the Canadian Goods Abroad Program. Under this scheme, products composed of Canadian inputs processed abroad are, upon importation into the home market, subject only to duties on the offshore value added. Canada's program also provides for duty relief on the temporary export and reimportation of goods repaired abroad.

The EC's version of outward processing is contained in EC Council Directive 76/119 of 1976. Only value added outside the EC is subject to the Common Customs Tariff, and goods may be moved among member nations after offshore processing. The EC reserves the right to withhold duty-free privileges for such operations if it ascertains that its interest would suffer as a result.

Japan provides reduced rates of duty for goods undergoing offshore processing and reimportation. Customs officials may exempt 100% of the Japanese-sourced components when establishing a product value for the purposes of levying duties.

Table 11-6. Number of Maquiladora Employees, Plants and
Value-Added Output per Employee, 1983 and 1990*

	1990**	% Total	1983	% Total	Yearly % Change 1990–83
Employment					
Electric and Electronics	171,225	37.4	82,690	54.8	15.3
Transportation Equipment	95,579	20.8	19,590	12.9	55.4
Textiles and Apparel	42,225	9.2	16,210	10.7	22.9
Total Above 3 Sectors	309,029	67.4	118,490	78.4	31.2
TOTAL All 11 Sectors	458,561	100.0	150,867	100.0	29.1
Plants					
Electric and Electronics	512	27.0	244	40.7	15.7
Transportation Equipment	157	8.3	47	7.8	33.4
Textiles and Apparel	288	15.2	94	15.7	29.5
Total Above 3 Sectors	957	50.4	385	64.2	26.2
TOTAL All 11 Sectors	1,899	100.0	600	100.0	30.9
Employees per Plant					
Electric and Electronics	344	—	339	—	(0.2)
Transportation Equipment	609	—	417	—	6.6
Textiles and Apparel	147	—	172	—	(2.0)
Average Above 3 Sectors	363	—	228	—	8.5
AVERAGE All 11 Sectors	241	—	251	—	(0.6)
Value Added per Employee ($)					
Electric and Electronics	8,001	—	4,958	—	8.8
Transportation Equipment	9,102	—	8,678	—	0.7
Textiles and Apparel	4,737	—	3,703	—	4.0
Total Above 3 Sectors	7,290	—	5,435	—	4.9
AVERAGE All 11 Sectors	7,794	—	5,780	—	6.2

*Figures may not add exactly because of rounding.

**1990 sector figures are estimates based on averages for the first seven months, as reported by INEGI. The total value added for 1990 is for the entire year, however.

SOURCE: INEGI; SPP.

Employment, Plant Development and Output Trends (Mexican Data)

By combining data on value added with an analysis of the growth patterns of maquiladora employment and new in-bond plant start-ups, it is possible to more fully appreciate the maquiladoras' contribution to Mexico and to US manufacturing companies. Table 11-6 provides these statistical data and figures on value-added output per employee for 1983 and 1990.

Table 11-6 illustrates the reason that maquiladoras in the transportation and electric and electronics industries have achieved dominance and why this trend is likely to continue. The yearly employment growth figures show that transportation equipment's 55.4% rate over the past seven years was almost double the industry average (which encompasses all 11 sectors). When combined with the data on new plant start-ups, it is clear that the plants in the transportation sector are twice as large as those in the electric and electronics industry and four times the size of textiles and apparel facilities. The significance of this superiority of the transportation equipment plants is that not only is this the fastest-growing major sector, but also the one that is most efficient, produces the highest value added per employee and also requires the heaviest capital investments. Although electric and electronics have lagged behind the explosive growth trajectory of transportation equipment, they have recently made enormous advances in generating more value added per employee as a result of greater capital investment and efficiencies.

Table 11-6 also dramatizes the overall impact of the maquiladora industry on employment. During 1983–90, employment tripled from 151,000 to 459,000 employees, whereas the number of plants more than tripled, from 600 to 1,899. By 1989, total maquiladora employment accounted for 17% of Mexico's manufacturing employment. Equally (if not more) important from a production standpoint, the value added per employee grew by 34.8% in the seven years from 1983–90, from $5,780 to $7,794, despite a series of severe peso devaluations. This indicates that maquiladoras are becoming increasingly sophisticated in their use of technology, rather than simply benefiting from Mexico's low labor rates.

The Future of Maquiladoras Under an FTA

In the past, critics argued that maquiladoras existed only to take advantage of cheap Mexican labor. The rapidly increasing globalization of industries, however, has shown that the Mexican work force can be trained to manufacture to the most exacting international standards. As a response to increasing competition for US market share from East Asian producers, most of the leading US manufacturers have utilized Mexico as an increasingly important supplier, integrating their Mexican subsidiaries into their North American and global marketing plans. Moreover, products manufactured in maquiladoras have become more capital intensive and represent the latest product developments in specific niches; they are not old products, using outdated technology, as may have been the case before. From the standpoint of US firms, offshore in-bond production has generated several benefits:

- **Maquiladoras have provided US firms with valuable competitive advantages.** This is true for manufacturers in transportation equipment (passenger cars, internal combustion engines and autoparts) and electric and electronics (television apparatus and parts, electrical conductors for wiring harnesses and tape players), as well as those in textiles and apparel.

- **Compared with other offshore production sites, Mexico's in-bond industry uses a significantly higher number of US-sourced components.** Under the US preferential import tariff scheme HTS 9802.00.80 (formerly TSUS 807), US content averages 53% of HTS 9802.00.80 imports from Mexico. By contrast, imports from Japan—mainly automotive—that come in under the same scheme use a fraction of US components (2%). This lends credence to the argument that in-bond production in Mexico is integral to many US industries.

- **Liberalization of maquiladora operating rules will enable US manufacturers to increase their exports dramatically** now that they are entitled to sell up to 30% of a year's production total in the Mexican market (1989 Maquiladora Decree).

From the Mexican point of view, additional advantages exist:

- Maquiladoras have provided substantial trade surpluses, and the sector has become Mexico's second leading earner of foreign exchange.

- Maquiladoras have furnished Mexico with its largest and fastest-growing source of manufacturing employment.

- Maquiladoras have provided Mexico with significant foreign capital and technology.

Despite all these advantages, there is a great deal of speculation about the impact of an FTA on the booming maquiladora industry. The consensus is that the positive trends are likely to continue, since they reflect increasingly integrated trade and investment patterns between the US and Mexico. Mexico has emerged as the US's third-leading trading partner, and liberalization of Mexico's restrictive foreign investment and maquiladora laws will accelerate integration between the two countries. It is generally believed that the signing of an FTA will only hasten these trends, which have been developing for the past several decades, as well as enhance the important benefits derived by both the US and Mexico.

A Growing Anachronism?

The differentiation between maquiladoras and other foreign operations in Mexico is likely to diminish, however. In-bond plants have existed largely because of Mexico's restrictive foreign investment laws. They provided a convenient and effective way for foreign firms to use Mexico as an export base, while prohibiting direct domestic competition against Mexican manufacturers. With protectionist trade and investment restrictions having been largely eliminated as part of the Salinas administration's reforms, the logic for maquiladoras is no longer as compelling, and the uniqueness of the industry has been eroded.

This will be even more true under an FTA. Under a free trade pact, maquiladoras will probably no longer have to be distinguished from other subsidiaries operating in Mexico. Presumably, the maquiladoras would be permitted to sell as much of their product in Mexico as they wish. They will perhaps no longer be called maquiladoras, and their imported content from the US, as well as exported value added from Mexico, will be duty free.

The status of the in-bond industry is already changing as investment options in Mexico increase. Two features that were once exclusive to maquiladoras—100% foreign ownership and concessions for the temporary, tax-free import of materials and equipment—now apply to most sectors. Changes in the foreign investment regulations made in 1989 paved the way for 100% foreign ownership in a majority of economic sectors, and in late 1988, officials extended temporary import concessions to all Mexican exporters.

On the other hand, the essential benefit of the maquiladora program—Mexico's supply of inexpensive labor—will continue to be a major drawing card for foreign investment under an FTA. Wage rates remain attractive and very competitive with the East Asian "tigers." In 1989, Mexico's average hourly rate for workers in the manufacturing industry was $2.32 (including benefits); this rate was 35% lower than in Taiwan and 25% below that of Singapore. Other East Asian countries with much lower rates, however, e.g. Malaysia, may still offer competition in selected electronics areas.

Some change foreseen

Industry observers say in-bond operations will be largely unchanged under an FTA, although they may be referred to differently. Some government officials are already starting to speak of maquiladoras in terms of "production sharing," rather than "in-bond industry."

With zero-tariff treatment expected for most Mexican products under an FTA, along with further loosening of investment rules, the idea of "maquiladoras" could become moot. The basic concept will not change in practice, however, with Mexico offering cheap labor as a complement to foreign capital in a cost-center, export-processing structure.

Although most experts say it is too early to predict the FTA's final form, several possible modifications to in-bond operating conditions are envisioned:

• **Shift to truer "border industries."** This implies a fuller utilization and integration of resources on both sides of the border.

• **Greater sales and supply options within the country.** Industry experts expect this to be explicit in an FTA. Although many maquiladora operators downplay the importance of the local market, they hope that a strengthened economy will lead to expanded possibilities.

• **Increased exchange of products between separate plants.** This will become easier under an FTA, eliminating the difficulties experienced by plants that must now export their product to the US and then reimport it for sale to other maquiladora buyers.

• **Further incorporation of local content.** Government efforts to promote the use of local inputs—which average only 1.8% of total—are likely to get a boost under an FTA.

Sticky areas

There are also some areas in which an FTA could bring about adverse changes for certain maquiladora operators. These include:

• **Third-country maquiladoras.** One of the thorniest problems to be addressed under an FTA will be the products exported from Mexico by Japanese and other non-US foreign subsidiaries. US-owned maquiladoras represent just over half of the 1,600 in-bond facilities in Mexico and account for a full 85% of the local work force and overall in-bond production. Most maquiladoras are affiliated with Mexican or US companies, and third-country operations represent only about 4% of the total. Yet the Japanese maquiladoras—owned by major companies such as Sanyo, Sony and Nissan—represent a key part of Japanese investment in the country.

The status of third-country plants under an FTA is being questioned—particularly in Washington, where legislators are apprehensive about opening a "beachhead" for foreign producers. Japanese maquiladoras use only minimal North American content; clearly, under an FTA, the exports by their Mexican operations would have to be subject to specific minimum North American content levels, and this could probably follow the precedent established in the US- Canada FTA (see next section).

• **Rules of origin.** According to the US Customs Service, two basic types of rules of origin could apply under an FTA. One is derived from the

---

Rules of Origin: How Sanyo Sees the Risk

Carlos de Orduña, general director of Sanyo's maquiladora operations in Tijuana, believes that Japanese operations will not have to worry about different treatment under an FTA, since most are subsidiaries of firms legally based in the US. The parent firm of Sanyo's five plants, for instance, is the Los Angeles-based Sanyo North America. Of the 20 maquiladoras designated as Japanese owned by the Mexican Secretariat of Industry and Commerce (several operate more than one plant), most (if not all) are owned by US-based firms which, in turn, are owned by Japanese parent companies.

Sanyo maquiladora management also downplays the importance of rules of origin, speculating that Mexico's lack of economic development will require a less strict FTA than the Canadian version. "I don't believe Mexico has the same technology or materials that Canada has," says de Orduña. "We're talking very different markets, capacities and products here." Still, Sanyo will be protected if tight local-content rules are imposed. In the early 1980s, 80% of its inputs came from Japan. Rising costs prompted the firm to look for new sources, however, and now nearly 80% of inputs originate in the US. Sanyo is looking at developing Mexican suppliers and establishing joint ventures as solutions to the problem of local supply.

Another manager of a Japanese maquiladora believes that stiffer rules of origin would cut both ways, since many US operations also rely on third-country sourcing. He stresses, however, that any FTA would include an ample phase-in period—10 years was provided in the case of US-Canada FTA—which would give companies time to adjust their sourcing strategies.

Generalized System of Preferences (GSP), under which the US grants reduced tariffs to select nations. The GSP calls for 35% minimum local content and "substantial transformation" in processing foreign inputs. Under the US-Canada accord, however, distinct local-content requirements were designated for many products, with a 50% value-added rule applying to items not controlled by specific requirements. Customs officials speculate that a combination of the two schemes might be worked out in FTA negotiations.

• **Tax treatment.** In-bond plants operate under a preferential tax structure in Mexico, but no one knows how tax status will be defined under an FTA. If plants reorient production toward domestic sales, a change is almost certain. One maquiladora expert believes that as long as the plants operate as cost centers, they will not have to worry about serious changes in their tax status. He notes that, in general, the industry is not considered a problem in the FTA negotiations: "I haven't come across anything yet that I'd consider a red flag," he says.

Using Maquiladoras to Build Competitiveness

Companies present many examples of how maquiladoras enable them to stay competitive in the US or world markets or, more broadly, how they play a critical role in global or regional integration strategies. The following are a few examples:

• **A large electronics MNC has built an integrated sourcing matrix utilizing operations along the US-Mexico border, the Mexican interior, the Caribbean Basin and key sites in South America.** The corporation's shift to a global organization based on world product groups has enabled it to create efficient sourcing structures to obtain the best products at the lowest possible cost. The firm's most strategically placed sourcing front is the US-Mexico border, where it operates a string of maquiladora plants in four cities, as well as one in the interior. The company also cross-sources between its Mexican and Brazilian operations, has several joint ventures with local Mexican firms to serve both the local and export markets and has manufacturing facilities in Puerto Rico and the Dominican Republic.

Maquiladoras became significantly attractive to this firm after the realignment of the Mexican peso in 1982. Only since then has product sourced out of Mexico been able to compete with components from the firm's Far East manufacturing sites. In addition to the advent of a realistic exchange rate, the company cites other key attractions: proximity to the US (which significantly reduces freight costs), lower labor costs and readily available technical expertise on the US side.

• **Major international automotive firms have made Mexico a global sourcing site.** General Motors (GM) is the largest investor in the country's maquiladora program. GM and its various divisions have a total of 27 maquiladoras, located in 12 cities, which turn out a wide variety of automotive components and accessories for reexport to the US. Eight of these plants are considered "megamaquilas," meaning they employ 1,000 or more workers. GM's plants employ some 24,000 persons, 6% of the industry's total work force. The firm has been a pioneer in locating new plants away from the border (eight of its 27 assembly production facilities are located in interior cities) and has been very influential in bringing supplier companies into the industry. Still, its first plant dates back only to the late 1970s.

Maquiladora operations are a major contributor to GM's cost-containment strategies for its worldwide operations and have enabled the corporation to stay competitive in the US market. GM management also notes that, had it not been for the maquiladora option, a number of major north-of-the-border facilities would probably have been closed and moved completely offshore (see Chapter 8 on the automotive sector).

• **In-bond operations have helped numerous US electronics firms stay in business.** One example of this is Chicago-based Zenith Electronics. Faced with a total loss of its consumer television market in the US, Zenith established its first maquiladora in Matamoros in 1971, with an initial employment of less than 300 workers. At that time, the overall prospects of Zenith's ability to remain afloat in the US were extremely bleak.

During the next 15 years, Zenith moved an increasing amount of its production south and expanded rapidly. It has plants in about six cities, including a large 560,000 sq ft facility in Ciudad Juárez. Zenith executives contend that their decision to move part of their operations to Mexico was a leading factor in the company's ability to survive and subsequently expand—in many cases into new higher-technology product lines in the US.

• **Smaller US electronic firms are using in-bond assembly to lower costs and bring production closer to the US.** Zircon International, a small Silicon Valley producer of electronic hand tools for home and professional craftsmen, has been conducting a portion of its manufacturing in Mexico since 1984. Until that time, the firm's main product was manufactured and packaged in Taiwan. Maquiladora assembly, however, has provided a significant cost savings and permitted the firm to bring production back—or at least closer—to the US. Costs savings have also enabled Zircon to hold the price of its leading product at the price for which it sold in 1981. According to the company's founder and chairman, the maquiladora arrangement met three objectives: "We wanted better control of production costs, a way to maintain the high-quality level of the product and a closer production location so we could initiate changes and product improvements immediately." At the same time, Zircon has brought jobs back from the Far East to its US headquarters, where final assembly, quality control, testing and calibration take place.

Zircon is a good example of the firms setting up in-bond operations in Mexico's interior as an alternative to the crowded border area. Zircon located its plants in Ensenada, Baja California, some 115 km south of San Diego. Among the most important benefits offered by Ensenada is a markedly more stable labor market than in the border area.

• **Japanese firms are setting up in Mexico to fend off competitive pressures from lower-cost Asian producers and to benefit from the maquiladoras' advantages and proximity to the US.** Japan has maintained an in-bond presence for years, but it has only been since 1987 that such investment has taken off. One Japanese firm that recently set up a maquiladora is Kyocera International. Kyocera is the North American holding company of Kyocera Corp, the Kyoto-based manufacturer of technical ceramics, computer hardware and electronic and photographic equipment. Kyocera established a beachhead in the US 20 years ago and has since grown to a total of nine subsidiaries and 2,400 stateside employees. The firm foresees tough and persistent competition, however, in many of its North American product lines from Taiwan, Korea and other Asian nations. Kyocera therefore seriously examines every possible option for cutting costs—and this is where Mexico fits in.

Kyocera Mexicana was established in Tijuana, near the firm's San Diego headquarters. The 100,000 sq ft plant assembles ceramic integrated circuit packages for semiconductors, which are used in a variety of applications. The Mexican facility duplicates work being done simultaneously in San Diego, where production capacity for the most advanced package design was recently expanded. Kyocera's plans for Mexico go beyond the Tijuana plant, however. Although the company does not have a timetable for expansion, it envisions shifting a wide range of more sophisticated labor-intensive activities to Mexico. The possibilities are limitless, given the firm's diverse product base, which includes audio equipment, marine electronics, Yashica cameras, personal computers and laser printers.

• **US, Mexican and Japanese investors have formed a strategic alliance utilizing Mexican labor, Japanese know-how and US raw materials in a**

new venture based in Mexico. The $30 million venture, Citra, produces chicken products processed in a maquiladora for distribution in the Asian market. The partners are C. Itoh (Japan), Provemex (Mexico), Promociones Industriales Banamex (Mexico) and Tyson Foods (US). C. Itoh wanted to diversify its base for chicken yakitori, a popular Asian food dish, which had become costly to produce in Japan because of the large labor component involved in its production. Provemex was looking to expand its Mexican business—raising and slaughtering chickens—to include other production processes, such as chicken deboning. Tyson Foods sought new markets for surplus dark chicken meat, which is less in demand in the US.

The Citra partnership highlights the fact that some firms increasingly eye Mexico, especially its maquiladora industry, not only as a springboard to the US but also as a base for exports to other regions. Moreover, the partners are moving into another innovative area in Mexico, that of forming joint ventures with small collective landowners (ejidatarios) for the raising of chickens (see Chapter 7 on agriculture).

Japanese Investment in Maquiladoras

Japanese companies are making strategic investments in Mexico's maquiladora industry with the aim of increasing competitiveness in the US market. They see considerable scope for expansion in the northern border zone, yet they are moving cautiously in setting up these projects. Like their US counterparts, Japanese maquiladoras are affected by inefficiencies in the sector, including inadequate infrastructure, poor raw materials and high labor turnover. The Japanese approach to setting up shop and tackling these difficulties is sometimes different from that of other maquiladora operators, and this has at times created tension within the closely knit industry.

The majority of Japanese maquiladora plants were set up by US subsidiaries of Japanese corporations. The Mexican plants generally produce for, or assemble components that are sourced from, the US facility. The components are then reexported to be finished and sold in the US. The temporary imports are free from Mexican taxes and

(Continued)

the reexported products owe US taxes only on the Mexican value added.

The Japanese approach

Japan's expansion in the in-bond sector is consistent with its traditional long-range approach to overseas investment, with firms moving slowly but deliberately in setting up shop. Unlike many US companies, Japanese operators prefer to build and own their facilities and have made a long-term commitment to manufacturing, not just assembly. No Japanese firm has opted for shelter or subcontractor arrangements, under which other operators handle the actual production. Instead, they have made direct investments, built their own plants and bought their own property. Another specific difference from other operators is the Japanese tendency to bring in their own contractors, landscapers, builders and engineers, instead of using local developers. This has been one source of tension with the locals.

The growth in the number of Japanese maquiladoras may not seem great when measured as a percentage of the total of approximately 1,600 in-bond facilities, but their impact is large in terms of size and employment. For example, Sony has about one million sq ft of space, and employs almost 1,500 workers in one plant alone. The average Japanese plant has 550–650 employees, double the industry average.

Japanese see multiple benefits

All of the Japanese maquiladoras count cost savings as the principal advantage of establishing operations in Mexico, where wages are still around $3 per day. At these bargain rates, labor costs in Mexican in-bond facilities are competitive with those of any other world location. For the Japanese, wages in Mexico are even more attractive because of the yen's appreciation vis-à-vis the dollar, to which Mexico's peso is pegged, in recent years.

Japanese companies also favor maquiladoras over direct investments in Mexico because foreigners can own 100% of the in-bond plants (although under the foreign investment rules revised in 1990, 100% ownership is also possible in many other sectors).

Another attraction is the access maquiladoras provide to the US market and the fact that the US is less likely to impose trade barriers against Mexico than against Asian countries. One potential risk is

(Continued)

that maquiladoras owned by Japanese subsidiaries in the US could be treated differently from those owned by US firms when the US-Mexico FTA is finalized. Most in-bond analysts think this is unlikely, however, since it would amount to a discriminatory trade practice that the US could not justify.

Dealing with supply, infrastructure and turnover problems

The Japanese confront the same problems inherent in operating in the sector as their US counterparts, including deficient infrastructure and services at many locations in the northern border zone and the poor quality and price of some locally supplied raw materials. Several Japanese and other Asian firms have responded to this problems with a new wave of investment in the sector, setting up supplier plants in Mexico—a solution that the Japanese are pursuing more aggressively than US firms. One example is that of Sumitomo Trading Corp, which has teamed up with another Japanese firm in the sector that makes copper wire for maquiladoras producing television sets.

According to maquiladora specialists, some Japanese operators are also more willing than others to improve road infrastructure and property surrounding their plants. In part, this is a function of the large scale of Japanese operations as well as their location. For instance, many Japanese plants are in Tijuana, where there are fewer industrial parks than in other border towns, and therefore more severe infrastructure and water and electricity supply problems.

Labor turnover—which can approach 50% a month—as well as productivity difficulties are the chief areas of concern in most northern border areas. Japanese maquiladoras often try to counter the labor problem, especially in Tijuana, by paying wages slightly better than market rates, while also offering bonuses for productivity and quality. Whereas the industry wage averages about 1.7 daily minimum wage plus fringes in Tijuana, the Japanese typically pay two minimum wages plus fringes.

According to one US operator, this practice has caused some conflict with US maquiladoras by pushing up wage rates at other plants. "From the Japanese perspective," he says, "wages in Mexico are minuscule compared to those in Tokyo. But US firms must compare wage rates not with those at home, but rather against those in other low-wage developing countries. For us, competitive pressures are much more severe." Still, labor turnover rates at Japanese facilities remain similar to those of other plants, which, as one analyst notes, "suggests that you cannot buy your way out of turnover."

12
Opportunities in Services

Although foreign investment in Mexico has traditionally focused on industrial sectors, especially manufacturing, services are sparking new interest following the liberalization of foreign investment rules and the easing of traditional suspicions among Mexicans about foreign participation in this area. Banking and financial services is one area in which foreign ownership is severely restricted, but regulations are likely to be loosened as a result of FTA talks. The reprivatization of the nation's commercial banks is giving added impetus to this process, and many foreign banks are eyeing the market for future opportunities.

Even though controls on foreign participation in retailing are minor, government officials have a history of being hesitant to permit foreign entry. Until recently, there was no legislation that specifically dealt with franchises, and the sector languished. Still, growth prospects are promising as the North American FTA moves closer to becoming reality.

This chapter reviews the changes under way, as well as the investment opportunities emerging, in the banking and financial services, retail, telecommunications, express shipment and tourism sectors.

Banking and Finance

The financial services sector in Mexico is experiencing rapid change and upheaval. The principal factors responsible are the government's decision, first announced in May 1990, to sell off its majority controlling interests in Mexico's 18 commercial banks and the implementation of new rules that permit the formation of financial groups in Mexico.

Legacy of Inefficiency

The commercial banks were nationalized in a controversial state-of-the-nation address on Sept. 1, 1982, just three months before former President José López Portillo left office. Accusing the banks of helping to organize the tremendous capital flight of the time, Lopéz Portillo hoped his dramatic measure would stop the dollar drain. However, the nationalization virtually erased local investor confidence and triggered a rise in capital outflows.

The decision taken eight years later to return the banks to private ownership signaled an aggressive policy by the Carlos Salinas de Gortari administration to broaden its campaign to attract investment capital, not only from foreign investors, but also from Mexicans who have as much as $80 billion worth of capital overseas.

Mexican bankers argue, however, that before the banking system is opened to direct competition with foreign banks, it must ready itself by improving efficiency and productivity. "Mexican banks simply are not competitive with international banks," comments a director at one of Mexico's leading banks. "We have learned how to create new instruments to attract funds, but we are in the Dark Ages when it comes to creative financing."

Local bankers predict privatization will undo much of the damage caused by state ownership. With a few exceptions, making political appointees heads of banks harmed their ability to implement growth strategies. Outdated technology survived because of budget constraints, and an inefficient bureaucracy grew. Some bankers blame poor government planning for the problems the banks experienced. "Once you put the politicians and government planners in control of the banks, you created all kinds of distortions," comments one banker at Bancomer, the second largest bank. "We were the leading bank before the nationalization, because the input of regional managers was valued. Since 1982, all decisions have come from Mexico City, putting us at a disadvantage with regional banks."

Some small banks, such as Bancreser, tried to expand during the years of state control and become seminational. "It was a misguided and poorly planned strategy based out of Mexico City," comments one banker. "The result was a bank that lost its regional strength but was unable to compete on a national level with the bigger banks." Bancreser eventually sold off its operations in the southeast to Banca Serfin, the country's third largest bank.

Privatization Begins

The bank privatization process was divided into two stages. The first stage began in late 1990, when the Bank Disincorporation Committee accepted detailed operating strategies from prospective bidders. The strategies explained how the potential bidders intended to operate the bank, what regions they planned to focus on, how present bank management would be restructured and who, including foreign partners, would retain visible control of the shares. The committee then decided whether a bidder or group of bidders qualified.

The second stage began when the first banks were put up for sale. This was in February 1991 for the first three (Banca Cremi, Banpaís and Multibanco Mercantil de México), and in May 1991 for another four (Banco Nacional de México, Banca Confía, Banco de Oriente and Banco de Crédito y Servicios). During the second stage, which was open only to bidders that qualified in the first, the government analyzed bids on the basis of price. "We wanted to avoid the two extremes in which state-owned banks were simply sold to the highest bidder or, alternatively, to investors appointed by the state," comments one high-level official.

Mexico's Commercial Banks Put Up for Sale

Banco Nacional de México (Banamex) is Mexico's largest bank. Founded in 1884, it is also one of the oldest. Until its nationalization, it had been administered by the Legoretta family and held equity in at least 120 companies. After losing its position as Mexico's largest bank in the late 1970s to Bancomer, it later regained its status as the largest and the leading bank in Mexico. It was considered by many bankers to be the "prize jewel" of the privatization process.

Bancomer, Mexico's second largest bank, is relatively young (founded in 1932). During the years of Mexico's oil boom, it pursued a policy of expansion, which provided it with more branches than any other bank. Following its growth in the late 1970s—when it added more branches and made strong investments in technology, permitting it to surpass even Banamex—Bancomer suffered during the first six years of its nationalization. Recently, the bank attempted to regain its momentum by acquiring a San Antonio-based bank and entering into a program with Bank of America designed to make it easier for Mexicans to send money from California to Mexico.

Although **Banca Serfin** is much smaller than Banamex or Bancomer, it is considerably larger than the other national banks. Founded in 1864 by British bankers, it is Mexico's oldest bank and was controlled by Monterrey-based businessmen from the Garza Laguera

---

(Continued)

family until its nationalization in 1982. The bank enjoyed strong growth in the years of state control, with its global operations doubling in the first six years of government ownership. It has also been the major actor in the recent privatization of state-owned industries. Factoring Serfin, the factoring branch of the firm, and Fonlyser, its international investment banking subsidiary, are among the bank's major holdings.

Multibanco Comermex, the fourth largest bank, was founded in 1934 by the Chihuahua group, a forestry conglomerate based in northern Mexico and led by Eloy Vallina. Although the bank focused on retail banking prior to nationalization, in recent years it has developed a specialty in trade finance. Analysts claim it suffered from a succession of political appointees to the post of director general.

Banco Internacional was founded in 1941 as a private bank but was taken over by the government in 1972 because of serious financial difficulties. Afterward it was closely associated with Nacional Financiera (Nafinsa), the government development bank (not up for sale). In recent years, however, the bank's dependence on Nafinsa has been reduced. It has been one of the key agents in the privatization program, responsible for the sale of Mexicana de Aviación, the national airline, and Teléfonos de México, the telephone company, and has developed expertise in trade finance.

Banco Mexicano Somex, like Banco Internacional, was taken over by the government prior to the nationalization of the commercial banking system. It was founded as a private commercial bank in 1932 and had a strong presence in the central states of Puebla and Tlaxcala before its takeover in 1979. It has suffered from a poor loan portfolio, but this has been improving in the last few years.

Banco del Atlántico, the country's seventh largest bank, is the result of a merger with Banco del Pacífico in 1983 after nationalization. It is headquartered in Guadalajara and is one of the largest multiregional banks. It has a strong client base among retail and small to medium-sized businesses.

Banco de Crédito y Servicio (Bancreser), also multiregional, is one of the weakest banks in terms of financial health. The government has succeeded in improving the bank's financial condition, but the turnaround has not been as spectacular as with BCH (see below). Prior to nationalization, it was owned by Antonio del Valle Ruíz, owner of Química Penwalt and Prime, the brokerage house.

Banco de Cédulas Hipotecarias (BCH), a multiregional bank, experienced a major turnaround as the government prepared to pri-

(Continued)

vatize banking. Plagued by internal fraud and loan portfolio problems—mortgages were BCH's primary business—performance has improved considerably, as shown by a sharp reduction in the percentage of nonperforming loans.

Banco Confia, Mexico's 10th largest bank, was founded in 1932. It was owned prior to nationalization by Rolanda Vega Iñíguez, current head of the powerful private sector group, Consejo Coordinador Empresarial (CCE). It grew most rapidly during the 1988–91 period.

Banca Cremi was traditionally closely associated with silver mining. Its owner prior to nationalization was Alberto Bailleres, who controls Industrias Peñoles, Mexico's dominant silver producer. Since government control, Cremi has continued to service a strong client base of mining concerns.

Banco Mercantil del Norte (Banorte), is a regional bank based in the northern industrial city of Monterrey. Its strength in northern Mexico, the area likely to develop most rapidly under a North American FTA, as well as its solid financial health, make it very attractive to potential investors. Banorte's profits in 1990 exceeded those of the large multiregional banks (e.g. Banca Cremi, Banca Confia, Banco del Atlántico, Bancreser, BCH).

Multibanco Mercantil de México is a multiregional bank based in Mexico City. It has traditionally had a strong client base of textile industries, which have been hurt by Mexico's trade opening. Because of its weak financial condition, it did not issue any stock to private investors until 1990, three years after most of Mexico's banks had been listed on the stock exchange.

Banca Promex is a very profitable regional bank, based in Guadalajara. Founded in 1940, it is the 14th largest (in deposits), but ranked eighth in net profits in 1990 and 11th in net worth. It has a very strong presence in the Guadalajara region and is expected to grow as a regional bank.

Banco del Centro (Bancén), Mexico's 15th largest bank, is also regional, with headquarters in the central state of San Luis Potosí. It is considered very healthy.

Banpaís, traditionally associated with the Monterrey group of industrialists, suffered after nationalization because of the troubles of its Monterrey-based clients. However, the government succeeded in making it a very profitable bank during 1990.

Banoro, founded in 1932, has remained strong in Mexico's central Pacific coast. It has headquarters in Culiacán, the capital of Sinaloa. Although it is one of Mexico's smallest banks, it has been well run

(Continued)

and posted net profits larger than those of the multiregional banks. It has developed strong ties to northern beach resorts and to the state of Sinaloa's important export produce industry.

Banco de Oriente (Banorie), founded in the city of Puebla in 1944, is Mexico's smallest commercial bank in terms of deposits, assets and net worth. It is considered to be in good financial health and to have much growth potential.

During 1991, officials had early success selling off the first of the 18 commercial banks. By June, the first three banks had been sold. Multibanco Mercantil de México went to the newly formed Grupo Financiero Probursa, a financial group linked to Probursa, the brokerage house, for $200 million (2.66 times the bank's net worth). The group should associate with a foreign banking concern now that it has the bank.

Commercial Banks: Vital Statistics
(pesos-billions)

	Assets*	Deposits*
Banamex	65,043	61,085
Bancomer	50,927	47,239
Banca Serfin	41,982	28,522
Multibanco Comermex	16,435	15,710
Banco Internacional	13,382	12,829
Banco Mexicano Somex	10,523	10,073
Multibanco Mercantil de México	7,048	6,819
Banco del Atlántico	6,812	6,544
Banco Confia	5,444	5,204
Banca Cremi	5,239	5,007
BCH	4,777	4,574
Bancreser	4,381	4,283
Banorte	3,569	3,141
Banpaís	3,316	3,181
Banca Promex	3,016	2,743
Bancén	2,206	1,929
Banoro	2,110	1,742
Banorie	1,016	949

*Through November 1990

SOURCE: Comisión Nacional Bancaria y de Seguros.

Banpaís, the Monterrey-area bank, was sold to Grupo Financiero Mexival, another financial group, for $180 million (3.02 times its net worth). The third bank, Banca Cremi, was sold for about $240 million (3.4 times its net worth) to a group of executives from Guadalajara and the state of Jalisco, along with Multivalores, the brokerage firm. The new owners plan to move Banca Cremi's headquarters to Guadalajara and form a group that will control the bank, Multivalores and other financial intermediaries.

All three banks were sold at prices higher than expected, well above their net worth—a trend which continued as the privatization process proceeded. The high offering prices for the earlier sales increased prices for other small and medium-sized banks subsequently up for sale. The privatization of the banks was almost completed by the second quarter of 1992.

New Financial Groups

The second critical feature that will have a strong impact on Mexico's financial system is the creation of financial groups. Although individual investors are prohibited from owning more than 5% (or as much as 10% with government approval) of a bank's shares, newly created financial groups can obtain up to 100% control over a commercial bank.

New legislation approved in 1990 permits financial services firms to join together under a single financial group. The subsidiaries of the group can use the same commercial name, work out of the same office as other subsidiaries of the group and share other fixed costs.

The new law provides for three types of financial groups to be formed: a group headed by a holding company, a group led by a commercial bank and a group run by a brokerage house. The first type is expected to be the most popular, since it permits a bank and a brokerage house to be owned jointly. Under the new law, a financial group headed by a commercial bank can own other financial companies, except for a brokerage house and an insurance company. Likewise, a financial group headed by a brokerage house can own other financial companies, except for a commercial bank and an insurance company. A financial group headed by a holding company, however, can jointly own a commercial bank, an insurance company and a brokerage house.

A financial group headed by a holding company may own one of each of the following: warehouse, leasing company, brokerage house, commercial bank, currency exchange house, factoring company, bonding company, insurance firm and mutual fund, as well as other intermediaries, e.g. real estate companies. No group can have more than one intermediary of any type, except insurance firms, if they cover different risks, and mutual funds.

In 1991, new financial groups were already emerging as Mexico's ex-bankers and other business and financial leaders began bidding on the banks and deciding which brokerage houses, leasing, factoring and insurance companies could form part of their financial group. Probursa, the financial group, now includes a bank, a factoring company, a leasing company and a brokerage firm and plans to acquire an insurance company. Grupo Financiero Mexival already controls a brokerage house (Mexival) and Seguros Constitucíon, an insurance company. Mexival, which lost in its bid for Multibanco Mercantil de México, joined up with Monterrey and Tamaulipas businessmen, Julio César Villreal and Policarpo Elizondo, to enter a successful bid for Banpaís.

Role of Foreign Players

Although foreign ownership of the banks now up for sale is limited to 30% per institution, government officials have privately conceded that more direct foreign competition is likely to become a reality in Mexico's financial sector, particularly in the areas of corporate finance and investment banking. Banking sector officials believe that retail banking, meanwhile, will probably be best handled by local institutions.

The free trade negotiations have further attracted the attention of foreign banks to Mexico, which believe that the opening of the economy to a greater foreign business presence under an FTA will almost certainly lead to the eventual granting of permission to foreign banks to set up in the country.

Some foreign banks have already submitted requests to the government for permission to operate in Mexico, despite the fact that no legal approval process yet exists. "We want to be as close to the front of the line as possible when the doors open," explained one European bank representative in Mexico. At present, the only foreign bank permitted to operate in Mexico is Citibank which, along with Banco Obrero, a small workers bank, was not affected by the 1982 nationalization decree.

Expressing a view typical of some foreign banks, Bank X has no interest in participating in the purchase of a minority holding in one of Mexico's commercial banks but would like to begin its own operations. "We have had our bad experiences in the past as a minority shareholder," comments a Bank X official. "We really want to avoid the deep-pocket syndrome." Instead, Bank X is interested in providing financial services to MNC clients in Mexico and entering Mexico's money market. "I don't believe that we could provide services for Mexican investors that they can't find elsewhere," adds the official. "But we could benefit foreign investors who still lack knowledge of Mexico's market and economy." Bank X would like to be able to trade the gamut of Mexican financial instruments currently available, from commercial paper to government securities (e.g. 28-day treasury certificates—Cetes).

Other banks, including one major US bank, are weighing the pros and cons of joining with Mexican partners to purchase a Mexican bank. They cite the obligation to be minority owners as the most serious drawback and warn that banks would probably be hesitant to bring their most advanced technology to Mexico when they would not ultimately control its use. Bankers also cite the difficulties that could arise in trying to establish a working relationship between parent and subsidiary. "If New York is approached by a US client who wishes to acquire a Mexican company, do I have to put the deal through the Mexican bank or can we handle it from our representative's office in Mexico?" asks one US banker.

US bankers also add that the "big vs small syndrome" can play havoc in a relationship between Mexican and foreign banks. "A deal that a US bank might think is doable may be much too large for a Mexican bank to want to get involved in. You could have great difficulties agreeing on what projects to work on," adds a US banker based in Mexico. In short, bankers argue that any equity participation would be likely to require a detailed agreement concerning "who brings what to the table."

Despite minority position, advantages exist

Regardless of the drawbacks, holding a minority share in a Mexican bank does offer certain advantages. Among these are the ability to obtain hands-on knowledge of Mexican banking, strengthen contacts with key financial and industrial leaders in Mexico and build local presence during the interim until Mexico opens to majority foreign bank participation. Bankers concur that having a more active presence in Mexico would provide added value for a US bank in dealing with companies planning to open or expand operations in Mexico. At the moment, Citibank, the only foreign bank authorized to operate in the country, clearly has an advantage over other banks. Other foreign banks are limited to representative offices.

"If the prospects of an FTA did not exist, I would argue that the bank privatization is a now or never proposition," comments one foreign banker. "But with the FTA, it seems inevitable that the free flow of financial services and capital will follow the free flow of goods. You can hold off entering into an alliance with Mexican partners now because the market will open up to foreign banks. But do you want to do this? The longer a bank waits to enter, the more the costs add up, not only in terms of lost opportunity, but also the costs of setting up operations."

"While we are not interested in a Mexican retail banking operation," comments a representative from Bank Y, a major US bank, "we are considering Mexico's pension system, and that would require retail operations. It would be a lot cheaper to buy a retail operation that exists now and modify it than to start from the beginning."

Some bankers argue that the choice is not simply whether to enter the market now as minority shareholder or wait for an FTA to go into effect. "There will be opportunities to buy into a Mexican bank after the initial sale," adds one banker, who predicts "reshuffling" on both the Mexican and foreign side after the initial privatizations are concluded. "Some people simply won't be happy with what they bought and will be willing to sell out." Bankers warn, however, that the price could be much higher. "Mexican groups want to team up with foreign bankers in order to strengthen their bid. Foreigners who come knocking on their doors later may be welcomed but can expect to pay a premium."

Although Bank Y is looking for a "focused" bank in Mexico, its representative in the country concedes that there is relatively little, other than participating in likely reforms of the pension plan, it would like to do in Mexico that it cannot currently do. The bank is presently involved in merger and acquisition (M&A) activity—a very large market already—as well as private placements for Mexican interests seeking to tap international capital markets, equity placements, structured trade and other areas of corporate finance. When foreign banks are permitted to operate in Mexico, Bank Y would like to be able to take positions in Mexico's capital and money markets.

New Shape of the Financial System

The privatization of Mexico's banking system underscores emerging trends that will alter the banking climate in Mexico during the 1990s. The following developments are foreseen:

• **New banks may open.** "What we need are more regional banks," comments a high-level Mexican official. "The former process of mergers and consolidation went too far." Officials claim, however, that new banks will not be permitted to open until the government has sold all its commercial banking interests.

• **Regional banks will become more important.** Government officials and Mexican bankers indicate that privatization will most likely serve as an impetus for strong regional banks, similar to those in the US. The sale of Banpaís, traditionally strong in Monterrey, to a financial group linked with northern businessmen, underscores the importance the government has given to strengthening regional operations.

• **Strong private financial conglomerates will emerge.** Although the government has apparently not made up its mind on how powerful it will permit these groups to become, officials are likely to allow greater concentration to help the sector face foreign competition. Evidence of this trend comes from the first privatizations, in which buyers were recently organized groups with multiple interests.

• **The government will regulate financial groups more closely.** Although the formation of financial groups has been given a boost by a law passed in 1990, investors will probably see additional regulations in the future as the government works out difficulties in their operation.

• **A shakeout among newly formed groups is likely.** By 1993, some of the new investors rushing to form financial conglomerates may drop out as their profit expectations are not met. As a result, opportunities for late comers will arise.

• **US banks will initially hesitate to buy into Mexican banks.** Although US bankers concede that an opening in Mexico's financial services sector is a good opportunity, the timing is poor, given the debilitated financial condition of many US banks. The likely candidates for eventual expansion into Mexico through a minority equity participation are institutions in California or Texas interested in a high-profile alliance with Mexican banks as a means to tap into business in the border area and places in the US where large amounts of Mexican workers reside.

• **European banks may demonstrate greater initial interest.** In particular, some state-owned financial institutions in Europe are likely to take a minority equity interest in the commercial banks Mexico has put up for sale. This will be a largely political move, done as a way to show support for President Salinas. Greatest interest is likely to come from institutions in France, Germany and Spain. Banco de Santador, one of the largest private commercial banks in Spain, is expected to join with Mexican investors in purchasing one commercial bank.

• **Foreign banks will be more free to provide corporate finance and investment banking services.** An opening in this area is likely before a decision is made on allowing foreign banks to enter the more politically sensitive area of retail banking.

• **There will be greater foreign participation in brokerage firms.** Foreign brokerage houses are now being authorized to open offices in Mexico. Barings Securities, Fidelity and others have been working in Mexico since late 1990 to study Mexican markets and provide more detailed information on local companies as requested by foreign investors. Mexican brokerage houses are adamantly opposed to permitting foreigners to compete directly and would prefer that the government allow some form of joint venture or other association between Mexican and foreign houses.

• **More opportunities are expected to emerge in the mergers and acquisitions market.** Even though foreign banks, through their representative offices, are already heavily involved in Mexico's expanding mergers and acquisitions (M&A) market, these types of activities will grow more rapidly as investment conditions improve because of the negotiations for a North American FTA. Some foreign multinationals will be interested in following the example of PepsiCo, Inc, which purchased Gamesa, Mexico's leading sweet snack food company, whereas Mexican firms are more likely to be interested in acquiring medium-sized enterprises to take advantage of economies of scale. In addition, breakups in large family conglomerates, wherein third-generation siblings choose a different business direction, are possible. In most cases, M&A will take place through the stock market. Gains obtained from the sale of stock in publicly traded companies are not taxable, whereas gains from the sale of privately owned businesses can be taxed. Consequently, taking a company public before selling it to another party can reduce M&A costs.

• **The cost of dollar financing will drop as foreign banks enter Mexico's financial services sector.** Although many US subsidiaries in Mexico are in a sounder financial state than quite a few US companies, they are faced with higher-cost dollar financing in Mexico than in the US. The presence of foreign banks should help lower these costs considerably.

• **Majority control of Mexico's insurance companies by foreign institutions is likely.** The country's insurance firms will probably be taken over as soon as majority foreign ownership is permitted.

Retailing

Mexico's retail market has been virtually unexplored by foreign investors. Although unexplored territory offers great promise, it also requires a great deal of initial study. This section does not promise to provide the details necessary for entering the retail market, but it does highlight some key characteristics of the market and sketch some of the attractive prospects likely to emerge once North American markets are united.

Nature of the Market

Although Mexico has over 80 million inhabitants, most of the population and its purchasing power is concentrated in a few urban areas in central and northern Mexico. One quarter of the population has 75% of the purchasing power. By far, the greatest concentration of population and disposable income is found in the Mexico City metropolitan area, which boasts 15 million inhabitants (1990 preliminary census results). It also generates a large part of the nation's wealth. Outside Mexico City, the cities of Monterrey, Guadalajara, Puebla and the border cities in the north are the principal targets for consumer goods and industrial sales, as well as for establishing large supermarkets and department stores.

Mexican distribution channels are weak for most consumer and industrial products. Channels to the more than 60 million people living outside the Federal District are not well developed. Most distribution is accomplished via wholesaling or a variety of unstable subrepresentative relationships. Many of these have been reinforced by an antiquated government-business client system that has served as a powerful influence against competition in certain regions.

Even in Mexico City—which has a population exceeding that of many countries—there are many areas in which no large supermarkets or department stores exist. In the eastern portion of the Mexico City metropolitan area, more than five million people live without access to any large commercial centers or supermarkets.

The lack of supermarkets is explained in part by the reliance of consumers on small street markets to purchase fresh produce and on small grocers to purchase other necessities. Other household goods are also sold in small stores and by street vendors. In addition, supermarkets and department stores in Mexico are usually costly to build and maintain. The higher overhead is reflected in pricing strategies that make them less attractive in low-income neighborhoods. The large tracts of land needed for the traditional supermarket or department store, with accompanying parking area, are scarce in Mexico City.

In general, Mexico's retail market is divided into the following types of outlets, listed in order of size (from largest to smallest): hyper-supermarkets; supermarkets and department stores; warehouse-style stores; small supermarkets; convenience stores; small stores; and unorganized, informal markets.

Warehouse Stores:
A Trend in Retailing

To meet the needs of large working-class and low-income areas, some retail chains segment the market and design a different model for much of Mexico City. The result has been bodegas, or warehouse-style stores, currently being used by Aurrera (Bodegas Aurrera), Blanco (Bodegas Blanco) and Comercial Mexicana (Bodegas Comercial Mexicana). Although the average tract of land for a supermarket, including parking lot, may be 10,000–15,000 sq m, a bodega may require as little as 4,000 sq m. Most of the land is devoted to sales space. Little parking is needed because population density (estimated at twice that of New York City, according to the United Nations) permits people to walk or use public transportation. One chain has been particularly successful in adapting existing structures (such as movie theaters) to bodegas.

Warehouse-style stores have much lower overhead than traditional supermarkets. They also provide volume discounts and stock a limited supply of items. Most sales are concentrated in general merchandise and clothing; perishable food items are generally not available.

Pricing Strategy

Pricing practices in Mexico's retail sector differ markedly from those in the US. In 1987, prior to institution of the PSE (the Pact for Economic Solidarity—precursor to the current price control program), many producers inflated prices substantially to protect their profit margins in anticipation of a more rigid anti-inflation shock program ("Azteca Plan"). Although this shock program never materialized, price controls or restraints still exist.

Retailers, like manufacturers, have traditionally had much higher profit margins than their US counterparts, in part in an attempt to protect themselves from market uncertainties. Faced with the likelihood of greater US competition, however, Mexican chain store retailers are accepting lower profits and focusing on higher sales volumes to compensate.

During 1990, the Aurrera chain instituted a price war, known in Spanish as la guerra de precios. The major chain repeatedly discounted prices on all merchandise and food by 30–40%. On other occasions, the chain discounted entire divisions, i.e. all housewares, clothing or general merchandise. The sales would last for one to three days, and stores would often remain open past midnight (until 5 a.m. in one case) to service the large numbers of customers. The result was a substantial rise in sales and an increase in market share for the firm. Although other supermarkets lowered prices on selective items, none were willing to compete with Aurrera directly by offering discounts on a similar scale.

Aurrera's discount policy has begun to change consumer pricing perceptions. Industry executives have noted a greater resistance by consumers to purchase many items, ranging from liquors to television sets, if they are not discounted. "I believe the real price on many goods in Mexico is the discount price and not the everyday price you see in most stores," comments one executive. "I suspect that in the coming years, you will see everyday prices fall closer in line with what today is being advertised as a discount price."

Retailing and Street Merchants

Any study of retailing in Mexico must consider the informal economy, which expanded tremendously during the 1980s. Although precise data is difficult to come by, the few studies that have been done
indicate that the informal sector plays a more dominant role in retailing than in the economy as a whole. Some analysts estimate that
tianguis, or street markets, street vendors and small family-run operations may represent up to 40% of the retail market.

The parallel economy can present numerous problems for consumer goods companies trying to design an effective marketing strategy for Mexico. Firms interested in setting up specialized retail
outlets may find that their product line is already entering Mexico
through the northern border and being sold through informal retail
channels.

Company M, a major US consumer goods manufacturer, has been
thwarted in its recent expansion drive in Mexico because of the large
informal market. Company M had achieved peak sales of its product
in Mexico in 1980–81, before Mexico's recession. In the 1980s, with
sales falling to one twentieth of the level registered in 1980–81, the
company withdrew from the market. With the beginning of economic reactivation in 1989, however, the firm reentered Mexico and
began selling its product in small boutiques aimed at the high end of
the consumer market.

After two years, the company has only reached sales levels of about
half those experienced in the early 1980s. Market studies show, however, that demand has not dropped to half the level of the earlier
peak period. Instead, the problem is on the supply side.

The company estimates that nearly half of the total sales of its
product occurs through informal retailing outlets: principally street
vendors and markets. The source of the products is clearly in the US,
where Company M has discovered unusually large sales to US distributors near the US-Mexico border. However, trying to confront the
problem by restricting sales to the border distributors would simply
"push the problem northward," according to Company M executives.

The informal retailing has limited Company M's marketing ability.
"How can you try to establish yourself as a 'status' consumer product
aimed at the high end of the consumer market, when consumers
know that they can purchase your product from street vendors?"
asked one executive in Company M's Latin American division.

"The Foreigners Are Coming"

One development that will force greater discounting and reevaluation of the pricing structure in Mexican retailing will be the arrival of US and other foreign retailers. "We believe the foreigners are coming sooner or later," comments one industry planning executive. "What we don't know is exactly how."

US companies will be attracted to two major markets in Mexico: the fast growing northern border area, which is forecast to continue enjoying rapid growth in the years ahead with an FTA, and the Mexico City metropolitan area—home of a population exceeding several Latin American and European countries. The advantages of entering the border area include utilization of existing distribution systems in Texas and the southwestern US, proximity to existing stores and the ability to take advantage of cultural synergies among similar Hispanic markets on both sides of the border. Furthermore, expansion along the border could be viewed as a first step in testing the Mexican market, before a company expands into the large population centers in central Mexico.

Mexico City has some advantages, including a large, concentrated market (15–20 million, depending on the estimates used) located within a relatively small geographic area. Disadvantages do exist, however. The distances between Mexico City and major US border cities in Texas and southern California mean substantially increased transportation costs, among others. Culturally, the Mexico City consumer market has less in common with the US Hispanic market than the US Hispanic market has with the border population. Also, tracts of land big enough to locate supermarkets or discount stores on are scarce in the capital city.

FTA and Chain Retailers

An FTA will substantially improve prospects for chain retailers in Mexico. Despite the acceleration of Mexico's trade opening since late 1987, few retailers have systemically studied the implications of more open borders. Even though retailers often actively sought out imported merchandise during the initial months of the trade opening, they now rely primarily on suppliers to introduce them to new products. "We went out looking at first," added one supermarket executive, "in order to get to know the products, but we have no interest in actually importing them ourselves."

Suppliers in Mexico have only been partially successful in importing new products. A cursory glance at the shelves in leading retail outlets in Mexico City will show that there are numerous areas in which US and other foreign products could compete in price, but these goods have yet to be imported into the country. Other items available at a substantial discount in the US are available in Mexico, but at very high markups. Transportation costs, existing duties (still up to 20% for some items) and smaller volume buying by Mexican suppliers and distributors explain these differences in part. The price differentials, however, are also a result of lack of competition and knowledge of the range of imports available.

Although Mexico represents opportunities in all markets, one of the most significant opportunities for US retailers may be in the discount retail sector. US retailers already know what US or other non-Mexican merchandise is available and at what price, and have strong relations with suppliers. In those product lines where US products could compete on the basis of price, a US retailer would have the further advantage of buying large volume and obtaining better prices and discounts than its Mexican counterpart.

One of the first foreign retailers to take advantage of the new opportunities presented by the prospect of an FTA is Wal-Mart, the US's largest retail chain. In early 1991, Wal-Mart—in its first foreign expansion—formed a joint venture with Cifra SA, Mexico's largest retailer. In 1991-92, the two companies opened a chain of wholesale clubs in Mexico to be known as Club Aurrera, beginning with five stores.

Like Wal-Mart's successful Sam's Wholesale Club in the US, Club Aurrera will sell electronics, stationery products and food, primarily to small-business employees and groups such as schools and trade unions. The clubs will require a membership fee of about $25 in exchange for the right to shop there. Most goods will be sold in bulk at discount prices.

Differences in Retail Systems

For US companies, entering Mexico's large chain store retail market requires a careful study of the differences between the two countries' markets, which include the following:

• **Only regional, rather than national, retail chains have had success in Mexico.** These include Soriano in the north and Cifra's Aurrera chain in central Mexico and Guadalajara. There are only a handful of cities with populations exceeding one million. Some large cities are isolated from other metropolitan areas.

• **Distribution centers are not widely used by many supermarket and retail chains, which prefer to have suppliers deliver directly to individ-**

ual stores. The exception is produce, where the large number of suppliers and great variations in product quality require supermarkets to set up distribution centers to monitor quality and select goods.

• **Mexican retailers usually require very little working capital.** They purchase products with liberal commercial credit arrangements and usually sell their products before paying suppliers. In many product lines, retailers are able to get 30-day credit from suppliers, sell the product in 15 days and earn interest on sales proceeds prior to supplier payment.

• **Computerized systems are still rare.** Although there has been rapid growth recently in the use of bar codes and scanners, their application is still not generalized.

• **Specialty stores have not been introduced.** The concept of high-volume discount stores that specialize in one product area, such as toys (Toys "R" Us), office supplies (OA) or drugstores (Drug Emporium), is still virtually unknown. Because these stores do not require tracts of land as large as supermarkets, however, it would not be as difficult to secure a location for one in Mexico City. In addition, their pricing strategy, which is based on volume, would be well suited for large population centers such as Mexico City.

Specialized stores are not guaranteed success, however. For instance, even though toys are purchased by essentially the same end-consumers as in the US, the Mexican tradition of consumer purchases of hardware merchandise differs. The "do-it-yourself" concept does not exist to the same degree in Mexico.

Prospects for Franchising

Although franchises are one of the most popular business forms in the US, until recently they were virtually unknown in Mexico. Even today, on the eve of the creation of a North American regional market, franchises are only beginning to be examined as a method of operating in Mexico. By early 1991, fewer than 100 international franchises were estimated to exist in Mexico, compared with more than 230 US franchises in Canada alone.

Revamped Regulatory Framework

One of the principle obstacles to franchises in the past has been Mexico's restrictive legislation. Prior to regulations on Mexico's technology transfer law published in January 1990, franchise agreements were considered technology accords and thus were burdened with requirements targeted primarily at hard-technology transfers. Royalty rates were restricted, required supply clauses were prohibited and confidential information had limited protection. Moreover, franchises were viewed negatively by government regulators, who saw limited value in providing protection for a foreign system of doing business.

The first change in this viewpoint occurred in January 1990, when new technology transfer regulations first recognized franchises by name and gave the parties to a franchise agreement the contractual freedom to set their own terms and conditions. Although a model franchise still had to be registered with the Secretariat of Commerce and Industrial Development (Secofi), lawyers working on such franchising agreements claimed that much of the government's discretionary power had been curbed.

A still more important legal change occurred in June 1991, when Mexico passed its new intellectual property law. The Law for the Promotion and Protection of Industrial Property not only repealed previous patent and trademark legislation, but also the former Law on the Control and Registration of the Transfer of Technology (1982) and its 1990 regulations. The result is twofold: (1) with the repeal of the former technology transfer regulations, franchise agreements no longer need to be registered with Secofi; and (2) under the new law, franchisors now have a disclosure obligation.

According to Article 142 of the Law for the Promotion and Protection of Industrial Property, a franchise exists when a license for a trademark or service mark is combined with technical information or assistance for the purpose of allowing the franchisee to "produce or sell goods or provide services in a uniform manner and with operational, commercial and administrative methods established by the holder of the mark, designed to maintain the quality, prestige and image of the products or services to which (the mark) refers."

The new law also requires company disclosure to potential franchisees prior to the signing of any accord. The scope of the franchisor's disclosure is not spelled out in the law, but left to forthcoming regulations. (Officials expect the new regulations to be ready by late 1992.) Industry experts who lobbied for the repeal of franchise registration and in favor of the new disclosure requirement expect the government to require franchisors to provide certain financial information, as well as trademark registration information.

The new interest in franchises is not solely a result of more favorable regulations, but of the overall opening of the Mexican economy. Franchises are growing, thanks to the sweeping changes in Mexico's policies, especially its commitment to liberalize trade and reduce the state's role in the economy—policies that will in turn be strengthened by an FTA. "If you couldn't freely import goods and equipment or set up the corporate structure in Mexico needed to initiate franchises, then the new rules wouldn't have helped much," comments an attorney in Mexico working on franchises. Mexico's recent economic recovery and projected growth in the years ahead have also spurred interest in franchise opportunities.

Franchise Growth and the FTA

Franchising in Mexico is still in its infancy. Of fewer than 100 franchises (national and foreign) in Mexico in early 1991, most had been in operation less than 18 months. In 1990, the number of foreign franchises setting up in Mexico was equivalent to the total number previously in existence. The first franchises range from fast-food restaurants and print shops to specialty shops and hotels. Agreements have been signed with Arby's (December 1990), Baskin Robbins (May 1990), Alpha Graphics (September 1989), The Athlete's Foot (April 1990), Subway (September 1990) and Domino's Pizza (December 1990). Most are master franchise accords that provide a Mexican entity with the exclusive right to grant additional franchises in Mexico and to open company-owned stores. The agreement usually establishes a minimum number of stores to be opened within a predetermined period, along with provisions for sharing of royalties and fees.

Although the variety of franchises entering Mexico over the last year is impressive, the market is still wide open. "Mexican consumer tastes have been molded by US retailing and advertising. A US franchise will meet those demands," explains a local franchising consultant. In addition, a franchise permits a company to market its services quickly and widely with limited capital outlay. This is especially important in Mexico, where geographic diversity and extension makes other forms of product distribution more complicated. As Mexico moves toward a North American free trade accord, the influence of US retailing and products is expected to grow, making foreign franchises more attractive.

"A franchise provides a company with a way to expand in a new market and at the same time obtain royalties," says one consultant. For major producers of food products, poultry and beef, fast-food restaurant and convenience store franchises can provide a new outlet for production. Even though most of the growth involves foreign trademarks and services, local franchises are also growing. Approximately 10 new Mexican franchises opened in 1990, including taco and tamale food services.

Obstacles Remain

Despite promising signs of growth, there are still obstacles to opening a successful franchise in Mexico. Although Mexican consumers are increasingly imitating their counterparts in the US, Mexican retailing and business practices continue to be quite different from those north of the border. In addition, the nature of Mexico's recent trade opening is proving difficult for some new franchises.

Franchisors in the footwear, hotel and food industries have complained about suppliers and distribution channels that have failed to keep pace with the needs of the more rapidly growing franchises. The director general of one master franchise involving athletic footwear had difficulties opening his first store because the merchandise he intended to stock was simply not available in Mexico. For the franchise's concept to work, a wide variety of mostly imported merchandise was required. In some cases, no one had distribution rights to provide the merchandise in Mexico; in other cases, the Mexican distributor supplied less than 15% of the models available in the US. "I am in the business of selling shoes and franchises; I don't want to get in the import business," explained the franchise holder.

In some cases, local financing has been difficult to obtain. Mexican banks emphasize hard assets, which are usually kept to a minimum in a typical franchise. Equipment and commercial space is often leased, and inventories are kept low. "We have to educate banks to look at a business's potential cash flow and not its hard assets in determining financing," remarks one industry executive. Some financial groups, however, such as Operadora de Bolsa and Probursa, have shown interest in developing financing needed for franchises.

Because many of the franchise agreements in Mexico are master franchises (which provide the holder the exclusive right to assign individual franchisors within a defined geographical area), the selling price has been high. This has often limited the pool of interested franchisees to large Mexican corporations. Large hotel, financial and construction firms appear to have the greatest interest in acquiring master franchises. Even in the case of individual franchises, analysts note that few individuals in Mexico with the amount of money needed to purchase a franchise are actually interested in operating the franchise personally. "Unlike in the US, where a franchisee can put down $25,000 or $30,000 and pay the rest of the fee over the life of the business, in Mexico you have to come up with most of the fee up front because of limited long-term financing available. That changes the nature of franchising," notes a consultant.

The Mexican group Xabre SA, owner of luxury hotel chains and a controlling interest in the airline Mexicana de Aviación, as well as sugar mills, has begun to apply franchising to both its Camino Real and Maeva hotel chains. "In tourism, perhaps 5% of the people want something new; most people want to know what they are getting in advance," says José Giral, managing director of Xabre. "With franchising, people feel comfortable with the knowledge that they know what to expect."

The Telecommunications Revolution

Mexico's telecommunications industry is undergoing a period of rapid growth and extraordinary change. Committed to the goal of bringing the country's antiquated and inadequate telecommunications infrastructure into the 21st century, the Salinas administration privatized Teléfonos de México (Telmex), the national telephone company (sold to a group of national and foreign investors in December 1990), and has opened areas such as cellular telephone service to domestic and foreign private capital.

At present, foreign investment in telecommunications is restricted by law to 49% and the industry is heavily regulated, despite the government's willingness to permit greater private participation. Still, the projected acceleration in the market's growth will provide telecommunications equipment firms with improved sales prospects. Also, the issue of expanded investor access to the industry is certain to be discussed during free trade talks.

The privatization of Telmex constituted perhaps the most important development in Mexico's telecommunications sector in recent decades. Two previous events—Telmex's international bidding process and Mexico's entry into GATT—have also played a major role in transforming the nature of the country's telecommunications industry. Free trade talks with Canada and the US could have an even greater effect on the sector.

History of Protectionism

The telecommunications industry in Mexico has been sheltered from competition for the last 40 years. Until Mexico entered GATT and began to adopt a policy of trade liberalization in the late 1980s, very little equipment could be imported, and those imports permitted were subject to steep duties. Under a national program, L.M. Ericsson (Sweden) and Indetel (a subsidiary of the US's ITT) agreed to produce in the country in return for special permission to import. (Only firms producing in Mexico were allowed to import.) Although other foreign companies had a limited presence in the country, including NEC (Japan) and NV Philips (Netherlands), the two leading Telmex suppliers—Ericsson and Indetel—formed vertically integrated operations and produced virtually everything Telmex needed with little regard to economies of scale. (Telmex was originally formed as a private company in 1947 when the assets of Ericsson and ITT were combined and acquired by Mexican investors. The government took over with a 51% equity stake in 1972.)

With no competition from abroad, Ericsson and Indetel had little incentive to introduce new technology. Modern technology would have represented an additional investment, and both firms pursued a strategy aimed at recouping the cost of their original outlays. The reluctance of both companies to upgrade technology led Telmex to request bids from other international firms, first in 1979–80 and then again in 1987–88.

Taking bids

Telmex's decision to place up for bid purchases for telecommunications equipment was probably the most important milestone in the industry's evolution before the privatization of Telmex. In the late 1970s, Mexico was enjoying economic growth, technology was changing rapidly and, most important, the life cycle of telecommunications equipment was becoming much shorter. At the time, Telmex bought basic equipment, central office switches, transmission equipment and telephones from Ericsson and Indetel. Despite the high level of protection in the industry, however, Telmex wanted to compare the products and prices offered by its principal suppliers with those of other firms throughout the world.

In its 1980 and 1988 bidding processes, or "requests for information" (so called to avoid complying with parastate procurement regulations), price requests went out to leading suppliers worldwide, including Siemens (Germany), AT&T (US) and Northern Telecom (Canada), as well as to local suppliers Ericsson and Indetel (now known as Alcatel Indetel). Ericsson and Indetel won both bids. Although the percentage of the contract awarded often did not match the actual work performed (problems with software development at Alcatel Indetel gave Ericsson the lead in digital installations in the late 1980s), Telmex management remained committed to having two strong suppliers receiving essentially equal treatment.

Long a source of comfort for Telmex's suppliers, this equilibrium has begun to change since the new owners took over. The change poses a serious challenge for Ericsson and Alcatel Indetel, and offers an opening for other telecommunications equipment manufacturers, an opening which AT&T has exploited best.

The other important change predating the privatization of Telmex began when Mexico entered GATT in 1986 and began reducing tariffs on telecommunications products. Since then, telecommunications has metamorphosed from an industry characterized by import permits, high duties and special treatment for local manufacturers to a sector in which, for the most part, imports are freely permitted and bear a maximum duty of just 20%.

New Owners, New Commitment

The first signs that Telmex would be privatized came during the 1988 presidential campaign. Presidential candidate Carlos Salinas de Gortari privately argued that the country simply did not have the necessary capital to invest in telecommunications growth. Industry observers countered that Telmex's problems—bad service, shortage of lines and widespread repair problems—resulted not from the lack of a growth strategy on the part of Telmex, but because the government would not let Telmex grow. "Telmex was a cash cow," explains one industry executive. "And the government was more interested in draining the company of revenues to resolve budgetary problems than it was in funding telecommunications growth."

On Sept. 19, 1989, Salinas announced that the government was selling its majority stake in Telmex. The sale hinged on a major commitment by the eventual purchaser to expand and modernize the telephone system. Under the terms of the privatization, the state retains regulatory authority over telecommunications. The new 30-year concession for telephone service will be reviewed every five years, permitting the government to make changes designed to improve Telmex's efficiency and international competitiveness.

In December 1990, a group of investors led by Mexican financier Carlos Slim, Southwestern Bell (US) and France Telecom's France Cable et Radio purchased a 20.4% controlling share of Telmex for $1.76 billion. In May 1990, over $2.1 billion worth of additional shares were sold in Mexico, the US, Europe and Asia.

The investment commitment made by the new owners of Telmex (estimated to be at least $10 billion over the first five years of ownership) to expand telephone service presents substantial opportunities to telecommunications equipment manufacturers. Under the terms of the privatization, Telmex is committed to providing long-distance service to all towns with more than 500,000 inhabitants; increase the present number of telephone lines from five per 100 people to 10 per 100 people by 1994 (and to 20 lines per 100 people by the year 2000); install four million new terminal lines during the first five years of ownership; substitute obsolete switching systems in urban areas with digital technology; double network capacity over the first five years through the digitalization of 8,500 km of microwave network, install at least 3,000 km of fiber optic cable and install additional 14 master stations for satellite services; increase the number of public telephones; reduce the number of lines out of order; speed up repair service; and, starting in 1992, provide basic telephone service to any town with at least 5,000 inhabitants within six months of a request.

An Unexplored Frontier

Business opportunities for telecommunications companies in Mexico are expanding at an accelerating pace. Among the trends in the market now evident are the following:

• **There are more players than ever before in the telecommunications industry—both government and private.** "You can no longer come down and talk with one person in the Secretariat of Communications and Transportation (SCT) and expect to find out what is happening in the market," says one industry observer. SCT projects are only a part of what is happening. Changes in the market make it more difficult to understand the operating environment, but also present firms with greater opportunities. Telmex is no longer the only potential buyer of telecommunications equipment: Cellular telephone companies without ties to Telmex now provide service throughout Mexico.

• **The Mexican market is growing rapidly.** Growth rates of 15–18% p.a. are likely in the sector in coming years. This contrasts with Europe and the US, where the market is saturated. In 1988, according to a government study, Mexico had only 1.9 telephone lines per 100 people, ranking 82nd worldwide, while its economy was the 14th largest in the world. The serious shortages in areas such as telephone lines are reflected throughout the telecommunications equipment and service areas.

• **More changes are on the way.** The 30-year concession granted Telmex does not guarantee exclusivity in long-distance telephone

(Continued)

service after 1996. Other long-distance carriers are likely to enter then. By that time, restrictions on foreign majority ownership in telephone services are expected to have been modified or removed entirely. Greater foreign participation in other areas of telecommunications may be permitted even sooner, and will be discussed during the free trade talks.

• **Rules of origin will be a key factor in telecommunications.** With stricter North American rules of origin expected under an FTA, equipment providers such as AT&T and Northern Telecom could certainly gain advantage over non-North American competitors. Still, companies such as Alcatel Alsthom (France) could invest through their North American affiliates to ensure that high North American local content rules are complied with. Telecommunications companies are advised to monitor the debate involving rules of origin in the FTA talks.

• **The dominant role that Telmex's two traditional suppliers have played may be ending.** To date, Telmex has purchased almost exclusively from two suppliers: L.M. Ericsson (Sweden) and Alcatel Indetel (France). With new management in Telmex, this long-standing arrangement may be over. AT&T has made important inroads in supplying most of the fiber optic and terminal equipment for an important $300 million, 13,500 km long-distance network in Mexico. Other firms, including Fujitsu (Japan) are also gaining a position in the market.

Beyond Telmex

Although Telmex's demand for telecommunications equipment will be great, there are many other opportunities in Mexico. These include the following:

• **Cellular telephone concessions** have been granted to two competing companies (one of which is owned by Telmex) in the four principal regions of Mexico: Central (Mexico City and surrounding areas), North (Monterrey to the US border), West (Guadalajara to the Pacific Coast) and Baja California. A single non-Telmex company received the concession for the country's five other regions. Telmex's subsidiary, however, is soon expected to enter those regions as well. Motorola (US) and Northern Telecom are among the suppliers of equipment to the cellular operating companies. By the end of 1992, at least 200,000 subscribers are expected nationwide. This figure should swell to as much as 400,000 before 1995, industry observers claim.

• **Data communications services** are expected to enjoy the fastest growth in the telecommunications market over the next five years. Over 1,000 private systems with nearly 37,000 terminals existed in 1989. Concessions for private data communication systems and private telephone line service with links to the national network and point to point with border crossings are granted by the Secretariat of Communications and Transportation (SCT). Although bypass telecommunications have been very popular with financial institutions and the maquiladora industry, saturation of the Morelos Satellite System and improved service provided by a Telmex overlay network have slowed down expansion. Once the first Solidaridad satellite is launched and begins operation in 1993–94, growth in bypass will again be possible.

• **Mexico's increasingly competitive environment** will fuel demand for telecommunications services and equipment. The newly reprivatized commercial banks are expected to spend heavily on telecommunications equipment and services from 1991–96. Moreover, the nature of new foreign investment in Mexico, which will place much more emphasis on integrating Mexican operations with other North American businesses, will also require much more sophisticated telecommunications systems capable of creating a stronger link between operations north and south of the US-Mexico border.

Case Example

Federal Express:
Servicing an Emerging North American Market

Federal Express Corp, the world's largest air freight company, first entered the Mexican market in 1987 to prepare to exploit opportunities presented by Mexico's role in an increasingly integrated North American market. The company is confident that growth in Mexico, linked to the country's entry into a free trade agreement with the US and Canada, will boost an already rapidly growing air freight business between Mexico and the rest of the world—especially the US.

The way in which Federal Express meets the challenges it faces in Mexico can provide invaluable information to companies interested in offering world-class service in a developing country. The firm's experiences also highlight issues that many service companies will encounter as they venture into the growing Mexican market.

From licensor to owner

When Federal Express first decided to expand operations to include Mexico, it entered into a licensing agreement with a Mexican company. At that time, Mexico's foreign investment regulations did not permit foreign firms to own more than 49% of local firms. The licensee agreed to deliver and collect all express shipments for Federal Express in 11 principal cities: Mexico City, Guadalajara, Monterrey, Puebla, Toluca, Acapulco, Puerto Vallarta, León, Mérida, Cancún and Cozumel. Although this arrangement permitted Federal Express to add Mexico to its global distribution network at negligible capital expense, it did not permit the company to meet its long-term volume and quality goals.

"Our commitment to providing the same quality of service in Mexico as we do anywhere else in the world meant we had to make a major capital investment in Mexico," says Melba Mullins Campbell, marketing manager. "In our business, a highly sophisticated communications system is key. Investments of that type simply could not be made cost effectively by a licensee."

In July 1990, after Mexico liberalized its foreign investment regulations to allow 100% foreign ownership, Federal Express bought its Mexican licensee. The purchase followed Federal Express's successful bid for landing rights in the international airport of Toluca, 40 miles west of Mexico City. (As part of a plan to reduce congestion in Mexico City's single airport, air freight and cargo destined for Mexico City are now being sent via Toluca. New passenger flights with a Mexico City destination are also scheduled to operate out of Toluca.) The acquisition of its Mexican partner also marked the beginning of the installation of a state-of-the-art communications network in Mexico.

Telecommunications challenge

Because of the nature of its business, Federal Express requires a strong telecommunications system. Complex communications capabilities are a must for interfacing with customers and keeping a constant watch on the status of all shipments. Customer service agents receive thousands of calls daily, such as requests for pickup service or up-to-the-minute status reports on a shipment from the time it is picked up until the moment it is delivered. In most parts of the world served by Federal Express, agents are equipped with small hand-held computers that send shipment status information via satellite.

In Mexico, however, poor telecommunications is one of Federal Express's greatest challenges. The country is making important strides in this area. Telmex, the national telephone company, was sold in 1990 to a group of national and foreign investors including France Telecom and US-based Southwestern Bell, which are committed to a multi-billion-dollar expansion program in the coming four years to improve service and launch additional satellites. At present, however, telecommunications infrastructure in Mexico is inadequate.

When Federal Express acquired its Mexican operations, it estimated that as many as 30% of all telephone callers to its numbers in Mexico did not get through to Federal Express's customer-service agents on the first try. "No matter how effective a marketing strategy you develop," comments Fernando Dueñas, director general for Federal Express's operations in Mexico, "if no one answers or customers cannot get through, you lose out."

To improve service for customers, Federal Express is setting up a special satellite system to handle customer calls from the US and Mexico, as well as internal Federal Express communications. A special line will allow customers calling from the US—or anywhere else in the world—to have immediate access to Federal Express agents in Mexico. The new line will eliminate the problem of lost calls or calls that do not go through and will permit Federal Express in Mexico to input data on shipments' status twice as quickly as before.

In addition, the company has set up a toll-free number for use within Mexico. Also, all vans are to be equipped with computers that allow up-to-the-minute tracking of packages and permit immediate on-line changes in delivery and pickup routes to optimize messenger travel time. The company is also relocating its Mexico City office to a site in the city that provides for optimum telecommunications transmission.

Coping with customs
Time is of utmost importance in air shipment. Indeed, it was Federal Express's commitment to provide next-day and next-morning service that dramatically changed the air express industry in the US. In Mexico, lengthy customs procedures are another obstacle to extending speedy service.

To ensure that air express service lives up to its name, the company has worked with customs agents in the Toluca airport to arrange for rapid handling of its shipments. It has placed its customs brokers and part of its own customer service division in Toluca as a means of more rapidly notifying customers if a commercial invoice or some other documentation is needed to clear customs. By working with customs agents and explaining Federal Express's needs, customs clearance has been improved.

Future plans
Federal Express currently operates in 11 of Mexico's principal markets and uses agents for delivery in other cities. The company guarantees delivery to the US from the principal markets by the following morning at 10:30 a.m. The company plans to expand in the near future, although this will not affect its world-class service.

"Mexico is our largest market in Latin America," comments Dueñas, "and one we expect will grow dramatically with increased trade and investment within a North American free trade agreement."

The New Face of Tourism

Companies in the tourism industry—like those operating in many other sectors of the economy—are having to rethink traditional notions of investing in Mexico. Although luxury seaside resorts continue to be popular, today they are less attractive as an investment option. Companies are turning their attention to many of Mexico's inland cities, which are expected to grow under a free trade agreement. A new focus on business travelers, domestic tourists and families is also likely to shape Mexico's tourism industry in the coming years.

For the traditional luxury seaside resort, operations in Mexico are much more competitive. On the one hand, Mexico is experiencing an oversupply of five-star and luxury hotels. The recent build up in Mexico is not the only reason for the more competitive market, however. According to hotel executives, the hotel glut extends throughout North America. Also, US destinations are now among Mexico's biggest competitors. (Hotels which enjoyed 35–40% gross margins in 1985 have watched them erode by half recently, to 15–20%, comments one executive.) The hotel oversupply, combined with the "back to basics" tourism trends of the 1990s—fewer trips per individual, more travel with the family and more trips to places close to home—will force Mexican resort hotels to compete more effectively.

The following issues are among the most important for the industry today:

• **There is a burgeoning focus on business travelers and city-based hotels.** Perhaps the chief change in the tourism industry is the way it is preparing for the growth fueled by expectations of a free trade agreement. Hotel companies are focusing on medium-sized cities in Mexico's interior, where few hotels catering to the business traveler can currently be found. The key strategy appears to be to open a chain of hotels that offers travelers similar facilities and services in each locale.

• **Joint ventures involving US partners are popular in this area.** The firm Park Inn International is associated with Hoteles Misión; Days Inn has allied with Romano; and Holiday Inn International has joined Corporación Hotelera Boyce to form Holiday Inn Express. Holiday Inn Express plans to open hotels in Mexico City and the states of México, Querétaro, San Luis Potosí and Chiapas. Posadas de México has announced plans to build 20 four-star Fiesta Inn hotels in the next 30 months, targeting business travelers to medium-sized towns such as Colima, Chihuahua, Aguascalientes, León and Zacatecas. Real Turismo, which owns Camino Real and Club Maeva, is expanding in the business-traveler market (see case example).

- **The stability of the Mexican peso is affecting profit margins.** "It used to be a better business to have luxury resorts in Mexico," explains one hotel executive. "Rates were essentially in dollars, whereas expenses were in pesos. The devaluations were good for business. Now, with peso stability, hotel rates have almost stabilized, whereas expenses have increased with national inflation. That has put a squeeze on our margins."

- **In the 1990s, travelers will make fewer trips and stay closer to home.** Changing tourist attitudes will require companies in Mexico's tourism industry to rethink their business strategies. "The trend in the 1990s will be back to basics, with less conspicuous consumption, less luxury, fewer total trips and more trips with the family," predicts one hotel executive. "Trips with the family are harder to organize and will be closer to home. That presents an important challenge and opportunity for Mexico's tourism industry."

- **Mexico's national tourism will grow along with the economy.** In some resorts, such as Acapulco, hotel chains are redirecting their attention to the national market. Industry experts agree that the country's tourism market will grow in line with the economy's reactivation. In 1990, 37 million domestic tourists spent $7.5 billion, whereas 6.4 million foreign tourists spent $3.4 billion.

- **The number of Mexicans residing in the US who travel back to Mexico is rising.** In 1990, foreign tourists (visitors) numbered 6.4 million, up from 6.3 million in 1989, but the increase resulted from Mexican residents abroad visiting Mexico. Passage of the Simpson-Rodino immigration legislation, which granted resident status to millions of Mexicans living in the US, was in part responsible for increased travel by returning Mexicans. Hotel executives argue, however, that the registered increase in visitors is not necessarily a plus for the industry, because Mexican residents in the US are less likely to stay in hotels.

Case Example
Real Turismo's Growth Strategy

Real Turismo, the Mexican tourism company, which along with Mexicana de Aviación, the airline, forms part of Xabre SA, has adopted a comprehensive strategy to deal with the changes in the tourism industry.

Its luxury hotel chain, Hoteles Camino Real (jointly owned by Real Turismo and Westin Hotels and Resorts of the US) is strengthening its presence in Mexico's cities to complement its strong resort presence. Camino Real has begun construction in Chihuahua. The company is also looking at Hermosillo, Mérida, Puebla and Oaxaca as key cities where "there is room to grow," according to Andrés Rossetto, chief executive officer of Hoteles Camino Real. "The quality of hotels in those cities is not that good. We expect to see greater growth in medium-sized cities due to the economic activity under a free trade agreement than we do in the resorts."

The company has also been busy selling off nonperforming assets in certain resort areas and restructuring its debt with lower interest rates. Expansion in resorts is still a part of Camino Real's strategy, however. A new resort in a secluded area of the Puerto Marques bay in Acapulco is expected to open in November 1992. Camino Real is also looking at expansion on Mexico's Caribbean coast.

Positioned to take advantage of changes in the industry, Real Turismo has decided to create a less expensive and more youth-oriented version of its all-inclusive resorts, known as Maeva. (Real Turismo has the exclusive right to use the name in Mexico, the rest of North America and South America. In Europe, Club Med controls the use of the name Maeva.) The Maeva group of resorts includes the family-oriented Club Maeva, which operates in Manzanillo and Puerto Vallarta; Royal Maeva, which operates in Huatulco and targets couples without children; and a less expensive version, known as Coco Club, which opened in 1991 with a total of 750 rooms.

"Coco Club allows us to maintain and expand Maeva, while providing something for a different market segment," explains Enrique Aguirre, Maeva's marketing director. "It will retain our all-inclusive concept but will be more youth oriented." The company is contemplating opening additional Coco Clubs in Acapulco, the coast of the Gulf of Mexico and possibly in a mountain resort area.

To meet the needs of the middle segment of the business traveler market, Real Turismo is planning to launch a new chain known as Casa Grande: Hotel and Club de Negócios (Hotel and Business Club). The first two hotels will be no-frills establishments with an emphasis on value for the price. The Business Clubs will have a library, fax machines and computers for individual use, as well as conference rooms and messenger and secretarial services. The first two Casa Grande hotels will open in the state of Jalisco and in the city of Guadalajara. A total of six such hotels should be operating by the end of 1992.

Index